THE THIRD AGE

THE THIRD AGE

*Six Principles of
Growth and Renewal
After Forty*

WILLIAM A. SADLER, PH.D.

PERSEUS PUBLISHING
Cambridge, Massachusetts

Many of the designations used by manufacturers and sellers to distinguish their products are claimed as trademarks. Where those designations appear in this book and Perseus Publishing was aware of a trademark claim, the designations have been printed in initial capital letters.

A CIP record is available from the Library of Congress
ISBN: 0-7382-0434-X

Perseus Publishing is a member of the Perseus Books Group

Text design by Jeff Williams
Set in 11-point Minion by the Perseus Books Group

1 2 3 4 5 6 7 8 9 10—03 02 01 00
First paperback printing, December 2000

Perseus Publishing books are available at special discounts for bulk purchases in the U.S. by corporations, institutions, and other organizations. For more information, please contact the Special Markets Department at HarperCollins Publishers, 10 East 53rd Street, New York, NY 10022, or call 1-212-207-7528.

Find us on the World Wide Web at http://www.perseuspublishing.com

for Sallie, cherished partner in life and growth

Contents

Acknowledgments

When people ask how long I have been writing this book, I often feel a bit uneasy in admitting that I have been working on it for more than a dozen years. Moving at glacial speed in the age of the fast lane can be embarrassing. I usually hasten to clarify that the book is based on a longitudinal study. In fact, I am glad it did not appear earlier, because it has changed so much and, I hope, improved considerably during its long evolution. Through the years, countless people have contributed to the research, the writing, and my own understanding of key ideas.

It is appropriate here to acknowledge just a few of them, those to whom I feel especially indebted and grateful: the several dozen individuals who have so generously given their time and shared their life stories for twelve years; adult students in several seminars and workshops who gently raised pointed questions that prompted me to revise every chapter they read; colleagues whose expertise and encouragement were indispensable at several stages, particularly the late professor John Clausen, who until his death coached my research efforts as well as my writing; Dr. George Vaillant, who at the beginning kindled my enthusiasm and offered advice about designing research; professor Arlene Skolnick, whose suggestions helped me interpret data pertaining to marriage and the family; and Professor Martin Lampert, whose technical assistance has been invaluable; Peter Willauer and John Huie, who generously launched pilot projects that eventually led to research on which this book is based; good friends, especially Jim Conlon, Cecilia Hurwich, Gilbert Leclerc, and Rowan Rowntree, who championed my efforts and offered keen insights from their own experience; and my sister, Sue McKibbin, who valiantly played the role of "general reader" for the earliest versions.

I am also indebted to the Kittredge Foundation at Harvard University, which provided a grant that made it possible for me to travel for one year to conduct several dozen focused interviews, to Holy Names College for a sabbatical leave that enabled me to focus on my research, and to the

American Sociological Association, which allowed me to present early findings at two annual meetings.

It is impossible to express adequately how much I owe and how grateful I am to the following four individuals: Laurie Harper, who has been all that I could expect of an agent and much, much more; Steve Lehman, a masterful editor whose comments pushed me to greatly improve the first rendering of this book; Marnie Cochran, an editor whose sympathetic reading and imagination brought me to this final version; and above all my wife, Sallie, whose love, belief in me and the project, critical intelligence, infectious humor, and loyal partnership have kept me on course and made this effort seem worthwhile. For all their magnificent assistance, however, those whom I have just counted in no way share my responsibility for any error or inadequacies of this book.

Introduction

Thirty years ago, as a young professor, I spent a summer in East Africa directing a program for American and Canadian university students who had signed up to live and work with Africans on an agricultural project. It was a summer of wonderful surprises. One of these, I now suspect, was the germ for this book. As I learned a little Swahili and became better acquainted with our friendly hosts, I found myself misjudging the ages of some of the African men I met by about twenty years. I remember once playfully bantering with a man who I assumed was a university student; to my embarrassment, he turned out to be a forty-year-old administrator. He could have been my boss! Several of our coworkers, whom I thought to be about my age, were actually about fifty. One host who led us on a brisk three-mile hike into town admitted, as we tried to keep up with him, that he was sixty-five. The African male youthfulness in midlife was expressed in attitude and outlook as well as vital physical condition and activities.

When I returned to the United States, it seemed to me that compared with African males I had met, many of my forty- and fifty-year-old colleagues were aging prematurely. I did nothing with this suspicion but sleep on it. Only after I began the research on which this book is based many years later did I critically question our culture's assumptions about "normal" patterns of adult development and aging. If other people can retain youthfulness and experience growth for decades longer than we have assumed likely, then why should we follow conventional patterns? Why indeed? What we expect to be normal is only what we are accustomed to.

Most of us have limited, inappropriate assumptions about how the second half of life is likely to go for us. These may be characterized by words like *degeneration* and *decline*. Obviously, our African male hosts did not share our assumptions. Through my research on alternative models of midlife and aging, I have come to realize that our ideas about what is normal for us as we grow older can become impediments to seizing and even recognizing a new opportunity to reshape the second half of our lives. We need to challenge our old ideas and assumptions and replace them with new ones.

I believe that our biggest personal challenge as we face the second half of our lives will be to discover and develop our hidden potential for a vibrant, more purposeful life than we ever imagined. Most of us will live much longer than we might earlier have suspected, yet we have not carefully enough considered what this greater longevity could mean. In preparing for a conference titled "Flying into the Fifties and Beyond," I suggested that a decisive question as we address our future is, Are we planning for a landing or a take off? The conventional view of life after fifty says, "Fasten your seat belts and prepare to touch down." We often think that after age fifty or sixty we should start to throttle down, to slow our approach so as to land safely in retirement. However, a twelve-year research project focusing on new growth within several dozen men and women between the ages of forty-five and eighty has shown me another option. As this book will show, the research suggests that as we look ahead past fifty, we should be thinking about taking off.

This book is for those who want to discover, understand, and develop a creative growth process that will transform the entire second half of their lives. At this time in history we have a chance not only to live much longer than most people ever did but also to initiate a new form of personal growth that will greatly enrich those additional years. This possibility raises a number of questions. How can we experience renewal and create new life designs? What is new growth after fifty like? What tasks need to be performed to initiate new growth? What benefits will be realized if we take advantage of this opportunity? These questions have driven my research and shaped this book.

As I completed my research, I thought about my parents and their generation. My mother died thirty years ago. She did not die of old age, though I believe the fear of it contributed to her premature death of a heart attack. Ironically, she died long before my father, who she feared might leave her to face a lonely widowhood, like her mother and grandmother before her. As a child I knew her to be a vibrant, caring, and fun-loving person. In midlife she seemed diminished by her years. Passing fifty frightened and unsettled her, as it does many people. Fifty, as Erica Jong recently put it, "is the time when time itself begins to seem short." For my mother it was both an awareness of less time and the idea of spending the last part of her life getting old that frightened her. As she entered her fifties, she saw only the prospect of aging. My parents lived with an old scenario for the second half of life. For one thing they did not anticipate a "life bonus" of any sort, as many of us can expect. And even if they had, they would have viewed it with mixed feelings. What might extra years offer? A lot more time to age. As they reached fifty my parents were preparing for a landing. They did not, I think, consider alternatives to usual aging. At that time, there did not seem to be any other options. In just thirty years, however, our life chances have changed dramatically.

The additional years that we can expect to extend our lifetimes are like winning the lottery. What will we do with this abundance? Newspapers recently reported on a fifty-three-year-old man who won $30 million yet kept his job as a garbage collector. When asked why he kept his job, he said that he needed to discover new ways to spend his time. Many of us now face that challenge, and many more will come to face it during the next twenty years. We have the chance to create a second half of life that is very different from what our parents or grandparents experienced. Instead of being diminished by time, our lives can become richer. It all depends on how we spend it.

When we look ahead we should perceive a vast, scarcely known region in the middle of our lives. This constitutes the third age, a new frontier with tremendous potential for growth. Our maps for adult life have not yet included this area. Experiencing midlife today is like reaching the top of a mountain, thinking we have finally achieved our goal, only to find on the horizon an enormous expanse of unknown terrain. For years we might have been expecting to reach the peak of our lives. Now, from the vantage point of increased longevity, we should see that there are more peaks for us to climb, if we choose to. This new third age frontier challenges us not only to go the full distance, but also to do so with style and a vital sense of purpose. I have more to say about this in Chapter 1 and in the afterword.

I discovered this human landscape with its amazing opportunities by tracking for twelve years individuals who chose to carve out unconventional paths in the middle period of their lives. The women and men who have shared their stories have been for me inspiring trail guides across the frontier of adult development. Although quite different from one another, and perhaps from you and me, they are alike in that they have not bought into the idea that growth comes to an end in midlife. All have been discovering hidden potential and initiating creative change. In their forties, fifties, sixties, and even seventies they have critiqued stereotypes of aging and explored new directions. The people you meet in this book are not exceptions to some supposed general rule of midlife crisis and decline. They show what is now possible within the middle stretch of our lives. In the new scenario that I will sketch out, the way forward does not go downhill.

The stories I share in the following chapters are not merely anecdotal. They are set within a theoretical framework that interprets the process I discovered and gives it meaning. This framework calls into question our previous assumptions about the second half of life, which until now has been subsumed under the heading middle age and aging. As I analyzed and reflected on their stories, I slowly began to see a new process at work. I have called this renewing process *second growth*. It explains how these people are reorganizing their lives to take advantage of a new option in the life course. If we come under the spell of aging, we will set aside ambition, anticipation, passion, idealism, and discovery. Based on what I have discovered in my research, I contend that we should not deny aging, but rather transform it with a new growth process.

You will learn from this book how second growth runs counter to the decline of usual aging, how it provides a new beginning with transforming power. Second growth differs from growth at an earlier age in that it is more complex, less predictable, and much more paradoxical. It is also more creative and better balanced. This renewing process is in fact filled with paradoxes—loss and gain, finishing and starting, reflection and risk taking, fear and optimism, liberation and attachment, caring for self and caring for others, growing older and growing young. As I have followed the lives of the people in this research project, I have learned how you and I can address these paradoxes by applying six principles. This book tells a different, more hopeful story of midlife than anything we are accustomed to. It will, I hope, help you become primed for the second half of life, ready to take off into a more fulfilling future.

Thinking about our future can be both enticing and unnerving. Our dilemma is that we face a new opportunity without appropriate knowledge or maps or role models to guide us. Even our vocabulary is inaccurate. Words from the old scenario get in our eyes, blinding us to what lies before us. We live on the boundary between the old and the new. Like citizens in the Old World, we hear vague reports about wonderful possibilities in new territory. We might feel that we do not know enough to be either confident or pessimistic. Should we really try something new in middle age? Should we risk living differently? Insights are needed and choices must be made. Growth beckons, but it is not inevitable. Old habits and narrow perspectives constrain us.

We may sense our potential to become a fulfilled, whole person in the second half of our lives only dimly and have trouble mustering the courage to alter our course. It is tempting to stay on familiar territory, to tread well-worn paths, or to relinquish ambition and just coast in retirement. The danger is that we could stagnate in this terrain and miss our opportunity, even though conditions are making it possible to redesign and enrich our lives. What will help us move ahead? Most likely it will be the examples of others who have been moving in new directions across this frontier, taking advantage of its opportunities by renewing their lives.

We will not find our alternatives to usual patterns and take off in new directions unless we first clear our minds of old ideas that program our feelings, attitudes, expectations, and behavior. We are all to some extent held prisoner by popular midlife myths. Many of us, for example, have assumed that midlife ultimately produces a distinct crisis. I have not found that to be true. We have also assumed that as we grow older, we shall feel lousy. That is due in part to media representations of aging; pharmaceutical companies, after all, invest fortunes to convince consumers that their products are needed. Most of the people I studied, however, are vitally healthy and enjoy life as much if not more than ever.

We might mistakenly assume that life after fifty calls for relinquishing what we enjoy. With a new perspective we can learn to create the results that we most desire. While some people think our lives should be stripped down and simplified, I see adults whose lives are unfolding in richer complexity. If we think of meaningful work occurring before fifty, then tapering off and stopping at retirement, we will want to explore the possibility of more meaningful work adding excitement and purpose to life after fifty. Instead of the stereotype that love and passion diminish, we should see the possibility of greater emotional richness and deeper relationships. Instead of cutting back and disengaging, we should consider adding value to our lives through greater engagement, expanded caring, and deeper connections. So many myths have blinded us to present and future possibilities. To take greater control of our futures we must dispel them.

The people I interviewed and whose lives I followed live more creatively than ever. We can follow them. Unlike individuals who try desperately to cling to a fading youth or who follow old patterns of what we now can call premature aging or who put off taking a new direction because they are unsure of what they really want, these adults have been thinking hard, changing perspective, and taking risks to initiate an extended period of new growth. They enjoy regeneration just when our assumptions would have them experience degeneration! I have been inspired by the way they are renewing their lives. I have written this book to share what I have learned from them about second growth in the third age, which promises to be the longest and best period in our lives.

This new scenario summons us to change our attitudes and how we think about our lives. It pushes us to rethink our plans, our values, our identities, and our purpose. It also points to new behaviors and relationships and to new possibilities for meaning, creativity, and service. A new scenario for the second half of your life, new ways of thinking, and new behaviors—these are what I hope this book will help you develop. We have so much more life to enjoy and so many more opportunities to develop hidden potential than our old assumptions, theories, and philosophies have dreamed of.

1

Making the Most of Your Thirty-Year Life Bonus

AN UNEXPECTED CHALLENGE

The lengthening life span of inhabitants of modern advanced industrial societies is both a challenge and a blessing. Our average life span has increased so tremendously that we are, in fact, experiencing a longevity revolution. Many people are living nearly twice as long as humans previously were expected to live. In eighteenth-century America, the average life span was barely forty. The Population Reference Bureau has described an unprecedented gain in average American life expectancy from 47.3 years in 1900 to 75.5 years in 1993. As we approach the twenty-first century, the average American life span is nearing eighty. In a few other countries it is already higher than that. The result of all this longevity is that many of us have something like a thirty-year life bonus.

It is not unrealistic now to think about living one hundred years or more. Dr. Walter Bortz of Palo Alto, California, who has specialized in vital aging, argues forcefully that we should plan on it. More and more adults already live a whole century. Between 1960 and 1996 the number of centenarians in America increased from 3,000 to over 55,000. In the next century millions will pass that milestone. Furthermore, Dr. Thomas Perls of the Harvard Medical School has found in his study of a select group of centenarians that, contrary to popular assumptions, the oldest of the old can lead active, independent, interesting lives until the very end. With more time ahead of us than we ever dreamed of, we have an unexpected opportunity to live vitally and purposefully for a whole century.

To respond to this longevity challenge, we need first of all to examine not only our goals and lifestyles but also our beliefs and attitudes toward becoming older. Even with good health and a pension a longer life span is a mixed blessing. Greater longevity has not been produced by a fountain of youth. More years could just mean that we have a lot more time to be old. Except for antiques and fine wine, the word *old* does not resonate with "value-added." In our youth-oriented society, being old has little going for it. Our challenge today is not primarily to stretch out our lives by adding more years. It is to learn how we can make the many more years that we can expect better.

The longevity revolution will have a tremendous impact on our society as well as on our personal lives. Social scientists now describe us as an aging society. Some 80 million Americans, nearly a third of the population, will soon be over fifty. This age wave is already starting to produce dramatic changes. Some forecasts of the aging society predict dire results. But the dismal forecasts we often read about are predicated on flawed assumptions about the second half of life. Alan Pifer, former chairman of the Carnegie Corporation Project on the Aging Society, has suggested that longevity gives us a new third quarter in our life span, which "should constitute a period of rebirth, with the awakening of new interests and enthusiasm for life, and new possibilities for being productive." Increased longevity presents us with both a personal and a social challenge: How can we tap our potential *and* increase social productivity? That is, how can we make the more years better not only for ourselves but also for our society? If we can find a way to respond to this more complex challenge creatively, not only will our personal lives be enriched, but the future scenario of our aging society can also take on an entirely different, brighter character.

THE NEED FOR A NEW MODEL

When considering the prospects of living longer, we should recognize that we are handicapped by what we have learned about "growing old" from previous generations. Our inherited beliefs about aging do not fit well with the possibilities in our future. A conventional paradigm of the life course and aging, with its assumptions and negative attitudes, can be illustrated graphically by a sigmoid curve:

After a brief dip in the learning curve during early adaptation to life, assuming an absence of catastrophes and disabilities, a person progresses towards a peak near the middle of life, reaches a plateau, and eventually begins a gradual descent. The poet T. S. Eliot at age seventy expressed a conventional view of the second half of life in unconventionally blunt terms: "I don't believe one grows older. I think that what happens early on in life is that at a certain age one stands still and stagnates." From this perspective our prime occurs in the first half of life. If we hold on to this view, then with a longer life span we can expect to spend a lot more time stagnating than did previous generations.

In the old model the second half of life also arrived sooner than it does now. Just fifty years ago middle age was thought to begin around thirty to thirty-five, as growth was seen to taper off. Now middle age seems to start somewhere in the forties. Yet even though our life span has expanded, the second half of life is still commonly perceived to be an unwelcome era inevitably marked by endings, loss, and decline. In his influential text, Dr. Theodore Lidz, former chair of psychiatry at Yale University, wrote about people in their forties:

> Middle age is initiated by awareness that the peak years of life are passing. A person realizes that he is no longer starting on his way, his direction is usually well set, and his activities will determine how far he will get. . . . The middle-aged individual becomes aware that ill health and even death are potentialities that hover over him.

About the same time Lidz articulated this view in the 1960s, the idea of a midlife crisis floated through the media and was often accepted as gospel. In our society middle age has rarely been appealing; it is usually perceived as a short transition from the prime of adulthood into a downhill process of aging.

Getting older has commonly been associated with five deadly *D* words: *decline, disease, dependency, depression,* and *decrepitude.* After these, of course, comes the sixth dreaded *D* word, which marks the end of the line. Everyday speech about the second half tells it all: we've "passed our prime"; we're "over the hill." In spite of all the "golden" rhetoric about life after fifty, middle age and aging have been generally viewed as "downers." Most of us are held hostage by the mystique of aging.

It is time to trade in our old model for a new one. My research has convinced me that we have the chance to transform the second half of life. It can be richer, more vibrant, and more meaningful—as well as much longer—than we have so far anticipated. If we hold on to old perspectives and assumptions we will miss that opportunity. But if we learn to take advantage of our life bonus, we can design our future so that it is characterized by vital *R* words such as *renewal, rebirth, regeneration, revitalization,* and *rejuvenation.*

NEW DISCOVERIES ABOUT ADULT OPTIONS AND AGING

Increasing numbers of psychologists, sociologists, anthropologists, gerontologists, and medical researchers have been finding that the usual patterns of midlife and aging in the old model are neither normal nor inevitable. Alternatives exist that most of us have not yet seriously considered. During a research project that stretched out over twelve years, I discovered how we can unleash our human potential for the second half of life.

Near the start of this research, I interviewed in the same month two middle-aged men who might seem to fit a recognized pattern of normal, healthy adaptation. Both of them at that time were businessmen. Their marriages were reported to be happy. Both had grown children, and one had grandchildren. Both had experienced peaks. They saw their lives as successful in many ways, particularly in work, love, and financial security. Neither had experienced midlife crises, health problems, or the feelings of stagnation and depression often mentioned in literature about middle age. Both exhibited traits of healthy maturity: strong on control, self-confidence, a sense of humor, and rewarding personal relationships. One difference between them was age—one is fourteen years older than the other. Another marked difference between these men, whom I will call Paul and John, is reflected in their outlooks and lifestyles. Do their ages explain this difference, as our conventional assumptions would predict?

Paul

Q: How do you feel about yourself at this time?

A: This is a great period in my life. All periods have been good, but the best is still to come. Life is getting better. I anticipate making some changes.

Q: Do you plan to retire?

A: No. But I do plan to develop my career in a different way. I have a good friend who used to be a workaholic, who has been talking with me about designing a lifestyle that will enable me to tap other aspects of my personality and spend more time with my family. In a few years I expect to make some changes.

Q: As people reach the midpoint of their lives, they become conscious of their mortality. How has awareness of your own mortality affected your life?

A: I know I have an end; but that makes me want to finish up what I'm doing and get on with the next phase of my life. There might be an accident or a stroke, so I am eager to get on with my life. I'm afraid of missing out, but deep down I think I have a lot of time left.

Q: How would you describe your marriage and family life?

A: We're a close family. My wife spends a lot of time at home, especially with our younger children. During the week my time is pretty much taken up with work. After a hard week, I need some time to be alone. I've learned that to be really giving in relationships to the family, I need some time by myself. I often take off Friday night to spend time alone on the shore or in the woods. On Saturday morning my family joins me, and we spend the weekend together. My wife is supportive of my need to be independent, though she tends to be more dependent. We're a close couple and still enjoy sex after years of marriage. I look forward to our upcoming vacation. She tends to get all wrapped up in children, and I like to have time with her when she is freed up to be more spontaneous.

Q: You have mentioned how important it is to be caring about your family. How do you take care of yourself?

A: I'm an active person and have learned it's important to be physically active, especially to work off tensions from work. I skip lunch to work out in our company's exercise room, and I spend as much time out-of-doors as possible—kayaking, hiking, playing tennis, and swimming. I'm more organized now to make sure there's time for me. I am careful about diet, especially since I learned I had a high cholesterol count. I don't smoke and drink only a little, mostly beer with my older kids or friends.

John

Q: How do you feel about yourself at this time in your life?

A: I feel good about myself right now. In some ways this is the best time, especially in terms of stability and financial security. I'm not "running for sheriff" as much as I used to; I'm more relaxed. I made a major change, leaving the company after more than twenty years. That was like separating from a parent. My new position is a good one, and I might soon move up to head of operations in the plant; but that isn't so important anymore.

Q: Do you plan to retire?

A: Sometimes I think about retiring. But really I've had the feeling that I won't live to see a pension. I just live from day to day.

Q: How has awareness of your own mortality affected your life?

A: The thought of death doesn't really affect me, except to be concerned about financial security. My children are grown and independent, so I am mostly concerned about my wife. She talks about retiring and moving up to Vermont, but that doesn't appeal to me. You can't even get television in some of those areas.

Q: How would you describe your marriage and family life?

A: We have a good relationship. When I was younger, I put in ungodly hours at work. Those were years where I often put in over seventy hours a week. It was hard on her and the kids. I used to tell myself there's a grander purpose being served, and it's good for you. I have a more intelligent balance now. I don't put in so much time, so I have more to spend with my wife. We work around the yard, and she drags me shopping. We eat out a lot. Often on weekends we look for antiques; that's a new interest. We still enjoy sex, though that's less important than it used to be—I'm less interested than I was when I was younger.

Q: How do you take care of yourself?

A: I do absolutely nothing to take care of myself. I don't exercise and was never into sports. I can't get myself motivated to exercise, even though I've got a growing paunch that bothers me a little. I probably eat fewer sweets and less meat; I've learned to like salads. That should help to keep the weight off, but I don't see any results yet. I still smoke a pack of cigarettes a day and drink occasionally. I'm slowing down, making life simpler. I have just about all I need, so I think I'm living a more balanced, easier life. I'm satisfied.

These two interviews might seem to support the conventional view about a supposedly natural life structure and progression of middle age. Paul is still energetic, with bold dreams and aspirations, taking charge of his life and preparing to move in new directions, thinking young and taking passionate interest in many different activities. Although he has reached one peak, "the best is still to come." John fits the stereotype of a man about to enter the later part of middle age: having reached a peak, he is slowing down, seeking simplicity and security, is less energetic and passionate, more complacent and stoic about what life still has to offer. With what you know so far, you might think that their different perspectives and experiences can be explained by age.

What challenges our assumptions is this startling fact: at the time of these interviews Paul was fifty-eight years old, and John was only forty-four! The younger John fits the old mold; the older Paul is breaking it. Surprising discoveries like this caused me to question conventional assumptions about what it means to get older. As I encountered a number of men and women like Paul, I started to explore their lives more deeply.

After interviewing about two hundred people in their late forties and fifties, I realized that some of them, like Paul, manifested qualities of exceptional growth just at the time we should expect degeneration. They were changing the way they lived and how they experienced aging. I chose to focus on them and began to ask, What is happening in their lives? What terms can I use to describe this phenomenon appropriately? At first, I saw a few salient characteristics; but I was not sure I was seeing anything but anomalies, exceptions to a general rule. I started to compile a list of traits and soon had over twenty of them. Yet I still did not know quite what to make of my discoveries. I wrote several chapters to see if I could clarify my thoughts; but clear insights would not jell. I was still trapped in the old paradigm. Eventually, I returned to the growing pile of interview transcripts and did a quantitative analysis. That helped me discover a real-life pattern outside the conventional adult development model. It also reinforced my hunch that I had found an alternative to usual midlife patterns, one that could be a model for the rest of us. I decided to get back in touch with about thirty individuals to learn how their lives were unfolding. I later enlarged the pool, adding people from different regions and countries as well as individuals in their sixties and seventies.

By tracking adults like Paul for over a decade, I at last came to see much more clearly what this alternative to ordinary middle-aging involves. Paul symbolizes an emerging potential within most of us. John, on the other hand, symbolizes the usual pattern of adult life described by Lidz—cresting in the forties before subsiding into an expected decline of aging. He represents an option we might follow. One reason John stalled was because his role models came from his past. In his midforties he already saw himself becoming more like his father, who died before reaching sixty. He told me he sometimes saw his father when he looked in the mirror and felt him in his stride. He saw life offering him fewer significant parts to play. As he put it, "I'm not running for sheriff as much as I used to." A major concern was for financial security. His ideas and attitudes directed him down a well-worn path. Paul carved out a different direction. He consciously decided not to follow the pattern of his parents and their generation. During his fifties he thoughtfully worked at building a different model, one that supported a positive change of direction and renewal.

As we face our futures, we could go either way. We now have a choice because the longevity revolution has provided us with what Europeans call our third age, a new period in our lives stretching from the late forties to age eighty. As I shall explain later, it contains hidden potential previous generations did not have. Not everybody believes we have this potential. Even psychology is divided. Some psychologists, like the late Swiss psychotherapist C. G. Jung, have agreed with the words of Robert Browning's character, Rabbi Ben Ezra:

> Grow old along with me!
> The Best is yet to be,
> The last of life, for which the first was made.

In this view our prime occurs in the second, not the first, half of life. However, the American psychologist B. F. Skinner asserted that Rabbi Ben Ezra was wrong; to expect that the best is yet to be would be a great mistake. On this point I side with Jung. There is now substantial research to support Browning's Rabbi, at least in terms of the possibility. If I am right, we need a whole new scenario for adult life, one that is open to creativity for the second half of life and aware of our growth potential in a new historical situation. And we need reliable insights to guide us in making this scenario a reality. Of one thing there is little doubt: if we hang on to old expectations, we are more likely than not to live down to them.

THE ALTERNATIVE TO MIDDLE-AGING: SECOND GROWTH

When you think about age, what does it mean to reach fifty or sixty or seventy? What does being any age mean? Do numbers tell the story? Are developmental experiences predictable? Are the depressing *D* words programmed into our DNA? Is biology destiny? Not quite! We know from natural science how powerful our genetic makeup is. Yet adult life is influenced, not controlled, by a biological clock. Chronological age does not predict what adults in the middle of life experience nor how they live. Culture, thought, experience, history, and individual initiative intervene. We have much more plasticity than we might previously have assumed.

Five years after the interview I just reported, Paul told me that his life was "sensational," better than ever. He had left the corporate world to start a variety of new projects and construct a different lifestyle. One of his role models was a vibrant eighty-year-old. Paul told me, "I want to be like that when I grow up!" At sixty-five he wrote that he was continuing on a path of renewal and self-actualization. "This is a fascinating and fulfilling trail," he reported, "and I'm having the time of my life." Paul has been stretching the boundaries of the prime of life well past conventional limits. I suspect he will continue to do so indefinitely.

Entering the second half of life is like being a farmer who discovers that his growing season has been extended by unforeseen conditions. Just imagine his surprise when he learns that changing circumstances have provided him for the first time an opportunity to grow a second crop. Until now, even with the help of science and technology, no matter how hard he worked he could still plant and harvest just once a year. Were he to maintain the conventional assumption of one crop per season, he would waste the potential provided by changes in his environment.

If we concentrate only on living longer, we are likely to find just more time in which to go to seed. Like our hypothetical farmer, we have the unexpected chance for second growth. That will not happen by just continuing what we have already done. We need to initiate a new process that will transform greater quantity of life and make the added years of our life better than ever. Our first task in midlife is to break away from the conventional perspective in order to renew our lives.

As I listened to this select group of adults, studied the transcripts of interviews, and reflected on their experiences and my own, I understood that I was witnessing not just a new growing season but a new form of growth. I have called it *second growth*, because it differs from the earlier growth we experienced as children and young adults. It is more complex and moves at a deeper level. Growth in the early years usually occurs in a linear fashion, moving sequentially, step by step, stage to stage. Some writers have even mapped out the adult life course as a series of steps. A result of this linear growth is increased attainments that are relatively easy to see and measure. Second growth operates differently; it is nonlinear and has distinctive principles that yield richer consequences. It actualizes our potential for personal complexity, which is easily overlooked and hard to measure.

The principles of second growth will enable us to reorganize the second half of our lives. As young adults we constructed our personal worlds using a variety of organizing principles: for example, careers, health, sports, looks, sex, friendships, personal identity, education, recognition, religion, belonging, love, and family. For some people one intention, such as success in work, becomes a dominating principle. Others struggle to balance several competing principles, such as careers, family, and service. Yet in the middle of life, regardless of gains made, many accomplishments are threatened by change and loss. Previous organizing principles are often retired to memories and photo albums as development seems to level off and even reverse. In this common scenario the disorganizing principle of aging sets in.

Unless met by a counterforce, aging overtakes previous growth principles. If we consider aging as a form of entropy, the natural principle of disintegration, then second growth represents a counterforce that resists entropy. It can retard and transform aging just when growth principles of young adulthood are challenged by decline, stagnation, and disorder. To counter aging we must do more than adapt, keep fit, and stay healthy. We need to initiate growth at a new level. That is a primary lesson I have learned from the people in this study.

A new scenario requires an image different from the single sigmoid curve. The English business writer Charles Handy has used two overlapping sigmoid curves to describe the developmental process of organizations that creatively address change. This model of overlapping sigmoid curves can also illustrate the alternative of second growth:

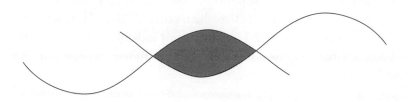

Ideally, second growth emerges before first growth has run its course; but as some individuals in my study showed, it is possible to start the process later. What matters is using our creative capacities to renew our lives and move in a new direction.

In the overlapping-curves model we see an individual initiating a new direction before reaching his or her peak. The ordinary descent expected in the second half is altered by the new upward curve. The shaded portion represents a period of creative uncertainty. In this situation an individual may feel torn by conflicting feelings—pride in accomplishment yet longing to go another way, achievement yet loss, satisfaction yet fear, confidence yet doubt, resignation yet hope. This new model suggests that our experience of uncertainty and conflict can lead us to discover new possibilities and options.

The second trajectory also contains a learning curve, descending through mistakes, trial, and error before rising toward a new peak. It would be wrong to assume that this renewing growth occurs painlessly, instantly, and steadily. This process involves ups and downs, twists and turns, fears and hope, bold initiatives and the cessation of initiatives; it is filled with paradoxes. Life along the second curve is often unsettling because it starts to move toward new goals before previous goals have been reached. As the second curve bends in a new direction, it does so by maintaining elements of the first curve, using them to set and fuel a new course.

One woman who has so clearly illustrated this new trajectory in second growth for me is Daphne, whom you will meet in Chapter 8. When I met her, she was starting her seventies, flourishing in a healthy, vital life filled with accomplishments, close relationships, new learning and interests, creativity, adventure, and meaningful service. Seven years later I noticed that although she had slowed down a bit, she was still blossoming. She often says that she is in the best period of her life. When I asked if she had always been so alive and productive, she replied, "Oh, no. I was very much stuck in my forties. But when I was fifty I just took off." Like the others in this book, she has consciously renewed her life, moving in new directions to reach new peaks.

SIX PARADOXICAL PRINCIPLES OF SECOND GROWTH

Second growth adds value to our lives just when we think we might be losing it. As we shall see in the following chapters it develops our hidden potential for human complexity. Part of the richness in this growth comes from developing new interests, talents, and different aspects of our intellectual capacity, such as emotional, interpersonal, and creative intelligence. As I reflected on the experiences of the people in this study, I discovered that much of the increase in complexity also comes from polar intentions that pull individuals in different directions at the same time. These polar intentions shape the paradoxical principles of second growth. Unlike the conventional linear model, the way forward into midlife renewal moves through paradox.

The notion of paradox has not figured prominently in the Western philosophy of life, which has tended to view life in linear terms. Like the classical concept of drama, life has a beginning, a middle, and an end. We think of before and after, of first and then second, of starting at one time and finishing later. An Eastern perspective sees life differently. I have found its appreciation of paradoxes in the life process very helpful when trying to understand our challenge in midlife. For example, the symbol representing the Chinese principles of yin and yang suggests that we integrate and balance two opposing forces, feminine and masculine, within the development of our personal identity. When addressing a challenge, the Chinese character suggests that we see in it both danger and opportunity. This ancient wisdom of paradox is actually in tune with advances in scientific understanding.

We are beginning to see paradoxes everywhere. In fact, they exist in the very fabric of reality. For example, we used to think that the shortest distance between two points was always a straight line; but the theory of relativity has shown that in the cosmos, because of the time factor, the shortest distance actually is a curved line. Similarly, the evolutionary process was thought to be a gradual, linear development; but now we see evidence that the cosmos, the earth, and life also evolve by exploding and contracting. The astronomer Martin Rees has described how our evolving universe has been governed by paradoxical principles such as gravitation and repulsion, diversity and homogeneity, structure and chaos. A modern worldview embraces both order and chaos, predictability and indeterminacy. These paradoxes do not constitute a problem to be solved. They suggest the nature of reality that must be understood and accepted.

Human life also needs the lens of paradox to appreciate its full reality. That is not a radically new idea. Religion has suggested this. To save your own life, you must first be willing to lose it. The first will be last, the last will be first, and the meek will inherit the earth. To receive love, we must first give it. To become happy, we must concentrate on the happiness of others. To discover the divine, we must focus on earth and our neighbors. Philosophy has also espoused paradox. Wisdom begins in recognizing our ignorance. Greatness lies in knowing and accepting our limits.

In today's upside-down world, even business is discovering paradoxes. For example, we have conventionally seen success in careers as golden; yet we know that it can have a dark side. Many people succeed in careers but lose in life. The challenge is to find balance. In developing organizations some leaders find that the surest road to profit is to concentrate on something else, such as total quality, customer service, and social responsibility. To meet growth goals, some companies are learning to grow bigger by getting smaller through outsourcing, technology, and employee empowerment. A new perspective for managers and leaders has emphasized the need to develop paradoxical thinking to manage the complexities and apparent contradictions shaping the workplace. Great leaders are finding that to increase power, they must learn to give it away. Successful leadership in business increasingly demands recognizing that we live in an age of paradox and then adapting accordingly.

Similarly success in the second half of life demands that we recognize and address paradoxical issues emerging in the core of our lives. As I listened to adults who manifested unexpected growth, at first I thought I heard contradictions; then I sensed that as they talked about their experiences, they were enunciating polarities, as though they were temporarily caught between opposites. I imagined their goal might be to resolve these polarities like puzzles or problems. Only as I reflected on the ongoing pattern of their development did I see paradoxes as the core of their reality. After an analysis of transcripts, I was able to reduce a confusing list of traits and identify six paradoxical principles. While there may be others, I focused on six that have consistently emerged from the lives I have studied. I did not expect to find this particular pattern, nor have I seen it in other materials.

Besides their demonstration of a capacity for vital new growth as an alternative to usual patterns of aging, the next most important lesson I learned from them lies in the six principles that emerged as they responded to and organized key paradoxes within their lives. These principles constitute the way of midlife renewal. You might think of these paradoxical principles, which are listed below, as second growth steps:

- balancing mindful reflection and risk taking
- developing realistic optimism

- creating a positive midlife identity—growing older/growing young
- balancing greater personal freedom with deeper, more intimate relationships
- creating more meaningful work and more play
- caring for self but also for others and for the earth

We shall explore each of these paradoxical principles individually in the following chapters. I will show how selected individuals learned to balance opposing tendencies rather than going toward a single goal. As I followed them for over a decade, I also saw how their lives became richer as they addressed one paradox after another.

You can see an example of the paradoxical principle of balancing freedom with intimacy in that portion of Paul's interview provided earlier in this chapter, when he described a regimen he developed during his fifties. His meaning comes from what he gives others, he told me. But he learned that to be really giving in relationships, he needed to be more organized, "to make sure there's time for me." As I listened to Paul tell his story, I was reminded of the paradox of freedom and relationship in the writings of philosopher Martin Buber, who insisted on the primacy of relationship in personal life. Buber suggested that to strengthen the quality and truthfulness of our intimate relationships, we sometimes need to set aside time to withdraw and be solitary. To be supportive of loved ones, Paul felt that he had to have special times by himself. At the end of a demanding week at work, he regularly went off on Friday evenings to camp alone. He deliberately chose time by himself not only to release tension and foster healthy independence threatened by heavy corporate responsibilities, but also to build a closer connection with his wife and children.

Midlife renewal through second growth evolves as we address these six paradoxical intentions. To choose just one intention without the other one will develop only half a self. The steps of this growth are generated by creative uncertainty, which often fuels significant learning and transformation. The process begins with searching, imaginative, critical reflection. I agree in part with authors who have emphasized the need to increase our self-awareness. We need to wake up to grow. Mindful reflection is a beginning. But then we must also experiment and take risks. Balancing reflection with risk taking forms the first principle or growth step. Most of us also need to become more optimistic; but our optimism must be balanced with realism. These two paradoxical principles underlie the others. Another major challenge in midlife is to redefine our personal identity. As our situations change, we cannot remain tied to the roles and traits that have served us in the past. We need to tap other aspects of our personalities. To build positive personal identities involves learning to cultivate emotional and intellectual reservoirs and also accepting our aging while at the same time learning to grow young.

These principles take us more deeply into the core of our personalities, but they also lead us outward. This growth is not just inward bound. After all, there are personal and practical realities to be addressed. In moving forward, we need to pay attention to tasks such as work and play, caring for others and for self, deeper intimate relationships and extended social involvement. These six paradoxical principles provide us with a foundation for renewal, meaning, wisdom, and integrity.

Leveraging the whole process of second growth is an underlying principle of *creative balance*, which integrates paradoxical intentions and prevents us from being pulled off course. This principle, like that of paradox, has also been recognized in ancient wisdom as fundamental to life and growth. Several years ago at an Earth Day liturgy, I heard a beautiful tale from Jewish folklore that recognizes a cosmic dimension of creative balance: Long ago the sun was having a dispute with the clouds about who was preeminent in caring for their offspring, earth. The sun said to the rain clouds, "I am most important and powerful. With my fire I can dry up your waters and make you vanish. Water is no threat to me." The clouds replied, "You underestimate the power of water, which can put out all fires. Not only that. We can prevent you from ever seeing earth again. There are so many of us that we can join together to hide earth from your sight forever. We will have earth all to ourselves." But then these two mighty and opposing forces came to their senses. Sun realized that if he dried up all the water, earth would become a lifeless planet. The clouds realized that if they hid earth from the fire of the sun, earth would die. So these eternal opposites, fire and water, agreed to share preeminence and to balance their powers for the sake of earth. Because fire and water achieve balance in caring for their offspring, earth is beautiful and life abounds. Wisdom recognizes the generative power of balancing seemingly opposing forces.

THE DAWN OF A THIRD AGE

As we think about the future, we are handicapped not only by a failure to appreciate paradoxes and new possibilities, but by the baggage of words forged in the past. Terms like *middle age, aging,* and even *life stages* imply old-paradigm assumptions that can become self-fulfilling prophecies of decline. We need new ideas and a different vocabulary to account for our future possibilities. Europeans have recently been talking about the life course as divided into four ages. The first age is for learning, the second age for work and family, the third age for living, and the fourth age for aging. Of course, learning, work, and family are important for all ages. This formulation is not entirely satisfactory. But it can be helpful. The really new element in this scheme is the third age. As I mentioned before, this term refers to a new middle period generated by the longevity revolution. I believe it is a helpful concept to think afresh about our option for midlife renewal.

Previous generations did not have a third age. Our fathers and grandfathers worked as long as they could. If they were lucky, they had a short retirement before they died. When the German chancellor Otto von Bismarck established sixty-five as a retirement age, he did so on the assumption that nearly everyone entitled to a pension would die before then. Although times have changed, most of us are unprepared for the third age. Peter Laslett, a retired English demographer, has argued that in mapping out our lives, most of us have drawn the boundaries within them badly. We have, in fact, failed to map out what should be the largest portion. The new opportunity facing adults today is a *fulfilling* third age. Before the fourth age of "decrepitude and decline," adults should create a fresh map of life in which self-actualization after fifty becomes a new norm. Unfortunately, the idea of a fulfilling third age does not yet show up on the life maps of most people.

Our life maps are like world maps used before Columbus sailed, with no acknowledgment of a "new world" lying between Europe and Asia. The map that most of us have unconsciously drawn has a dark middle area defined by the dreadful *D* words. Now, however, we can draw a new map that contains a meaningful middle period. Within it lies our potential, which is defined by *R* words that resonate with the excitement of renewal. At this point in history, we have reached a watershed in adult development. The third age sets the stage, representing an unparalleled opportunity to initiate new growth. What prevents us from stepping boldly across that stage to make the most of our thirty-year life bonus?

SHREDDING OLD SCRIPTS THAT
BLOCK SECOND GROWTH

Different circumstances can promote but not cause healthy change. It takes a conscious effort to design and develop a new map for vital, creative renewal after fifty. Even if we sense the potential for new growth, most of us are very uncertain about how best to design our futures. We may sense that the way forward has serious obstacles. That is not so surprising. In addition to inherited notions about aging, we live in a world that puts "being young" at the top of a hierarchy of values. As the world mourned the death of Lady Diana, the Princess of Wales, one astute commentator suggested that the world's grief could in part be explained because she symbolized youth wedded to beauty. Her death marked both a tragic loss of a person and devastating damage to one of our most cherished symbols, that of youth and beauty. In a youth-oriented society, age is a deficit. Trying to locate prime time in the second half seems like the ultimate oxymoron.

Compounding a pejorative perspective, we have inherited what social scientists call an age norm. An age norm is a cultural fact, not a biological one. But especially in middle age it can feel like a biological fact and have equivalent consequences. When we are tempted to try something new, we might hear a faint voice deep within our consciousness that says, "You're too old for that. You had better not even think about it. Act your age! Find something else to do." Such thinking obviously can diminish the possibility for creative change.

Age norms were embedded long before our third age arrived. They pervade our society. Just a quarter of a century ago a national survey indicated that Americans viewed the best times for nearly everything important as occurring under the age of fifty. Though men and women differed slightly in the ages they named, there was a general consensus about best times. The range was between the early twenties and the late forties. Fifty was then an accepted standard for entering decline and settling for less. For many it still is. The big five-oh signifies to many individuals that it is time to board up their lives in preparation for the long winter of aging. The psychologist Ellen Langer has suggested that one reason people experience aging as decline is that they "have been taught to grow old inadequately." Growth is often "blocked by premature cognitive commitments about old age that [they] make in their youth." Age norms can act like photographs of information that freeze action and development.

How can we overcome our cultural bias? We might learn from women's discovery thirty years ago that traditional sex roles are artificial. Age norms are as artificial as gender stereotypes. Both age and gender norms are cultural artifacts, not genetic givens. As women have critiqued and redefined sex roles more appropriate to the realities of modern life, so all of us can challenge midlife age norms and free ourselves from their formative influence. I see the age norms that we have internalized as old scripts that both freeze our behavior and provide misinformation about how to age. Perhaps we need to start a campaign to promote "aging liberation" and commence shredding these old scripts that block new growth. Throughout this book I will show how a variety of creative men and women have stepped boldly onto the new stage and increased the quality of their lives. The third age sets the stage for renewal; the six principles of second growth generate it.

HOW LONG CAN THIS GO ON?

Although I first focused on people in their late forties and fifties, I have seen second growth continuing in the lives of people in their sixties and seventies. An eighty-year-old who has been both a mentor and a role model to me summed up our conversation about this topic in a memorable epigram: "You don't grow old. You get old when you stop growing." His renewal in his sixties and running through his seventies left those of us thirty years younger breathless. He and the oldest members in my study have shown how it is possible to experience and sustain renewal well beyond the conventional boundaries of old age. As the two overlapping sigmoid curves of our model for second growth would suggest, most of them got started on a new direction well before reaching sixty. But a few, like Irene, initiated a new spurt of second growth in her sixties.

Seventy-six when I met her, Irene has been an inspiration and role model for hundreds of students enrolled in an adult-education program for elders. For most of her adult life, she was a wife, mother, and teacher. When she was sixty her husband, a school principal, became seriously ill. Both of them retired and she devoted her life then to caring for him. When he died a few years later, she was devastated. What was she to do? Well into her sixties, she could have withdrawn quietly into comfortable retirement. Somewhat to her own surprise, she took another route.

She returned to education as part of an experimental program for adults at a local college and became involved in several learning programs. Responding to the challenges of new learning and self-discovery, she blossomed. As she turned seventy, the program was flourishing and needed a president. She did a great deal of soul searching and reflection before she risked taking on the executive responsibilities of an innovative college program. Six years later, having been a great success in that role, she was beginning to think about retiring again.

In addition to her challenging new work, she has made new friends and has participated regularly in community and cultural events. She has developed her potential complexity in many ways. She has filled her life with new learning and interests, lifestyle changes, work, and friendships. She continues to nurture her musical talent. At the time we met, she would join her one-hundred-year-old mother and two other friends once a week to play chamber music. Realizing in her sixties that she had much more life to live, she was determined to live it to the fullest.

Irene told me she had been reluctant to be interviewed for this project, but her friends persuaded her. "One friend said, 'Irene, by all means be interviewed. You show what's possible.'" Her friend's comment captures the intention of this book: to show what is now possible in the third age. Irene specifically illustrates how second growth can occur through one's sixties and seventies and how it can transform the aging process. In her late seventies Irene was beginning to sense that she was on the verge of aging. As she approached eighty, she felt that she was turning the corner of a new middle age to become a young-old citizen. As she has broken the conventional image of the middle years, she will undoubtedly be a model of successful aging in her fourth age.

Irene's growth also shows something else. It extends beyond herself. Her friends and her community have benefited immensely from the increased richness of her personal life, which has been more, not less, invested in public activities. Like others in this study, she has expanded her capacity to care and be helpful. Creative people like Irene point to new possibilities for both adult personal growth and a healthier, happier, more responsible and socially productive aging society in the twenty-first century.

Until now, the cause of personal growth has not pointed to a renewal of society. Twenty years ago, the culture of personal growth got a bad name because in its apparent self-centeredness it seemed to ignore the needs of community. Second growth is different! As one of the men in this study put it, "My purpose is to become the person I am and to share." As he grows, sharing and contributing to others become increasingly important; his community has benefited because of his personal renewal. He, Irene, and the others whose lives I have studied symbolize a new potential for building a better society. As we shall see, this renewal adds value not only to their personal lives but also to their communities, because it involves balancing a proper self-centeredness with caring and responsibility.

If we learn to promote the principles of growth described in this book, society and individuals will benefit. The lives I have studied have shown me not only how to realize personal potential but also how to make meaningful contributions to a variety of good causes. Their growth benefits their families, friends, institutions, communities, and our natural environment. The good news from my research in adult life is a story of change and discovery, of extended personal renewal and social enhancement, of greater sharing and hope.

2
Principle One: Balancing Mindful Reflection and Risk Taking

In America I have forgotten my age. I feel like I'm getting my youth back.
—Professor Lin, while on sabbatical

THE SURPRISING APPEARANCE OF SECOND GROWTH

During the past twelve years, as I have tried to see more clearly just what second growth is like and how it starts, I have had the opportunity to watch it emerge at close range. In 1988 several Chinese educators arrived to spend a year as part of an exchange program at the university where I was then serving. After a few months I became intrigued by the senior professor, whose appearance and demeanor were changing. I wanted to interview her because she was manifesting the kind of growth I had been trying to understand. As she shared her story, I learned that during her sabbatical she had been experiencing changes that she would not have dreamed possible. Her experience provides a window into the initial phase of second growth.

Professor Lin was fifty-six, married with two sons, and a teacher of English at a university in China. When we first met, I had guessed her to be close to sixty. Gradually, I noticed inhibitions fading as her serious composure was broken by a sparkling smile and an infectious laugh. After six months I sat in on her class in Chinese language and culture and observed a dynamic teacher briskly moving around the classroom, keeping up a lively dialogue with all of the students, and encouraging their learning with open-mindedness and humor. Strangely enough, she seemed to be growing younger.

In one interview she described her life in China and how it compared with the changes she was experiencing on sabbatical. As a teenager she had been devoted to the Communist Party and its promise of revolutionary change. She saw her life then in terms of a noble and exciting sacrifice; everything was for the party. Her twenties were the high point of her life. She completed a graduate program in Russian and in advanced studies in science. By the time she was thirty, she had a career in publishing that combined her expertise in science and Russian. At thirty-one she married a scientist and within the next few years they had two sons. Then, in her late thirties, her career was crushed by the Cultural Revolution. Academics and intellectuals were out; for over ten years it was a crime, she told me, even to read a book. Her life during that period was extremely harsh; many of her friends died.

Positive changes in China allowed her to resume a position in the university, but as a teacher of English. How did she see herself at the time I met her? Her response was tinged with remorse:

> I've been getting older, and I sense my abilities fading. Good times are returning to China, particularly for those in universities. But I'm too old, and I regret that I didn't have the chance to develop when I was younger. For over ten years I lost an important part of my life. I love to learn, but there was no opportunity. When the Cultural Revolution was over, I felt it was too late to embark on an important academic career. We envy the younger generation.

In this response she portrays herself as an aging woman who sees herself in decline, too old for promising development. Quite understandably her adverse social situation as well as her disappointments had had a negative impact. Social and psychological forces had been pushing her down. She felt that the best part of her life had been stolen from her; it seemed to be too late to make a fresh start.

But another side of her personality emerged in response to other questions, a side that I had detected as I saw her walking briskly around campus, engaging in animated conversations as well as teaching and managing her affairs with youthful vitality and enthusiasm. Instead of withering, she seemed to be blossoming.

What was she learning about herself on this sabbatical? How had her experiences in America been affecting her life? She told me that "many people my age are starting to plan for retirement. I don't want to do that now. I would like to continue working." She felt that she was recovering a sense of vitality and felt in better health.

She made an observation that I sensed was particularly significant:

> While I have been in America I have forgotten my age. If I were in China, there would be so many things that would remind me of my age. Here, nothing reminds me of how old I am. The secretary even refers to us as "girls." My life here has allowed me to study as much as I want, to learn, to communicate openly with many people, and to wear what I want.

She was beginning to experience greater personal freedom and with that a new sense of herself. She was learning about her potential for a fresh start in middle age. She was forgetting her age and letting go of an old self-image. As we talked, I witnessed her making a conscious critique of her old script, which had been imposed by cultural standards. Recently, she was learning to think of herself and her age in more individual terms. As she reflected on desirable possibilities, she began to move onto a second curve of new growth. She was renewing her personal world by embracing several paradoxical challenges.

Professor Lin was both experiencing rejuvenation and accepting her aging. I could see a youthfulness in her face, her movements, and her appearance. She began to dress in colorful blouses and fashionable skirts, far different from the drab outfit she wore when she arrived. The outward change reflected an inner transformation and the creation of a more positive identity. "In China, I would not wear bright colors like this. Here, older people can wear colorful clothing, but in China people my age wear only gray, brown, or blue." Her sabbatical had provided an unexpected challenge. She found in it an opportunity to discover new possibilities about herself, to reject her old scripts, and to change her perspective and her lifestyle. Contrary to her own conventional expectations, she was initiating unexpected growth at fifty-six.

This was a fascinating discovery for her and for me. How did this new growth feel and what did it mean to her? She explained:

I feel like I am getting my youth back. Here, I look younger, feel younger. I'm starting to become more courageous. I used to fear making mistakes. Now I am taking more risks. Coming here was a risk. When I return I cannot imagine retiring, staying home, and giving up on vigorous activities. Hard work stimulates a person—at least it does for me. I am becoming more open— more open with people and to possibilities for myself. I'm more optimistic and feel much more in control of my life than I did ten years ago. My goal when I go home is to continue what I've started here.

She seemed committed to renewal through new growth at a time when she had thought she was too old for it. She would continue this growth process, she told me, even though she would encounter considerable resistance. She was determined to strive for more quality in her life when she returned home.

GETTING STARTED

What can we see in Professor Lin's experience? Halfway through her sabbatical, she had two different views about herself and her life chances. The first was that of an aging woman who regarded herself as too old for new opportunities. She thought of accommodating herself to decline and operating on a reduced level. The second view was that of a reflective, vital woman who was experiencing rejuvenation. In a different context she had discovered buried potential. With a dawning awareness of alternative possibilities for her life course, she started to move onto the second curve of new growth. I sensed that her life from then on would be very different from what it might have been had she not had this experience and chosen this option.

How did she manage to exploit her sabbatical so richly? One trait that stands out in her conversations with me is what I call mindful reflection. As she reflected deeply on her life and recent experiences, she found her self-awareness expanding. She was not hemmed in by old standards and images. She seemed to move into a personal space in which age does not matter very much. With the customary signs of age removed, she could listen to the creative power within, a power we have tended to associate only with youth. She began to ask probing questions about what she really valued and what she wanted to do with her life in contrast to what was expected of her. She challenged her old scripts, which included cultural standards and social expectations. Then she was free to explore possibilities she would never before have considered.

As she saw herself differently, she became more willing to risk experimenting to achieve what she valued. This experience represents more than just growing awareness. Her transformation illustrates the first principle of midlife renewal as she creatively balanced mindful reflection and risk taking.

I have come to better understand this principle in second growth by drawing upon two different concepts from modern psychology. The first has been developed by Ellen Langer, a professor of psychology at Harvard University who for two decades has conducted studies on mindfulness, a mental trait that turns lives around. She focused on elderly Americans, especially those who had been placed in situations that inculcate mindless behavior, such as nursing homes. Langer has observed that many people, especially as they get older, operate as if by remote control. She has found that much routine behavior is guided by a mindset that is narrow, inflexible, repetitive, and automatic. She calls this pattern mindlessness, a common but dangerous state of mind that blocks development and interferes with healthy adaptation. Mindlessness, the opposite of mindfulness, causes us to shortchange our potential.

Older people have no monopoly on mindlessness. We can see mindless behavior everywhere, as when we say of someone, "You can't talk with him, his mind is made up. He'll never change." Because it inhibits open questioning, mindlessness is detrimental to learning, as when we pass through a new situation thinking we know exactly what to look for only to discover afterward that we missed everything of importance. Rigid stereotypical thinking and prejudice are also common forms of mindlessness. We behave mindlessly when we try to force whatever may be new and different into old categories. A more subtle form of mindlessness becomes particularly powerful as we age. We endanger our growth chances by mindlessly assuming after five or more decades of living that we have little new to learn from our experiences. We also block our progress if we follow old scripts. The kind of self-awareness I saw in Professor Lin, when she portrayed herself as an aging woman, was a form of mindlessness. Everyday comments and jokes about middle age and aging resonate with mindlessness.

Langer has been showing how mindfulness can overcome mindlessness, especially with elders. She has recruited people in nursing homes for simple experiments. Control groups have continued with life as usual while those in experimental groups have been encouraged to break from routines, to think creatively about everyday possibilities, to make decisions instead of allowing decisions to be made for them, and to take charge of their daily lives. Once, she radically changed the context for several elders for a week so that they could relive the time when they were twenty years younger. With a different context, they broke free from old categories, saw themselves in a new light, experimented with nonroutine activities, and experienced rejuvenation. Her experiments have shown that elders who break mindlessness with mindfulness have greater life satisfaction, live longer and more creatively, enjoy greater vitality and health, and even appear younger to objective observers. What we have considered a normal process in aging can be reversed.

What Langer has been learning from her experiments, the adults in my study have demonstrated with their improved lives. Mindfulness can jump-start significant personal renewal. Professor Lin had mindlessly accepted the conventional assumption that she was old and wearing out. A different situation prompted her to question her old script and to draw upon her creative resources to see herself and her life chances in a new light. She was freer to experience her repressed youthfulness and to experiment. If we change the way we think of ourselves and our personal worlds, we can start a creative process that will carry us in a new direction.

Professor Lin used the new context in America as an opportunity to break mindlessness and change her way of thinking. What can we learn from her? What did she do?

- She became more aware of the full scope of her personality and the rich complexity of her potential.
- She critically questioned both her own old script and her society's traditional expectations of older women.
- She clarified her values and visualized what she really wanted to do with her future.
- She set long-term goals and took risks to reach them.
- She became more optimistic about her possibilities.
- She began to develop a new self-image and assume more control over her life.

These are ingredients in the initial phase of second growth.

A PARADOX OF MIXED MESSAGES

Mindful reflection, in which we step back from habitual perception and practice reviewing and questioning our lives, is crucial. This expanding awareness and critical thinking must be joined with risk taking. But these two intentions seem to run counter to each other. How can we integrate them? The paradox of these two traits becomes more sharply drawn if we consider an ancient Eastern form of mindfulness.

Behind the powerful concept explored by Langer lies a long Buddhist tradition of mindfulness. Both views provide insight into the creative power of the human mind to break free from common assumptions and expectations so as to increase our self-awareness, frame different perspectives, and achieve new understanding. Mindfulness in both approaches calls for cessation of current practice and encourages altering our perspective on life. If we make the time to develop a new perspective of our potential and our possibilities, we can achieve greater control of our lives. This is a powerful lesson of mindfulness.

There are various ways to interfere with ordinary activity in order to develop mindful reflection. Langer's experiments changed context and broke routines. Professor Lin took a sabbatical; some in this study took an Outward Bound course. Traditional Asian mindfulness recommends disengagement by going on retreats or setting up a special time and place to suspend ordinary thinking and activity. In contrast to the familiar activist command, "Don't just sit there, do something!" a motto for mindful reflection might be, "Don't just do something, sit there."

Especially today, with our materialistic, highly active, competitive lifestyles, we often need to stop doing and planning in order to be quiet, open, and attentive to the other dimensions of experience that become drowned out by action and daily routines. We need a break from *doing* to regain a sense of *being*. With mindful reflection we can withdraw from active engagement and our practical preoccupations to become open to deeper dimensions of our feelings and thoughts. Reflection enables us to get more in touch with our spirit and become clearer about our values and who we want to become. Our imaginations can be freed to explore untapped potential and new possibilities. That is one part of the first step in second growth.

The other part has to do with challenge and risk taking. Professor Mihaly Csikszentmihalyi, a University of Chicago psychologist, has for thirty years researched people's sense of happiness and well-being. He has noted the irony that despite their increased affluence and leisure time, average Americans do not enjoy life more than their ancestors. They could, but they do not know how to translate their opportunities into enjoyment. He has found that people become self-fulfilled and happy when they are fully engaged in an activity that provides them with an appropriate challenge, neither too great nor too little. With a minimal challenge, they become bored; with too great a challenge, they experience anxiety that is even worse than boredom. In the moment of total engagement with the right challenge, they experience what he calls flow, a form of expanding consciousness that can emerge with a good match between a challenge and one's competence. Active engagement and total involvement in a challenging task propel us into a higher, more creative and vital state of consciousness.

Csikszentmihalyi's studies of optimal experience provide a perspective on growth slightly different from Langer's. His explorations with many different kinds of people in diverse social settings have demonstrated that we need to take on daunting challenges if we are to grow significantly. The motto for flow might be, "Go for it." To experience vital, fulfilling growth we need to take risks and become actively engaged. Another motto for us might be, "Flow to grow." We enter a flow experience by recognizing opportunities for action, responding to the challenge before us, developing the requisite skills, and integrating those skills with the rest of ourselves. Such a response should not be an isolated event. If we extend flow for a lifetime, Csikszentmihaly believes, we will fulfill our potential complexity.

Here we have two powerful ideas with what appear to be opposite directions. One says stop, while the other says go. Which way is correct? The answer is not one or the other but both. The way to start second growth is to embrace the paradox of both ideas by holding them in creative balance, to engage in mindful reflection *and* risk taking, and to integrate these two qualities into the expanding scope of our lives.

That is much easier said than done. New insights into our potential complexity can be disconcerting, even confusing. Risking total involvement in a new challenge can be positively scary. We might sense deep potential and new possibilities but have difficulty taking the risks necessary to realize them. As Langer has pointed out, there is a danger as we become older of resisting change. The writer John Steinbeck observed that "it is the nature of man as he grows older to protest against change, particularly change for the better." It might not be in our nature, but Steinbeck's opinion is consonant with the old scenario of aging. Fear of change and risks can hold us in place so long that we miss an opportunity. A major task for all of us aiming for renewal in midlife is to learn how to live with these fears, taking them along with us into the risks of the creative process of new growth.

After acknowledging fears and our natural tendency to resist change, how might we begin? It helps to make a careful assessment of our current situation and then contrast that with our desired state. Significant personal change usually requires such a double vision. We saw that Professor Lin had two views of herself, as a declining old woman and as a person getting her youth back. Both views together fueled her determination to change her direction and recast her future. Just developing a critical view of where we are at present will not motivate us enough to change, because change usually begets resistance regardless of age. We need to activate our imaginations and sketch a mental picture of where we want to go and what we want to become. Our dream of a desired future will help pull us through resistance. This movement, however, is neither smooth nor easy. The double vision emerging from critical analysis and dreaming about the future can be a discomforting motivational force because it includes a creative tension between what is and what could be. We have to endure this tension and move with it. If we let the tension go, our sails will luff and we will stall.

This double vision also entails some personal accounting that often seems hard to bear. We might first assess the pain and costs of making a significant change. But then we should recognize the pain and costs of maintaining the status quo. As we reflect on all that is involved in staying put or changing, the intensity of this perception can become nearly overwhelming. The status quo may be comfortable albeit stifling. At least it is a known quantity. Change is filled with unknowns, and steps into uncharted terrain are usually frightening. Unless we see that the costs and pain of our current state exceed the costs and pain of the transition, we shall not likely find the courage and resilience needed to risk a change. Making that calculation can build our determination for risky initiative. At this point in the process, Professor Lin said of her socially prescribed future, "I don't want to do that now. . . . My goal when I get home is to continue what I've started here. Now I am taking more risks. I am starting to become more courageous."

KEEPING GOING

After clarifying what we want, we have to choose, to take on challenges posed by new directions and risk the ambiguity and uncertainty involved in an open-ended process. Our personal transformation results from a variety of acts: how we think, the choices we make, and the actions we take. The two paradoxical intentions of "stop" and "go" enliven, sustain, and complement each other like independent lines in musical counterpoint. Clear vision starts us; then we need to make choices and keep the process going. Second growth can be very hard work.

Sometimes my research has turned up instances of withering possibilities. If the vision fades, a person loses resolve and flow slows to a trickle. Old scripts can reappear and take over a life. Tom is an example of a person whose midlife was initially energized by changes and then curtailed by a conventional assumption about aging. At fifty-five this one-time psychology professor was enjoying his tenure as a college dean. He had been living a productive, active life, but then went through a life-review process that led him to this conclusion:

> I suppose the best years of my life have been the last ten. I've loved my job and the respect it brings me. And I enjoy being with young people. I've always been physically active, but I realize the need to slow down. I no longer think of myself as middle-aged. You know the literature—I'm at the stage where I am entering old age. I think I'll give myself another five years in this position and then perhaps do a less demanding job in the college.

Tom's perspective expressed in this interview startled me. When I had spoken with him just three years earlier, his outstanding trait appeared to be a youthful sense of adventure. His story of change in his late forties reflected second growth. In his early fifties he had seemed to me to be brimming with renewal, vitality, and hope. A few years later an old script had apparently caught up with him.

Several years after this last interview, I learned that he had in fact started cutting back in significant areas of his life. And his second marriage failed. It seems that he has not mapped his third age well. Old scripts reinforced by conventional psychology prompted him to settle for less and prepare for decline in what could otherwise be the prime of his life. Knowing the "literature" that espouses the old paradigm can be dangerous! Tom could have challenged the mindlessness of an old script and composed a different kind of life. Contrary to the literature that Tom referred to, we know that a midlife of diminishing expectations is neither inevitable nor necessary. Old scripts are not bred in the bone.

TAKING THE FIRST PARADOXICAL STEP

Ginny: *Life for me began when I was forty-six.*

An African American woman the same age as Tom illustrates how to start and sustain a long process of second growth. Unlike Professor Lin, her growth was not prompted by a different geographic or cultural context but by a dawning, discomforting double vision. She became aware that her life could be much better than it was. Ginny continues to live in the same small southern city where she was a factory worker for thirty years, but her personal world has changed dramatically.

Ginny was recommended to me by a university administrator who had known her for eight years and was greatly impressed by her character, accomplishments, and growth. She was fifty-four when I met her, a very thoughtful, articulate single mother who had worked on an assembly line while raising her children and had recently received a bachelor's degree. Very early in the interview she surprised me with a comment about her middle age. I had asked how she felt about herself now and if she wished she could be twenty-five again: "No, I wouldn't want to be twenty-five. At that time I was having a rough time as a young mother, divorced with four kids and having to work full time. Life for me began when I was forty-six. That started the best time in my life."

What an extraordinary, unexpected response. What had happened at forty-six? She explained that she completed her high school education and after that enrolled in a local university. She had tapped a previously undetected reservoir of creative potential that put her on a second curve in her development.

What happened during that year?

After the children had left home, I found myself in a rut. I would go to work, come home, fix a meal, flop on the couch and watch TV, party on weekends, shop when I wanted. Then I said to myself, there must be something else I can do with my life. I was just lying around and in the biggest rut. Then I got into a hospital volunteer program that turned my life around, spending two hours a day with people. I started to ask, You feel sorry for yourself? I questioned a lot. Most important, I asked, What can I do with my life?

Ginny's answer to this existential question gradually came to her. She could get an education and prepare for a new career in geriatric services. For a working-class black woman raised on a poor farm in the rural South and who was already a grandmother, this was not an easy answer to live with. But the discomfort of the status quo exceeded the fear and uncertainty she would have to endure in making a transition. She was determined to learn how to make more of her life. All significant learning begins and continues with questions. She got under way by raising a lot of probing questions about herself. With mindful questioning she embarked on a new path of lifelong learning.

After she enrolled in a nearby state university, she, like many adults returning to school, soon had to confront mixed feelings and doubts about her chances of success. Although mindful reflection had indicated rich potential and possibilities, the realities of tough courses and different circumstances raised intimidating new fears. In her pursuit of a higher education, she was tested often and in many ways. I have learned that her challenges were formidable.

As if the challenge of higher education with minimal preparation was not enough, she realized she had to take risks in other areas as well to make her dreams come true. Her emerging vision of herself clashed with some old habits. While pursuing a university degree, she eventually changed her lifestyle and herself. Here is an extended portion of the interview; it indicates her remarkable character, her resilience, and her impressive growth:

> I changed and I'm still changing and learning a lot about myself. I feel good. Things I never thought I would do, I've done. They've been hard on me mentally and physically, but I'm the kind of person who easily gets bored with routine things.
>
> After I came to the university, I became ill and had to lose a whole year. I came back, and there were courses that were really tough. I asked, why am I beating my brains out at my age? There were times I wanted to quit. But I'd tell myself, if you never try, you'll never know what you can do. I didn't want to be a failure, but I'm not afraid of failing. I'd tell myself, that teacher has

something you want. I'm going to do whatever it takes to get it. I'll walk the extra mile to achieve my goal. Along the way, I've learned to ask for help, which I couldn't do before.

I've also developed a new philosophy. I'm much more probing and ask many more "why" questions. I used to think everybody is entitled to her own opinion. Now, if I don't agree with them, I'll ask why they feel this way.

I also realized I had to have a different mentality to deal with fears. The thing you fear, you can conquer it if you have an open mind. I've learned that when you go into something with a "what if" mentality, it holds you back. You have to put that mentality aside. Like swimming. I always had a fear of the water. But I had to learn to swim to complete a college course. So I took survivor lessons in swimming at the Y. Then in the course I learned to reinforce my willingness to swim. I got rid of the "what if" mentality and have adopted the "why not." Now I consider my options and ask, Why not?

After this interview, I knew why Ginny had been recommended to me. She is a person who has certainly not experienced the luxuries and privileges enjoyed by some adults I interviewed. But over the years I have learned that her life is one of the richest I have encountered.

In midlife, in very constrained circumstances, Ginny made some dramatic changes that increased the complexity of her personal world. Continuing to work full time on the assembly line, she applied herself to a rigorous academic program that stretched out for eight years. By the end of that time, she had been promoted at work and was preparing for a graduate program that would train her for social work with the elderly. By her midfifties, education was an essential component of her life; she had built a commitment to learning. When I last spoke with her, when she was sixty-three, she reported that she was continuing to take courses at her community college to learn new things.

In addition to work and education, Ginny has remained close to her children and grandchildren, but she has learned to balance time with her family with time for herself. Her growth has extended into the paradox of freedom and relationships. While negotiating new patterns of relationships with her children and grandchildren, she also changed her circle of friends. Previously, her friends were mostly those with whom she partied on weekends. At parties she often smoked and drank too much. She realized she needed to cultivate different kinds of friends, people with whom she could share her emerging values and interests.

While developing her mind, she also started taking better care of herself physically, paying more attention to nutrition and exercise. As she gained confidence in her ability to succeed in many different areas, her attitude toward her life chances improved. Her mentality toward taking risks altered, as expressed in her "why not" philosophy. As she has taken on more challenge, she has become more optimistic and feels much more in control of her life. She is also having more fun. When I last spoke with her, she could not resist telling me about leading a friend from Latin America on some challenging hikes in the mountains of Pennsylvania. My guess is that she is in better shape in her sixties than she was at forty.

The changes I witnessed go beyond what is commonly thought of as self-improvement. Job enlargement, continuing education, emerging new career, close relationships with family and friends, greater social involvement, healthier lifestyle, and leisure activities that are physically challenging or culturally enriching are visible new features in her increasingly complex personal world. The internal changes of self-awareness and a venturesome spirit have launched her on a course she previously would never have imagined.

Ginny's second growth expresses her potential complexity; it also benefits others. In her personal world, there is a dynamic interplay between what happens *within her* and what happens *because of her*. Her internal changes have contributed to improvements at work, in her family and friendships, and in her community. As she has grown older, she is clearer about her priority of caring for people. When describing her continuing education, she said that she was particularly eager to learn when it meant she could use the knowledge to help others. She is composing a life that enriches both herself and others.

As I followed her steps through second growth, I noticed her addressing other paradoxical challenges. For example, while caring more for herself through education, leisure activities, and a healthy regimen, she has become even more involved in her community. She became active in a church as well as in a community educational program for the poor. For a while, she both tutored in and coordinated a local tutorial program called READ. A few years ago her community recognized her as "celebrity for the day." She is also very involved in her growing family. When I last talked with her, she had a dozen grandchildren who lived no more than a few minutes away.

For over a decade Ginny has reported continued growth. Her mindful reflection and risk taking have often focused on plans for both work and service. She has not given in to conventional expectations of aging but has continued to question, learn, and try out new alternatives. Her growth has not been without difficulty and setbacks. As planned, she had enrolled in graduate school at fifty-five to become a social worker. However, she developed back problems that required surgery and a six-month convalescence. During that time she decided she would instead become a geriatric nurse. She completed courses for certification as a nursing assistant as well as a Red Cross lifesaving course, which would move her closer to her goal. While working full-time in her industrial job, she also continued to do volunteer work with the elderly in a hospital. Just before her sixtieth birthday, the industry closed its plant, which coincided with her retirement. When we last talked she was continuing with her plan to serve as a certified nursing assistant, but she has also expanded her volunteer work in her community. For nearly twenty years she has volunteered in hospitals; she now also serves in a hospice. Ginny, like others we shall meet in the chapter on work and play, has redefined her work to include learning and service. While her work has become more important as she has grown older, she paradoxically places more importance on leisure and play. She once told me: "I put more emphasis on leisure time. After fifty-eight years, I think I owe it to myself." Her play has often been linked to vacations, which include travel to foreign places, something she never had the chance to do before.

Ginny's second growth has been initiated and sustained by mindful reflection and a willingness to risk new ventures. This first step has led to other paradoxical intentions. She has consciously developed a new scenario for the second half of her life with a growth-oriented philosophy: "I think about my options and ask, Why not?" She has transformed her third age into the prime of her life. In doing so she has enriched not only herself but also the lives of others. She has helped countless individuals and become a role model for others, such as her niece, who at fifty-nine is completing a university degree program in English literature in order to become a teacher. I can now understand why, after nearly twenty years of impressive growth that has overcome many obstacles, Ginny believes that her life began at forty-six.

Theresa: *For the first time, I have been really in control of my life.*

Growth doesn't just slip-slide along. Everyone encounters intimidating obstacles and some impediments. Sometimes a tough situation at work, the loss of a job or loved one, or conflicts at home can get in the way and hold us back. For many people impediments are not physical but psychological, such as anxiety, fears, or old scripts. For some adults the most formidable obstacle to sustained personal growth has been a life-threatening illness. Several of the people I interviewed have encountered that obstacle and overcome it with remarkable personal growth. Theresa is one of them. Her story also powerfully illustrates the first paradoxical step of mindful reflection and risk taking.

When we met, Theresa was fifty. A tall, blond, vivacious, and attractive woman, she exuded confidence. She reported that she was happily married with two grown children. She appeared to be one of the most vibrant and venturesome adults whom I had interviewed. I had trouble registering the fact that just eight years earlier she had endured the harrowing ordeal of breast cancer. In fighting it, she not only recovered her health but also changed her personality and personal world to exemplify extraordinary second growth. She told me that fifty was the best time she had known. She described her life at that time as more exciting and fulfilling, more adventurous and unpredictable, more complex and rewarding, and her relationships deeper and more loving, than ever. Like Ginny, she seemed to be telling me that her life really began in her late forties.

Theresa had been raised in a conservative, traditional home, socialized to play the roles of suburban wife and mother. As she put it, "I was dedicated to being the perfect *Good Housekeeping* wife." Her achievement was satisfactory, but there were negative consequences. She felt that she was never quite good enough in her role as wife and mother, and she sorely lacked self-confidence. She was timid and afraid to go out alone, even to drive alone into New York City. Shy at parties she felt she had to drink to loosen up and carry on a conversation. Increasingly, she became housebound. When she made a date to play tennis, she was relieved when a weather report forecast rain, so she could cancel. She was dependent on her husband, letting him make major decisions, even planning details of family events and vacations. As I review the transcript of her report of her earlier life, it reads like a mindlessly routine existence, with narrow and rigid boundaries. She was hardly a candidate for midlife growth. The worst thing she could then imagine happened when she was forty-two: she developed breast cancer.

The contrast between how she described herself in her early forties and what she has become is astonishing. Her story tells of more than just recovery; it conveys an inspiring account of significant, unexpected growth in her forties and fifties. How could she account for the change? How did she respond to the assault of breast cancer and the powerful fears it unleashed? She said that she was terribly frightened by the discovery of cancer, yet she was determined to fight it. Her fight included chemotherapy and a regimen designed to promote health and a healthful lifestyle. She set goals and developed her capacity to take risks to reach them. Her coping strategies are a model of the creative balance of mindful reflection and risk taking.

Achieving a healthy self-awareness was neither easy nor immediate. "I felt despair at first, especially when I was in chemotherapy. But I didn't feel like giving up, even though I was depressed. I had a job I loved, and that helped. I also learned to put things in perspective and set priorities. There were so many things to distress me." She was battling not only disease but an old script. Her recovery and growth involved recognizing unhealthy patterns in her life, discarding them, and then redefining her identity as a healthy and productive woman.

Theresa described vividly both her reflection and her response to challenges. What did she do in mindful reflection? She talked about building a broader perspective and setting priorities. But first, she raised critical questions about herself and practiced visualization, seeing herself as the woman she wanted to become—healthy, active, and competent—rather than as the woman she had been:

I learned the art of visualization from a book about getting well. I believe it's practiced in other fields like the arts and athletics. When I started visualizing myself seven years ago, I would see myself as healthy and active, like running and doing physical things. I clarified what I really wanted—eventually it came true. I'm not athletic, but in my new lifestyle I wanted to be physically active and to expand my limits through challenges.

I also learned to set goals. I make lists of long-term and short-term goals. My daughter makes fun of me—especially when I start making lists when we're together. When I'm alone I take stock of myself and ask, Do I really like what I'm doing? If not, how will I change it? I write down a big goal, like wanting to get more pleasure out of life. Then I make some concrete goals to realize the big one. Do I want to go to the movies once a week, to go into the country once a month, to go hiking? Write them down and then do it!

That last comment indicates her realization that her vision had to be followed by courageous action. As she explained,

Does all this goal setting make life too controlled? Well, I need a lot of structure. But when you structure your life with priorities and goals, you get out in the world and find life gets very unpredictable. After planning, you have to jump in. Like when I decided to sign up for Outward Bound, I had to send in the check.

Theresa's comments illustrate the paradoxical complexity of mindful reflection and risk taking. After taking inventory on herself, she has followed up with risk-taking decisions and assumed responsibility for her actions. She admitted that her decisions sometimes frightened her, but living with the status quo was even more frightening. She has learned that she has to take risks, a trait that is new to her. As she put it, "You have to jump in." That seems to be her own motto for flow.

Theresa's second growth models not only mindful reflection and risk taking, but also the principle of realistic optimism that we shall explore in the next chapter. I mention it here, because it is usually closely linked to the first principle. At forty Theresa was certainly not optimistic, nor did she exercise much control over her life. Her optimism was at a low ebb. She has deliberately developed her optimism by taking on challenges and learning to settle issues of personal power and control as she realistically faced her mortality:

Realizing I will die has made me relax about a lot of things. I can set priorities and not worry so much as I used to, because in the long run, once you've faced death, it changes the way you think about things. I used to worry about money or marriage. Someone would say, "Your husband might meet some younger woman and leave you." I don't worry about this now. You do the best you can. By relaxing, you're giving up trying to control everything.

There is also another paradox here, for in relaxing control over individual events, she has developed much greater control over the direction of her life. She has come to know the things she can and can't control. "If I get sick or something happens to my husband, I know now that I can start a support group and find a way to learn from this experience to keep going."

A key factor in her optimism is self-confidence. Before her illness, she apparently had little of it. How ironic that when struck by an illness that can shatter confidence, she was able to use that experience to build what she lacked. She converted a disability into an opportunity. A significant increase in self-confidence has bolstered her self-image and self-esteem: "When I was doing things I was supposed to do and didn't particularly want to do, it made me feel bad. Now I'm feeling better and am in more control of my life."

In everyone's life, certain events stand out as turning points. Theresa's encounter with cancer was certainly one of hers. It marked a significant occurrence that led beyond recovery to unexpected, mature growth. She also considers an Outward Bound sailing course in Maine that she took after her recovery another turning point. It had an effect on Theresa that was similar to the sabbatical's impact on Professor Lin. Being in a radically different context freed Theresa to discover untapped potentials of her character. It offered the necessary break from a secure, comfortable setting to strengthen her self-confidence and her readiness to seek out and respond to challenges:

> After the Outward Bound course and the incredible confidence it gave me, for the first time I have been really in control of my life. I can look into things I want to do and have the courage to do them. Before my illness, I wouldn't have done anything, even go out to dinner with a friend. I felt I had to stay home and be the perfect wife. The turnaround was Outward Bound. I was able to do my own thing, and my husband and kids got along fine. I learned I could be attentive to me!

Actually, I think the Outward Bound course augmented her already growing self-confidence rather than instilled it. The way Theresa entered the course is itself a story of self-confident initiative. She learned of Outward Bound through her children, each of whom took a course. She never considered such an experience for herself; after all, she had had cancer and was afraid of the outdoors. But the program's impact on her children and the philosophy of its founder, Kurt Hahn, attracted her. One aspect of his philosophy that certainly applied to her was contained in his aphorism, "Your disability is your opportunity." She was trying to turn a life-threatening situation into an opportunity for impressive personal growth.

As she thought about taking the Outward Bound course, Theresa conceived an extraordinary idea. Acting on it showed evidence of mindfulness and a willingness to risk adventure. She went to the producers of the television program *60 Minutes* and proposed that they film a group of ten women, all of them recovering cancer patients, taking an Outward Bound course. Theresa had formed a support group for women battling cancer and was involved in building networks of women who could assist one another in their endeavors to become well. *60 Minutes* liked Theresa's idea and put her in a leadership position: to plan, organize, and recruit the women who would take the course. The resulting segment was a great success and has been presented on national television several times. This is just one example of how Theresa took charge of her growth and her life.

As her job and volunteer work developed, Theresa's life assumed much greater complexity. She learned to balance diverging responsibilities to work, community, self, family, and friends. While committed to taking much better care of herself, she has extended her care for others. She has been involved in caregiving, fund-raising, and community and educational projects. More recently, she helped launch a nonprofit funding institution to assist indigent children in the New York area. This expanding arena of work and service has also led her to enlarge her network of relationships. Previously, her friends were women like herself; now her many friends include women whose backgrounds, experiences, and traditions are very different from hers.

While her commitments have expanded in many directions, a major component in her growth has been a firm commitment to face challenges and take risks. When I once asked her to illustrate how she was open to risks, a list started to develop that left me in awe. After a number of years her work propelled her into a role of community leader. No longer shy in social gatherings, she plans, organizes, and makes fund-raising presentations to groups small and large. Sheltered in a secure suburb for twenty years, she and her husband moved into the center of New York City. Once afraid to go into the city alone, she began moving through New York on her own easily. In her midfifties she even led a fund-raising march through Manhattan. She also has gone alone occasionally into the country or woods to hike, something she would never have done before. Once on a wintry night returning home from cross-country skiing several years ago, her car broke down on the FDR Drive. Rather than wait for an unlikely rescue during a blizzard, she put on her skis and went skiing through the snow-covered streets of East Harlem in search of help.

I have felt awed and humbled by this formerly timid woman's stories of adventure. For all the impressive daring I see in her accounts, Theresa is modest about her risk taking. She described a first effort in experimenting and risk taking when she was fifty:

> My risks are small, not like a corporation president. They enable me to become more independent. For example, I used to let my husband do all the planning for our vacations. Now, I'm willing to do it. Last summer, I took total responsibility for a camping trip to Yellowstone. It was my decision, but together we planned the trip, organized it, bought the equipment, and then went camping on our own. This wasn't the end of the world, but I certainly would never have done this before.

This simple example illustrates how she started to combine mindful reflection about the life she wanted to create with risk taking. This principle has remained a central feature in her life.

The remarkable transformation of second growth that started during her forties has continued through her fifties. I know of no reason why it should diminish in the next two decades. Nearly twenty years after she had cancer, Theresa is not only healthy but also vitally creative and richly cashing in on her life bonus. To sustain her growth, she regularly seeks challenge and adventure.

Growth-promoting challenges do not have to be physical. A major challenge for her in her midfifties was switching careers to develop an innovative fund-raising institution for needy children. However, physical challenge remains important to Theresa, because it is an integral part of her self-image as a healthy, active woman.

She remains committed to expanding her "limits with challenges." When I talked with her at fifty-five, she had just returned from another wilderness experience, this time in the Everglades. She then told me that during the previous four years, she and her husband had gone on several outdoor adventures, which included climbing in the Himalayas in Nepal and camping in Joshua Tree, a desert park in southern California. Five years later, she and her husband had again just returned home from an adventure, and she had another story to tell:

> We started our vacation with river rafting. We probably should have waited to get oriented, because we spilled over on the first day, got soaked and a little shaken. Perhaps that was too great a risk. I'll soon be sixty . . . but I will still keep doing things like this. I still seek adventure.

These experiences of rigorous challenge nourish her growth: "I need this so that I don't get too comfortable with my life and where I am." Now in her sixties, she continues to be both mindful and daring in her search to expand her limits.

LOOKING AHEAD TO A MORE ABUNDANT FUTURE

Theresa, Ginny, and Professor Lin are very different in terms of personality, background, interests, and lifestyle. Their experiences growing up and as adults are highly dissimilar. They are not typical women of this or any other time and place. They have a few things in common: more than half a century of experience and good prospects for sustained growth and fulfillment. One impressive similarity is that as they entered middle age, they did not anticipate experiencing new growth. In fact, each described her early forties as a down time. Each life was in part shaped by an old script. While some individuals, like Paul, have been fairly steady growers through their adult years, Ginny and Theresa were not. Their most impressive growth came late.

In their stories we have seen principles that play a crucial role in second growth. In particular, we have learned how they got started combining mindful reflection and risk taking. This principle has led them to address other key paradoxes and to integrate several key themes into vibrant new lifestyles. Their lives are evolving into ever greater complexity. As they experience new growth just when conventional assumptions predict decline, they show us that supposedly inevitable processes of aging are reversible.

In his famous longitudinal study of Harvard men who had reached their middle fifties, the psychiatrist George Vaillant noted that the healthiest, best-adapted participants had become stoic, masters of suppression, sublimation, and control. As a way of life, stoicism is admirable. But it is not enviable. It does not fulfill our dreams. At the close of his study, Vaillant interviewed an ebullient, idiosyncratic poet, who manifested a passion lacking in the other men. He raised an intriguing question. Is it possible to transcend stoicism by integrating creative passion with healthy adaptation? I believe my research answers that question for adults in the middle years with a resounding "yes!"

The unfolding lives of the people in my study are enviable as well as admirable. They show that, among all the possible ways through the third age, we have the option of transforming our lives by second growth. From individuals as diverse as Paul, Professor Lin, Ginny, and Theresa we learn that the middle period of adulthood can open wide to new possibilities. When we enter midlife the die is not cast. We can change our future and renew our lives. To get started with the first paradoxical principle in second growth you can

- put yourself in a situation where you can step back to review and question your life
- listen to your creative potential and imagine/visualize how you want to live
- clarify your values and reflect on the meaning/purpose of the second half of your life
- break away from constraining cultural norms and critique your old scripts
- find the challenges right for you and clarify your expectations
- take the necessary risks to experiment
- be open to the creative tension emerging from the double vision of yourself as you are now and as you want to become
- develop the competencies needed to respond effectively to your chosen challenges
- commit yourself to the results you want.

As we move onto the second curve of new growth, our lives will expand into a richer, more fully developed maturity. This abundance of life cannot be attained in one's twenties or thirties. Ripeness comes later. The men and women in this book illustrate that at forty-five, fifty, sixty, even seventy, the ripeness we aspire to is ahead of us. Their renewal reveals both the hidden potential in each of us and the way to tap it.

3

Principle Two: Developing Realistic Optimism

I know that at times
I will be troubled,
I know that at times
I will be belaboured,
I know that at times
I will be disquieted,
but I believe that
I will not be overcome.
　　　　　　　　—Julian of Norwich,
　　　　　　　　"Revelations of Divine Love"

ADDRESSING THE DILEMMA OF OPTIMISM AND REALISM

One of the most fascinating areas in modern science is the intimate relationship between health and the human mind. As a graduate student I devoured books by Freud and other psychoanalysts because I wanted to understand more clearly how mental processes could produce dysfunctional behavior, troubles, and even illness. In the last two decades there has been a different, more positive emphasis in psychology, exploring how the mind functions in healthy adaptation and healing. One of the most powerful, positive mental traits in this relationship is optimism. Medical and social scientists are learning that optimism is crucial to health, coping, and recovery from illness. The body seems to need messages of hope from the brain to heal, adapt, and stay well.

I believe that we also need hopeful messages to initiate and sustain growth, particularly in midlife. Pessimism and cynicism certainly do not prompt us to look for new alternatives and to keep moving when the going gets tough. Optimism encourages us to be open to alternatives, to become more mindful, to take risks, and to stay on course. It fuels the resilience needed both to initiate new growth and to respond to setbacks. To use a sailing analogy, in order to tack we need wind to come about and point in a new direction. Optimism acts like a fresh breeze that lifts our sails on a new course and keeps us under way.

To recognize the importance of optimism is one thing; to renew and sustain it after half a century of downs and ups is something else. A common response to the experience of growing older is to lower expectations and settle for less. While some individuals appear to be unshakably confident, most of us enter the second half of life with battered optimism. Eight centuries ago the poet Dante, as he began his *Divine Comedy*, compared the experience of middle age to entering a dark forest where the light of youthful hope disappears. Looking for illumination, he became conscious of greater darkness. This dilemma persists for many of us, even though we live in a setting that is radically different from Dante's.

At the least we might sense that our optimism needs tuning up. When we realistically take stock of ourselves, we recognize that we are more vulnerable and that life is more difficult than we had been led to expect. Personal disappointments may shake, even shatter, youthful hopes. Current events also buffet our perspectives. Social turbulence impinges on everybody's personal world. Unprecedented worldwide violence, the seemingly hopeless plight of billions of people, unforeseen changes in work and family life, and the disastrous impact of modern civilization upon our planet are enough to darken the vision of all who are attentive. We live in a world that we often cannot understand, and the past is insufficient to forecast the future. The management guru Tom Peters is reported to have remarked, "If you're not confused, you're not paying attention." The journalist Bill Moyers has observed that "our secular and scientific societies are besieged by violence, moral anarchy, and purposelessness that have displaced any mobilizing vision of the future except hedonism and consumerism. . . . There is a widespread sense in the country that everything that is tied down is coming loose." To find optimism in a world where we sense everything coming loose is no small feat. Some might think it foolish to try. When asked if he was an optimist, Peter Drucker, the great management sage and interpreter of our time, said, "For any survivor of this century to be an optimist would be fatuous."

One important insight that I learned from reading psychoanalytic literature is that healthy adaptation requires courageous realism. Denial can be dangerous and unhealthy. Yet choosing realistic assessment of our situation as we look ahead creates a dilemma. On the one hand we can see a bright horizon offering us new options. On the other seemingly insoluble global problems and personal disappointments, uncertainties, and losses suggest that the second half of life may be too tough to make significant improvements. A variety of fears may understandably darken our perspectives. We might at times feel caught. How can we increase the optimism needed for growth without denying reality?

An experience I once had on a dark afternoon provided me with a helpful analogy. Atop Nob Hill in San Francisco sits Grace Cathedral, impressive for its Gothic majesty within an eclectically modern environment. As I entered the nave and looked toward the chancel, I had to strain to see details because of the darkness. But midway down the aisle, as I turned and looked toward the great entrance, I had a very different experience. The back portion of the nave, which is a later addition, was bathed in bright, colorful light, even in a thick San Francisco fog. How could this be possible? In extending the cathedral, the architects were challenged: How could they find a way to let in more light while retaining the Gothic style, with stained-glass windows high above the ground? They had to overcome structural darkness. They did it very creatively, by using faceted glass in the windows. The thicker, unevenly cut glass picks up more light waves and makes the extension of this cathedral unexpectedly bright.

This place sent a message unintended by its builders. Like the architects who designed the cathedral's extension, we need to be creative in designing the unexpected extension of our lives. In doing so, we need to bring in more light as we face darkness. Our challenge in designing our lives for the second half involves integrating two seemingly different perspectives: realism and optimism. A realistic outlook might suggest that the odds against renewing and enriching our lives may be too great for us. Yet optimism says we can beat the odds! Learning to integrate this paradox into our lives constitutes another important step in midlife renewal. It is the second principle of second growth.

When I interviewed Professor Lin, I learned that the Chinese have a wonderfully appropriate term for optimism: *sunny view*. She told me that as a young person, she had a very sunny view, believing that her society was evolving into an unprecedented era of justice and that her career as a scientist held great promise. The Cultural Revolution in China smashed her optimism by destroying her youthful faith in justice, ending her scientific career, and wasting her talents. Only during her American sabbatical did she recover her sunny view. Without losing her critical, realistic perspective, she learned to let light back into her personal world while acknowledging the dark that persisted in her situation back home. Many of the adults in my study have done the same.

The medieval English contemplative Julian of Norwich has encouraged people for generations, because her perspective is so realistically optimistic. She admitted that forces seemed to work against her: "I believe I will be troubled, belaboured, and disquieted." But she held on: "I believe I will not be overcome." How could she be so optimistic? She developed a vision of positive outcomes: over and over she affirmed that "all things shall be well, all manner of things shall be well." The way she spoke to herself in adversity shaped and strengthened her vision, which in turn gave her hope. She provides another illustration of how we might address our dilemma without being undone by it.

WHAT REALISTIC OPTIMISM MEANS

The kind of optimism needed for second growth is a grown-up trait. It is informed optimism rather than the unrealistic optimism of youthful inexperience, which believes that life, like fairy tales, will always have a happy ending. Realistic optimism is not a Pollyanna view that no matter what happens, one's wishes will be fulfilled. It should not be misconstrued as wishful thinking. Several decades ago, an optimistic viewpoint was promoted as "the power of positive thinking." This approach, however, involves a strong dose of magical thinking, telling oneself that if one wants something badly and prays hard enough, one can expect to receive it. Such a strategy resembles the call to enter fantasyland in the musical version of *Peter Pan*: "Believe! Believe!" Uninformed optimism can become make-believe, which denies reality. Healthy human development requires clear vision and realistic assessment. We cannot grow if we practice denial.

We need to develop an expectation that is tough, responsible, *and* hopeful. Recent work by Martin Seligman, a University of Pennsylvania psychology professor and authority on cognitive behavior, can help to get us started on this task. He has described optimism as a positive rational perspective that effectively counters pessimism. Seligman points out that the crucial difference between optimism and pessimism is how we talk to ourselves about our failures. Optimism is a way of explaining how things can work out in spite of difficulties and setbacks. It is basically a hopeful perspective; and it can be learned.

A growing body of research into optimism provides good news. Optimism and pessimism are not for the most part built into our genes. We have options, even in the most frustrating situations. While we could become pessimistic, most of us can begin to build optimism by changing our mental outlook and developing positive expectations. We have to see the good with the bad, emphasize the positive, and build a long-term view that is open to the best possibilities. But more than this is needed for the long haul.

The people I have studied have shown me several important qualities that are also elements of optimism. Two of them are hope and belief. Hope affirms a vision of what can be. For example, Theresa's vision of herself as a healthy, vital woman was strengthened by hope, which in turn fueled her healing process and her growth. Her optimism also includes belief. Optimists believe that they can find the means to respond successfully to challenges so as to realize their visions. They say, "I'll find a way." Theresa was determined to change course and become healthy. The basis of her determination was a belief in herself. Self-confidence undergirds her new initiatives and resilience. Faced with a tough challenge, a pessimist says, "I can't do that." "Can't" then becomes a self-fulfilling prophecy. An optimist like Theresa, on the other hand, says, "I can and I will." That is the kind of outlook that can turn a life around.

The Harvard professor Rosabeth Moss Kanter made a prediction regarding business leaders that applies equally well to our growth: "The years ahead will be best of all . . . for those who learn to balance dreams and discipline." This is no time to put aside dreams. On the contrary, now is the time both to dream hard about what we really want and to work hard to make those dreams come true. It is no tragedy if we fail to realize a particular dream; it is a tragedy if we fail to dream at all or fail to respect a dream and act on it. Individuals in this study have shown me several constructive activities that will help us build realistic optimism to turn our dreams into reality.

GETTING A LITTLE HELP FROM YOUR FRIENDS

Nancy: *One of the first things I learned was to ask for help. There's always someone there to help you.*

Nancy was a forty-three-year-old widow, mother of two daughters in college, and a partner in a prosperous real estate firm in New England when we met. She seemed in many ways a picture of success on the threshold of middle age: healthy and active, she owned a beautiful home and had a lucrative, highly satisfying career; she was a seasoned traveler who had a broad circle of good friends and looked ahead to a bright future. Had I interviewed her five years earlier, I would have found her struggling in a very different situation.

After Nancy finished college, she married and believed her dreams were coming true. Within a decade her life had become a nightmare. Her husband became an alcoholic. She spent many days alone raising two young girls. She became uncertain of everything and too afraid to drive alone even to get away for a day. Idealistic as a girl, she was depressed and despairing in her thirties. Raised in a strict religious home, she had been taught to submit to her husband. Divorce was not an option. She felt trapped. Then her husband died of an alcohol overdose. Her plight seemed grim.

In the intervening years she repaired and redesigned her life. The first thing she mentioned when explaining how she had been able to transform her outlook and her life was the importance of good friends:

> One of the first things I learned was to ask for help. That hadn't been allowed at home. I was told to carry my cross and think about others, to give and not to receive. I got so depressed; but I haven't felt that way for years. There's no more throwing up my hands and saying, "I give up." It was important for me to learn that I could receive from other people and that I can share deeply with them.
>
> It was so lonely living with someone who was never sober. I have some really good friends now. I confide in them. They can tell me I'm off base and

can be very reassuring. They have helped me enormously and kept me from going off on a tangent.

Her testimony to the strength received from friends points to one of our most important resources for developing a realistic optimism that will support second growth. Their support gave her the lift she needed to tack, then stay on course.

Nancy went on to describe how her improved optimism had affected her growth:

> One of the things I know is that I've changed a lot. In fact, I'm struck by the constancy of change that has occurred during the past five years. I had an attitude problem at first and couldn't express it. I'm an optimist now—not an idealist like when I was younger. I feel better about myself than I ever have. I've done a lot of exploring and a lot of creative things. My feet are on the ground, and I am more appreciative of what happens on a daily basis.
>
> My life has become more complex—this is good for me. I've learned to manage pretty well. I'm much more in control of my life now; I sure wasn't five years ago. I think my life is just beginning. In fact, I don't feel I'm middle-aged. I've got another forty-five or fifty years, and I want to keep moving ahead.

She made positive changes not only in her outlook and thinking, but also in her lifestyle and situation. As I read through the transcripts of interviews with Nancy and the others, I perceived that an outstanding characteristic of these changes was the emergence of an optimistic expectation that was grounded in reality and that looked hopefully toward the second half of life.

Nancy provided me with numerous examples of how her optimism helped her to overcome fears and build a vital personal world:

> My risk taking has catapulted compared to what it was ten years ago. Then, I was afraid to drive into the city alone. Now, I travel all over the world. There's a strength I sense coming from within but also from what I learned. Before, I didn't travel anywhere because I was afraid of getting lost. But you can't get lost. There's always someone there to help you. I've been helped to find my way. And I've learned to walk through my fears. I know now I can get through.

I have a philosophy that we create our lives by the choices we make. What makes the difference is knowing there are options and having the courage to make choices for what I want and believe is best. That's new for me.

Her discovery of the link between her options and getting help from friends has served her well. It proved to be something she could fall back on when her circumstances changed.

Four years later, I was stunned to learn how her good fortune had slipped into reverse. A year after we met, the real estate market that had contributed to her financial success collapsed as the economy suffered a severe recession. These economic events carried away nearly all of her material assets. She lost her investments, her job, and then her lovely home; eventually, she filed for bankruptcy. During this traumatic two-year period her mother died, and Nancy was involved in three car accidents. Her realistic optimism was so severely tested that it nearly broke. Quite understandably, she again became depressed.

She was in shock for a while and then again sought help from psychotherapy and friends. Gradually, she started redirecting her life. After a couple of years, she started to feel more positively about her chances. She saw that she could make things work. Her daughters received scholarships to continue in college. She moved to a new community and took a new job. She maintained a healthy lifestyle and a circle of good friends. She even planned to develop a new career: "When I turn fifty, I want to prepare to work in the health field. I'm even considering applying for medical school." This display of renewed optimism nearly knocked me over.

How could she manage to recover her optimism? "I have a broad network of good friends who have been sympathetic and supportive," she told me. "When I reach out, someone is there to help me." The optimism radiating through this story of misfortune and turnabout reflects not only her resourcefulness but also the quality of the relationships that have sustained her. Her remarkable story illustrates an easily forgotten truth: often we can stand strong because we have been supported by significant others.

Learning to ask for help has been a turning point for Nancy and for others in this study. It has given them the boost needed to build optimism and take initiatives. On the surface, learning to seek and receive help seems like discovering the obvious. But in the United States, where success is defined in terms of individualistic achievement, asking for help is not viewed positively. We are a do-it-yourself nation. One of our major industries is self-help. Nancy had been taught to rely only on herself. In interview after interview, I heard people tell me how difficult it was to learn to genuinely care for themselves by asking for help. We have idolized self-reliance and competitive individualism. Americans are encouraged to dream big, to hitch our wagon to a star, and, when the going gets rough, to tough it out on our own. Asking for help is thought to be a weakness.

One consequence of exaggerated individualism is widespread loneliness. Twenty years ago after a long study of contemporary loneliness, I concluded that Americans often seem to be in pursuit of loneliness. By demanding the right to "do our own thing" and protecting a private self, we neglect relationships and community. Loneliness can have serious negative consequences. In contrast to people nurtured by supportive relationships, those suffering from extended, profound loneliness have more ailments and are more likely to develop a pessimistic outlook and become depressed. They are more likely to suffer heart attacks and to attempt suicide. While people may not die of loneliness, it seems to aggravate health problems, contribute to premature death, and inhibit growth. It can also have a devastating impact on optimism.

When people experience long stretches of loneliness, they are likely to lose their optimism and find it very difficult to rebuild it. Housebound with two small children, living with a man who was never sober, Nancy was "so lonely." In her loneliness she became depressed and felt powerless. To break out, she first had to find and receive help from caring people. Nourished by supportive relationships, she found the resources she needed to broaden her outlook, learn optimism, and renew her life.

To overcome a tough situation requires courage. But where does courage come from? I believe there are two sources: one's self-confidence and determination, and significant others who give encouragement. We acquire a self-confident optimism in part from experiencing the confidence and hope others have in us and by receiving their encouragement. The courage needed to meet intimidating challenges is nurtured by the encouragement we receive. Nancy's optimism emerged both as an accomplishment and as a gift from her friends.

Since turning fifty, Nancy has continued her new growth. She left New England and moved to Denver, the place where she most wanted to live and work. In Denver, her first experience living in a city, she shares an apartment with her sister and has found a new job. After exploring the breadth of her options, Nancy decided that going to medical school was unrealistic. Instead, she entered a master's program in psychotherapy to work toward a new career as a counselor. She has been designing a life that she loves with realistic optimism nourished by the help of good friends.

GAINING SELF-CONFIDENCE BY ASSERTING WHAT YOU WANT

Karen: *I have changed my attitudes towards hills. . . . I can affirm what I want. And I can get to where I plan to go.*

Some people never develop much optimism while growing up. That does not mean that they cannot do so later, as Karen's story so clearly illustrates. Karen was forty-seven when I met her, married eighteen years, with a child of her own and several stepchildren. She had been raised in a working-class family troubled by alcoholism. Her expected life pattern was to finish high school, go to work, and get married. She followed that script, but became dissatisfied:

> It was difficult to break out of this rut. My family raised me on "shoulds." I had a hard time thinking of what I wanted. Eventually, I got up the nerve to attend college at night while I was a secretary. I had thought I wasn't very bright, but good grades and a scholarship suggested that view wasn't right.

Continuing with college, she graduated; she then divorced and moved away. In a new city, she met a widower and married again, this time happily. She became the mother of a large family that grew even larger when she and her husband had a son. Having discarded her original script, she assumed the role of middle-class housewife. As she entered her forties, she began questioning this role and the "shoulds" that still circumscribed her life. She wanted to affirm her own needs and rights, "but I still didn't think of myself very well. Others always came first. If I felt that something wasn't right for me, I avoided confrontation. I didn't want to offend people. I wanted them to like me."

Although in many respects Karen had significantly improved her situation, she felt that she was missing something important. Even after she had experienced success beyond her early dreams, she still felt corseted in "shoulds." She could not assert what she really wanted. She became increasingly frustrated and confused. Like Nancy, she chose to risk asking for help and entered therapy. There, she learned that she had many positive qualities but was too pessimistic to express them:

> I used to think there was nothing I could do to make a significant change. I'd give myself pep talks: "You can do it. Things will work out." But that didn't make much difference. I'm a survivor and kept plugging away, but I wasn't able to make changes. I was so self-critical.

Only when she learned to silence her self-critical voice could she affirm other inner voices and make new choices.

A turning point for her occurred on a nine-day bike ride that was part of an Outward Bound course in the mountains of western Maine. It rained every day. She had never done any sustained strenuous activity before and hated it at first. On the third day, she was about to quit. She summoned the courage to say to her group, "I don't need this in my life. I don't enjoy this at all. I don't want to ride up all these hills and never see the country." To face this group was scarier than signing up for the course. Why? It represented a break from her past; for the first time, she dared to stand up for what she felt and wanted.

In that experience she found the self-confidence she had been missing. For the first time, she said, she confronted others directly and forcefully. Much to her surprise, she discovered that they accepted her and responded to her needs and strength. That experience was pivotal for her:

> I gained so much self-confidence there. I found that I can do this. I have since changed my attitudes toward hills—they've become a metaphor of my life. I can manage. I can confront. I can affirm what I want. And I can get to where I plan to go. What was so surprising was that after that incident we altered the course so that we could break up the rides and enjoy the scenery more and develop friendships. I am still developing qualities that I discovered then.

When I spoke with her four years later, she said she returns to that moment, when she learned to affirm herself when confronting a challenge.

Instead of being controlled by "I can't," she is sustained by "I can." But it is not an "I can, because you think I should." Daring to assert what she wanted and to affirm herself engendered the self-confidence needed for an optimism rooted in her inner resources. This optimism has enabled her to make significant changes in her life, one of which was to enter graduate school for a counseling degree:

> I'd rate myself a seven or eight on a ten-point optimism scale—and the same for having a sense of control over my life. Several years ago I was a real pessimist. As I gained in self-confidence, I decided to enroll in graduate school. I believe I can do this. I'm finishing a program that will enable me to work with teenagers.
>
> My family has learned that I also have needs that have to be cared for. I'm working on making choices and getting more power in several aspects of my life. I've developed new interests. My life's more complex. I've started something for the future and am concentrating on making a constructive beginning.

What she started then has continued.

Now in her late fifties, Karen maintains her commitment to growth through personal exploration and the pursuit of new challenges. She continues to fill the roles of wife and mother but has gone beyond them to pursue her own interests. Having completed graduate school, she embarked on an intensive training program in psychotherapy. She then started a career in a helping profession, focusing on indigent women. She maintains a small practice but has branched out to do various volunteer jobs. She is preparing to become an outdoor guide. Her stepchildren have married; she particularly relishes her new role of grandmother. Ten years after our initial interview she wrote to me about the pride she feels about her growth: "During the past ten years I have gone even deeper into my process to make more discoveries about how I am in the world." Her self-confident optimism, developed after years of lingering pessimism, has sustained her second growth for more than a dozen years.

PLANNING FOR PURPOSE

EI: *I realized we could have what we've really wanted.*

In addition to supportive relationships and self-confidence, we have to do some planning in order to express our optimistic expectations. Dreams must be balanced by discipline. By planning I do not mean making a blueprint with lots of details, but learning to frame a perspective in which our dreams can become a reality. Without a practical perspective we will too easily become discouraged. One of the most frustrated individuals I interviewed was an architect who, for all his creativity, was finding it increasingly difficult to organize his time. In a situation he could only complain about, he felt stuck in a midlife rut.

El was different! He showed me how to develop realistic optimism by integrating a purposeful plan into the strategic organization of one's life. A former executive, El switched careers at forty-eight, a year before we met. He had worked for a major corporation for more than twenty years, moving steadily up the corporate ladder. He was happily married to his high school sweetheart. Two of his sons had completed college and his youngest son was halfway through. The family gathered one New Year's Day to discuss his desire to make a significant change. He shared his thoughts and clarified his needs that had not been attended to. He said he was ready to leave the corporation and create a new lifestyle, including a new career as a woodcarver. He asked his wife and sons to work through this dream with him. Together they explored their resources and options and formulated their plan.

The corporation, however, was not ready to lose El. It offered him an even higher position and more money. He was tempted, but his decision to leave was firm. The man I saw in blue jeans and a flannel shirt in a city park not far from the corporation's headquarters was very different from the "model" three-piece-suit executive his company had known. "People were so surprised when I announced that I was leaving," he told me. "Everyone saw me as the ideal company man, a committed workaholic, completely devoted to the company, totally rational. They weren't aware that behind the company image, there was a person who was feeling hemmed in, feeling unfulfilled by his job, and discovering creative potential that called for a totally different outlet."

By conventional American standards El was a success. But in his forties he had found his successful lifestyle wanting. He was dreaming about a change that would lead him to another kind of success. For years he had developed a hobby of woodcarving. As he started to receive some recognition for his work, he sensed that this craft more than his corporate job would nourish his creative side. His reflections led to a plan that included making his avocation into a vocation. The plan linked discipline to his dream. Ten years later his planning continues to guide him toward a new model of success and the fulfillment of his dreams.

What led him to quit the company to develop a new lifestyle?

Several things started me thinking about the meaning of my life: a wellness program and a company seminar focused on purpose in life. As a planner I had always been good at working out strategies, but I never asked why. What's it all for? I just hadn't considered the purpose of my life.

I did then, for the first time. My purpose was formulated as becoming the person I am, to realize my potential, and to share with others. I sensed I had been getting too closed in at work—all work and no play, little sharing, and no fun.

He concluded by setting this change process within a meaningful perspective: "I left the company because I wanted to focus on purposeful living through personal growth." Six years later El reconfirmed and clarified this goal: "I was seeking a broader approach to change, trying to find a more creative lifestyle that corporate life did not allow. More important now than it was then is sharing. I find a lot of satisfaction in that."

The decision to leave his corporate career and start a new one was not as easy as it might sound. It called for great risks, especially financial ones; as a corporate financial planner, he had always tried to minimize such risks. His willingness to take risks had been tempered by a conservatism strengthened by years of prudent fiscal planning. To risk an entirely new direction required realistic optimism, which he expressed in a livable plan.

His growth plan evolved as a practical family plan. He and his wife, Stephanie, together planned the steps, and they have continued to do so. By setting aside enough money for the youngest son's education, Stephanie realized that she could also start to think about a new career. She had long wanted to open an antique shop. She and El decided to form a business partnership. They then found a new home and moved to a place they had both dreamed about. They relocated to a lovely lakeside community in Maine where they opened their new business. Both it and their new life have flourished. As partners they continue to share in creative life planning.

El's plan exhibits other paradoxical principles of second growth. For example, purposeful living calls for greater independence but also aims at strengthening relationships and caring for others. The new life he has been creating evolves through sharing. In addition to close ties with family and friends, he has become very active in volunteer activities and causes. "Why is sharing so important?" I asked him. "Because it is closer to where I'm at," he said. "I'm giving back after years of not being able to share in the corporate world." El, like all the others we have met in this study, has been affirming what he deeply wants by balancing this self-regard with giving himself to others.

El once said of his transformation,

> I feel great now, better than I did at twenty-five, though that was also a good time for me. I'm starting a new life. I like being where I am. I'm not thinking about growing old but of having opportunities to pursue interests for perhaps the next forty years. This is a growth period, not a decline.

Seven years later he made nearly the same assessment. In his late fifties El reported that the benefits of the changes he and his wife made exceeded their expectations. "We did exactly the right thing. I remember saying to my wife years ago, 'I think we can have what we really want.' It's happening. Life keeps getting better. We enjoy each day. What's next? We plan to continue what we're doing."

I have been impressed by how El's realistic optimism has sustained his growth through the past ten years. He and Stephanie have designed a life that fulfills their dreams. Both are freer to pursue what they want, and their marriage is stronger than ever. Their dual-career marriage has also become integrated into a prospering family business. El still carves and wins prizes, which he modestly displays in a corner of their shop. His life also extends outward into church and community organizations, where he shares his expertise in management. But work is balanced by play. Increasingly, he devotes time to fishing, which is becoming an avocation. When we last spoke, he was starting to write a book about fishing in Maine and had presented several local lectures on the subject.

As he reflected on all of these changes, he commented, "I am still awed by the realization when I wake up that the day is mine to structure. This is so different from my life in the corporation." Like others in this study, El learned to measure success differently than he once did, not by corporate title and income but by the extent to which he translates his goal of creative and purposeful living into a lifestyle of growth and sharing.

UTILIZING DETOURS

Evans: *Rebuilding an old house became a metaphor for my life, something with hidden potential that with imagination, commitment, and hard work could produce a positive result.*

With new vision, determination, and bold self-confidence, we might nevertheless find ourselves unable to maintain our desired course. Instead of smooth sailing, we might get knocked about by an unforeseen storm or delayed by a thick fog. What then? What can we do when the plan seems not to be working and our optimism falters? One man in particular showed me.

Evans, a fifty-year-old entrepreneur, was the president of a small company that he had started a few years before I met him. At the end of a busy day, Evans was still vibrating energy and enthusiasm. He exuded self-confidence and optimism, and he obviously loved his work. He pointed to a motto hanging on his office wall that revealed his attitude: TGIM (Thank God It's Monday). He told me that he had now reached the high point of his life:

> I'm more confident, more directed, more accomplished, more into believing that dreams will come true, more into chasing rainbows. I'm giving myself permission to do things I had wanted to do but held back. My wife and I are both achieving our potential. We feel so much better about ourselves than we ever did.

He sounded like a person moving upward on the second curve of new growth. In work, family, lifestyle, self-actualization, and social contributions, he felt more successful and content than ever. But this happy state was not a predictable outcome from his previous life course. When he entered his forties, he had begun to feel dissatisfied with his job in the corporate world; he thought he could not combine fun with work. He concluded that he had to leave. Why?

> I was frustrated, bored, not in love with myself, not making as much money as I thought I should, champing at the bit and feeling I was cheating myself and the world. So one day I just said, "Screw it. I'm going to leave." I did it all by myself, which I know now is not the best way to go. That's one reason I've started this business, to help others move in new directions.

Evans realized that it was time to set a new direction. At that point in his life he had a double vision, one of what he was becoming by holding the course he was on and another of what he could become if he changed direction. As he visualized his second option, he developed a strong belief in the validity of this possibility and in his potential to make his dream of a new career and a different lifestyle a reality.

Yet the second option did not lead quickly to his goal. Evans learned the hard way that important life goals set in an optimistic moment are not instantly attained. After starting off on his own, he found himself getting poorer rather than richer. He used up most of the savings that he had carefully set aside. Then he took out a second mortgage. One evening he came home to find his young son had opened a stand selling old golf balls to help his dad get started in his new business.

> At that point, I just about cracked up. I had known anger and despair before; but this situation was the worst. I felt so low. I kept on, though. Why? Because I believed in myself and I believed in the product. This was my mission. I was totally committed and felt this would develop my potential and make a contribution. I was sure eventually it would work.

His dilemma was that he felt stuck on a well-chosen course just when he should see progress. He had thought of himself as optimistic; but he was losing it. What should he do while waiting for things to happen? He decided to take another gamble:

> I had just enough money left to buy an old wreck of a house down at the shore. I took long weekends to go there and tear it apart and then rebuild it. Eventually, I resold it for a good profit. That house gave me the feedback I needed. It became a metaphor for my life, something with hidden potential that with imagination, commitment, and hard work could produce a positive result. If you saw that house, what it was before and after, you'd know how much it gained in value. Rebuilding it not only gave me a vent for frustration and anger, but it supported my efforts to set new goals and achieve them.

Evans was not giving up on his vision but finding a way to rechannel his energies and reinforce his hopes of establishing his own company and a more satisfying lifestyle. One advantage of this new activity was that it could be completed in a short time.

Personal growth is often portrayed as a journey. Encouraged to set off toward a new destination, we sometimes find our journey delayed. Friends speak encouragingly: "Don't give up hope. Things will work out." But when nothing appears on the horizon, even their support seems insufficient. We understandably become discouraged when we stall.

At such times, some people advise patience. The words of John Milton, the blind English poet, have encouraged many: "They also serve who only stand and wait." That philosophy does not work for everyone. Americans especially do not like to wait. We expect quick happenings: instant coffee, fast food, and immediate results. Waiting is hard for us. Professor Csikszentmihalyi has some different advice:

> When adversity threatens to paralyze us, we need to reassert control by finding a new direction in which to invest psychic energy, a direction that lives outside the reach of extended forces. When every aspiration is frustrated, a person still must seek a meaningful goal around which to organize the self. Then . . . that person is subjectively free. . . . It does not matter [what we do] as long as we are in control of what is happening.

That is what Evans did. He sublimated his energy by finding a substitute goal to focus on temporarily and remained in control of his life. Cutting a path to a new destination in midlife takes time. Intellectually, we know that. But when our prospective timetable is off, it is important to learn how to use the time intervening between resolution and result, especially if we are to sustain optimism. Evans learned to wait out the delay by taking on an alternative project, which he interpreted as a metaphor for life renewal. In doing so, he developed skills needed for a new direction by taking a minor detour.

Sailors have learned a similar lesson when facing unexpected delays. Regardless of how carefully a trip is planned, there may be days when you wake up and can barely see the bow of the boat because fog has settled in and with it complete calm. You have to stay anchored. Ingenuity is tested as you are forced to wait for the fog to lift and the wind to pick up. You use this time to repair lines, work on the engine, or fix something on the boat, or to read a novel, learn a new game, or go ashore and explore a new terrain. This "sailing lesson" suggests that when waiting hopefully for improvement in one area, it helps in the meantime to redirect one's interests into a substitute endeavor over which one is in control. When our journey gets fogged in, we can wait out delays and disappointments by rechanneling our energies.

GROWING A SENSE OF HUMOR

Another important way to improve optimism is to develop a sense of humor. Some of the individuals I interviewed have wonderful senses of humor and kept me chuckling during the long stretches of our interviews. Others, however, admitted their serious nature and said that they were trying to put more laughter into their lives. Being too serious and self-absorbed can stifle optimism. Karen has realized that as she builds optimism and self-confidence, she has needed to lighten up:

> Humor is important. I believe something physical happens when you laugh. It's good for you. I'm a serious person, not like my husband who can find a joke in almost any situation. I'm learning to see the funny side of a situation and find that when I laugh at it, it doesn't seem so dreadful or important anymore.

Karen has learned that laughter, like optimism, is good for both body and soul. So has Theresa, who said she had forgotten how to laugh in her terrifying battle with cancer. Quite unexpectedly, she found herself laughing at a situation:

> I noticed the first time I had laughed after getting cancer. How good it felt! I knew then that I needed to laugh more, not only to feel better but to develop a positive attitude that was crucial to getting well.

The journalist Norman Cousins discovered the restorative power of laughter while suffering from what was diagnosed as a rare, incurable illness. With his doctor he designed an unusual therapy that included massive doses of vitamin C and laughter. He developed a daily plan to watch old comic movies that he knew would make him laugh. Hearing laughter down the hall, people wondered what kind of medicine was being administered in Cousins's room. He later wrote a book about his remarkable recovery. Exactly how the cure happened is still a mystery. But it seems that laughter fed into his determination to beat the illness and supported an optimistic, self-affirming attitude that more recently has been attributed to unexpected healing.

One way to develop a sense of humor is to recognize the incongruities and absurdities in a situation and laugh at them. Another is to learn to laugh at ourselves. Sometimes situations become so egregiously awful that there is no other sane response but to make fun of them. Trying to get this chapter written produced one of those situations, which eventually reminded me of this valuable lesson.

After spending several weeks rewriting an early version of this chapter, I saved it on the hard disk of my computer. In a hurry to make an appointment, I told myself, "I'll make a backup on a floppy disk later." When I turned my computer on again later, it would not boot up; not one program would run. After frantically calling for technical assistance, I learned that the computer had a system error. When I brought it to a service department, I was told it had suffered the equivalent of cardiac arrest. The hard disk had failed beyond the point of repair. The "life" of the machine had ended. I needed a new computer. All files were lost.

Immediately I bought a new computer. Then I looked for a rough draft of the chapter on paper to copy. But where was it? Just in time, I recalled that my only copy was in with the household trash, waiting for the weekly pickup. I was lucky to find it, stained and messy but usable. For the rest of the week, I reentered and rewrote this chapter. One evening, I cut my finger when I knocked over a wine glass while preparing dinner. I resumed typing the next day with difficulty because of a clumsy dressing on my index finger. When I at last came to the end, a strange message on the screen told me that the computer could not save the chapter. Was I threatened with another total loss? Were sinister cosmic forces trying to defeat me?

Technical assistance came to the rescue by phone. By Friday afternoon, I had the chapter printed and saved on both hard and floppy disks. My wife and I had long before planned a weekend of skiing at Lake Tahoe. We arrived at our rented condo in time to prepare an elegant dinner. Within a couple of hours, I came down with the flu. So much for plans to ski and enjoy a holiday.

"Certainly," I thought, "fate doesn't want my chapter on optimism or an optimistic me." I was in fact feeling somewhat depressed and discouraged. At such times, when Murphy's Law seems to be controlling our universe, we might be tempted by pessimism. An alternative is to laugh at the outrageousness of our unusual situation. Anything less than that might increase paranoia, which is hardly supportive of mental health, let alone optimism. When I later told my adult children about this upsetting episode, I heard them chuckle, as though I were telling a sequel to the news from Lake Wobegon. Through their eyes, I saw a funny story. Learning to laugh, especially at ourselves, can give our optimism a much needed boost.

TAKING CHARGE OF YOUR LIFE

Cathy: *I feel more powerful . . . knowing my limits yet recognizing I am a cocreator of my life, being what I want, doing what I want, and achieving those goals.*

Another crucial ingredient running through each story of optimism reflects an increasing sense of control over life. An optimist believes, I can and I will. Cathy's story illustrates how a person can gain a greater sense of control. Fifty-eight when I met her, Cathy had for most of her adult life been a wife and mother. She was employed in a science laboratory as a technician when she jumped onto a curve of second growth. When she was fifty-three, she left her marriage to become independent and start a new life. Within a ten-year period she has changed the pattern of her life and manifested extraordinary renewal.

How did she get started, and what prompted her to make such a remarkable change?

> When I entered my fifties, I began to sense that I was dying inside. I had not really been listening to my feelings. I was a robot, doing what I should. I had been the "good wife" and the "good mother"—just the way I was raised. I was devoted to others. But where was there room for me? I decided it was time to change—not just change a situation but change me! During the sixties I was too busy raising my kids to hear the message about being yourself and personal growth.
>
> But as my children started to leave home, I started to listen to it. I just wasn't happy, and I didn't know why. It took me a long time to find out. I wasn't meeting any of my goals. I couldn't stay just a housewife. I tried to talk about this with my husband, but he was rigid. Still is. At that point I felt I had no control over my life. I was angry and hurt. I had to work through these feelings and my fears of taking risks.

Aware that her home situation was stifling her, Cathy became attentive to an emerging creative energy that had previously been suppressed. She "started to listen" to messages about liberation and personal growth that she had been too busy to think about. Without a sympathetic audience at home, Cathy joined a women's support group, where she was able to clarify some of her suppressed feelings and needs. Her new friends helped her confront the fear she felt as she contemplated moving out on her own, and they gave her a boost of much needed self-confidence. She soon was "ready to experience anything."

Her growth presents a story of impressive liberation. She has freed herself from both inner and outer constraints. She had felt trapped in conventional roles of wife and mother, roles in which she was subservient. Like Karen, she felt ruled by "shoulds" rather than by "coulds." She had tried to find alternative ways to meet her needs but felt blocked by the rigidity of her husband and an abiding sense of anger. Her anger affected her outlook and even her humor, which then was mostly sarcastic. With the help of her women's group and counseling, she discovered that her underlying anger had really been directed against herself. Only by understanding, confronting, and ultimately transforming that anger into positive energy could she develop a positive attitude:

> I was angry at myself for not being what I thought I should be—for not being the perfect wife, the perfect mother, the perfect employee. It took me a long time to figure out my anger. I'm not sure I have it right yet, but at least I can identify targets of anger now. Back then I looked through my anger and found out that underneath it lay a fear that I wasn't really lovable.
>
> Fortunately, I have a broad network of friends and some really close friends. They and the support group helped me love myself. I realized I was missing a balance in my life. I hadn't learned to love myself. I came from a dysfunctional family and always had to watch out and do what I was told. I've been learning to love myself and know that the more I love myself, the more I can love others, not because I should but because I want to. This has made such a difference in my life, and my relationships with my children have never been better.

Since making this discovery, Cathy has significantly changed. She has overcome anger and its hold on her life. "What do you do if you feel angry now?" I asked her. "I admit it, express it, and get on with what is important," she said. "Also, I have a punching bag in the basement, which I'll hit for a while to make sure the anger gets out." I detected a thin smile, suggesting she had also developed a sense of humor about her "unladylike" way of harmlessly getting anger out of her system.

Her growth has had noticeable external results. Her personal world has become more interesting and complex. While working full-time in the science lab, she started training to become a licensed massage therapist. Like El and Evans she had formulated an important goal over which she could exercise control. She felt both freer and more empowered. Within a couple of years, she retired from the lab and started this new career. At sixty-two she was branching out even further, working as a masseuse but planning another career as a writer. She has established a new home with her good friend, a grade-school music teacher. Each year they take vacations aimed at enlarging their personal boundaries by challenging themselves physically and emotionally. When I last spoke with her, they had started to build a small vacation home in the woods and had completed the first part of it. Cathy also keeps in close touch with her children and is devoted to her first grandchild.

Her internal changes are greater and more important than the external ones, she told me. For the past ten years she has seen herself on a journey of self-discovery and self-realization. She has developed a positive personal identity by becoming more aware of her feminine qualities and balancing them with a strong will, a sense of autonomy, and control over her life. Another big change in her self-image is her increased optimism. To become an optimistic person she had to discard an old script in which she saw herself as a victim. She replaced that image with one of a competent woman who could become the person she really wanted to be. She once reported,

I don't like the word *victim*. But that's how I saw myself back then. We allow ourselves to become victims, and that's how we get stuck. I couldn't move. I was a victim of anger and "shoulds." That made me rigid. As I worked through my anger, I found a return of self-confidence and self-respect.

I addressed my fears and increased my sense of power. It's not power over others. I don't want that. I am developing power by affirming myself, affirming my goals and the changes I'm making. I have an image of myself being what I want, doing what I want, and then I start working on the skills needed to achieve those goals. Like what I'm doing now, learning and practicing the art of massage.

Her optimism has so increased that she rates herself near the top of a ten-point optimism scale. For half a century she was laced up with expectations others had of her. Attending always to the needs of others, she found no room left in her world for her own self-realization. The second half of life looked then like a desert. Only in midlife did she break free to begin her journey toward a more authentic self. Like Daphne, she also "took off at fifty." By no longer allowing others to shape her self-image, she has boldly affirmed the person she wants to become, developed a new life plan, and taken charge of her life.

Now in her sixties, she is more open both to her feelings and to the world, asserting her values and wants with freedom and vitality. Cathy thinks she is more vibrant now than at fifty. She refuses to acknowledge "that growing old means to have less vitality." She reports that most of her sixty-year-old peers are cutting back, while she searches for new answers to questions surfacing from active self-reflection and experimentation. Her reflective openness to change has fostered personal growth; realistic optimism has fueled it. As she told me, "I feel more powerful, but in a different sense—knowing my limits yet recognizing I am a cocreator of my life." Because she no longer adheres to her Presbyterian heritage, her portrait of herself as a cocreator suggests that she feels in accord with and empowered by an evolutionary principle of life. Cathy provides another illustration of how an adult over fifty can take a firm hold of the helm and set a new course for the second half of life's voyage.

STRATEGIES FOR REALISTIC OPTIMISM

Optimism is a tremendously powerful force in human development and renewal as well as in healing and well-being. It acts as a motivator in creativity and learning, an enabler of change and growth. Optimism is not a fixed quantity; it can diminish or increase. If we are intent on growth, we have to learn how to develop it. The stories in this chapter have shown us how several adults have increased their realistic optimism. They met distress and were not overcome. They learned to face adversities and turn them into opportunities. Tested and troubled, they nevertheless allowed positive factors to outweigh negative ones. They learned to hope and believe that at least in their personal worlds, all shall be well.

To employ the strategies we have learned from them to rebuild and maintain your realistic optimism, you can

- honestly assess your situation and develop a perspective that admits obstacles and fears but highlights your strengths and other resources you can tap
- learn to see failures positively, as learning opportunities
- visualize desired outcomes—emphasize what you can do, and develop an "I can" outlook
- receive help and encouragement from family, friends, and a support group or counseling, or both
- welcome challenges that can build self-confidence and learn to assert what you deeply want
- express your dream in a purposeful plan
- when stalled, use intervening time to rechannel interests and develop alternative outlets
- develop and enjoy your sense of humor
- take charge of your life by making choices that bring you closer to desired outcomes

The people in this study have had the courage to follow directions that lead to the unknown. We, too, face uncharted terrain that calls for courage, commitment, and a derring-do that is new to most of us. We have seen by their examples how the principle of realistic optimism will enable us to step forward into the adventures of second growth. With the strength gained from the first two steps, we shall be ready to take on the third challenging task: building a new, positive identity that will be more appropriate for our third age.

4
Principle Three: Creating a Positive Third-Age Identity

My journey has been to go the edge, and as I do I find amazing dimensions to myself.

—Barbara

WHY THINK ABOUT IDENTITY AT THIS LATE DATE?

Rebuilding a vital personal identity represents one of the most daunting yet exciting challenges presented by the third age. Until recently forming a viable personal identity was viewed primarily as a major task of youth. Only by achieving a healthy personal identity can a young person be ready for the challenges of adulthood. As the American Express motto says, "Don't leave home without it." The psychologist Erik Erikson, who so brilliantly illuminated the often tortuous adolescent identity process, in his later years suggested that forming a personal identity should be a continual process. As our lives unfold in a complex, fast-paced world, it is appropriate for us not only to take on new traits but also to enlarge and redefine our sense of self. Continual self-redefinition is increasingly recognized to be a normal element of healthy adult development.

Some research has found adults who have renewed and even transformed their identities. For example, in the famous Berkeley longitudinal study, which stretched over seventy years, the sociologist John Clausen

discovered somewhat to his surprise that the identities of healthy, successful adults evolved over the years. While most studies of the life span had
shown more constancy than change in adults, Clausen and his colleagues
found some men and women who were moving in unanticipated directions. By becoming more intellectually alive, more sensitive and emotionally expressive, and more interested in developing new lifestyles, they were
also developing new identities. Sometimes individuals surprised themselves when they discovered dormant qualities and developed new directions. They questioned long-held roles and habitual patterns and gave
themselves permission to change. Their identities evolved as they shed social roles, recovered youthful traits, and combined them with their adult
strengths.

Ironically, what holds many of us back from developing a new personal
identity is our previous success at constructing the one we have. We can
become locked into the mental models, habits, and roles that until midlife
guided our lives. Coasting comfortably on our past socialization process,
we grow oblivious to new possibilities. We often fail to see broader hori-
zons because we are mindlessly committed to roles and norms of the past.
Many of us tune out novelties. Building a new, more appropriate identity
for our third age involves freeing ourselves from attachment to some previous achievements.

The psychologists Robert Kegan and Lisa Lahey have made a tantalizing
suggestion about our task in midlife: we should construct a post-institutional identity. In our youthful socialization process our identities were
formed largely in terms of the roles we acquired in a variety of relationships and institutions, especially family, school, work, and community.
The result was a compromise between self and society. Instead of identifying with social roles, as we tended to do in youth, we should transcend
them to become more autonomous and self-actualized. With longer lives
and healthier lifestyles, we have an opportunity to go beyond the earlier
compromise and create a richer, more idiosyncratic identity. That is what
the people in my study have discovered, often more by accident than by
intention. One woman phrased the challenge this way: "It's time to make
myself a person again." These adults have left behind or redefined a variety of roles as they moved into uncharted terrain where they are freer to
create more uniquely individual selves. They have been learning not to
take their roles so seriously, realizing that personal worth extends beyond
any particular role.

I have found that in creating a post-institutional identity, we will confront several challenges. The first has to do with defining our age. Satchel Paige, the legendary baseball player and first black pitcher in the American League, is said to have phrased our challenge this way: "How old would you be if you didn't know how old you was?" Are we still young or old or in some other category? We have to accept the reality of growing older, but we do not have to live down to the old expectations of chronological age. We can also grow young. We might address this challenge by doing some upside-down thinking about the meaning of our expected longevity. Recognizing that we probably have the equivalent of a thirty-year life bonus, why should we see it coming at the end of our lives? Why not insert the bonus in the middle? If we see our thirty-year bonus emerging in the third age instead of at the end of our lives, how old are we then? Who are we? Are we landing or taking off, finishing up or starting anew? Or both? The paradox of growing old/growing young presents an unnerving yet enticing challenge to our task of self-definition. With respect to most of our important interests and efforts, age could become irrelevant.

A second challenge involves gender. Sociologists have observed that maturing men and women experience gender crossover. As they become older, men often take on feminine qualities, and women add masculine traits. In my study I saw something a little different. In second growth women often deepen their feminine sides while becoming more independent and affirmative, whereas in adding gentler, feminine traits, men have enriched their masculinity, not lost it. Creating a new identity requires us to rethink what it means to be a whole woman or a whole man in the second half of our lives.

A third challenge lies in the process of self-actualization itself, which includes both greater autonomy and a sense of deeper connectedness. The late Abraham Maslow described a paradoxical commitment in self-actualization—to autonomy and to ego transcendence, in response to "something bigger than we are." In a truly self-actualizing experience we both center on ourselves and forget ourselves in appreciating and serving a larger reality. The unfolding lives of some adults in my study suggest that in second growth one's emerging identity will incorporate one's awareness of his or her unique potential *and* one's inherent connectedness with others and the universe. As we shall see later, an important part of our self-actualizing, post-institutional identity also emerges in response to several key questions involving our personal boundaries: Whom do I love? What do I care about? What connections provide meaning? What purposes do I serve?

A fourth challenge requires that we rethink our definition of success. In our third age, what standards should we use to measure that success? Our previous definitions, often shaped by specific roles and extrinsic social standards, may be inappropriate for our new identity. We need some up-side-down thinking in this area as well. I like the suggestion provided by Professor Fritz Roethlisberger, when he addressed a graduating class at the Harvard Business School fifty years ago. Knowing that the young men had their hearts set on goals of fame and fortune that could be achieved with their superior education, hard work, and connections, he encouraged them to look at success and ultimately their lives differently. He suggested that instead of viewing the present instrumentally as the means to the future, they might reverse the arrows of time. Think of the future as the means and the present as an end, he told them. I doubt whether those young men could follow his advice. The message came twenty-five years too soon.

Roethlisberger was, of course, affirming the profound importance of purposes and values in constructing an identity and setting a life course. But wasn't he also suggesting that personal success will best be measured *intrinsically* by who we are becoming rather than *extrinsically* by what we might obtain or achieve? Live more fully in the present, for it is all that we have for sure. Perhaps success in our third age depends on how well we respond in the present to the opportunities provided by the longevity revolution. As we take stock of who we are becoming in the second half of our lives, what matters most is not so much any external achievement but the quality of our personal complexity. I'll say more about redefining success in Chapter 5.

DETECTING AND DISLODGING
THE STEREOTYPES OF AGE

Building a new identity can be tough work; our society is not kind to maturity. If, like the stepmother in *Snow White and the Seven Dwarfs*, we ask, "Mirror, mirror on the wall, who is fairest of them all?" the answer we get is, "No one over fifty." No wonder we have difficulty in forming a viable midlife identity. Our youth-oriented society tends to assume that age coexists with attractiveness and value in inverse proportions. The more of one, the less of the other. Commercial images chosen by the media also show how much we idolize the twenties.

This cultural devaluation of maturity confounds our efforts. Maturing adults often sense a discrepancy between the self they inwardly talk to and the person they see in the mirror. They often do not like what they see. At fifty, one man said, "I know I'm getting older, but I can't believe I'm as old as the guy I shave every morning." Another man in his early fifties told me how disturbed he was when a young woman characterized him admiringly as a grandfatherly type, while he imagined himself as still fatherly. A man who has enjoyed feeling attractive to young women experienced shock when they began to pass by him as if he were invisible. An attractive woman expressed her shock when she noticed that a former lover was more drawn to her twenty-year-old daughter than he was to her. This was more than an awakening; it was an identity-crunching experience. I have often heard women ask friends a question they are afraid to ask the mirror: "How old do I look? Do I look as old as she does?" In this case friends are not expected to tell the truth, the whole truth, and nothing but the truth. As we mature, we do not particularly like our looks and find it hard to accept our age. Our attitude can become a major roadblock to our progress.

As I suggested earlier, we need to critically examine our attitudes and beliefs about age. Why is this so important? Dr. James Birren, a leading gerontologist, succinctly described the danger of assimilating the wrong ideas about aging. What we take in is stored in our neurons; the brain sends these learned messages to the rest of the system, affecting our behavior and development. If we have acquired a negative view of being older, we are much more likely than those with a positive view to experience our increase of years as degeneration. Dr. Gay Luce, founder of SAGE (Senior Actualization and Growth Exploration), has astutely observed that it is not the years that reduce us but how we have learned to live them, giving up a little of our true selves at each step. Our unwitting acceptance of negative stereotypes about age and growing older threatens the development of a rich, vital, creatively unfolding identity. That is why we should free ourselves from myths of aging, or what Betty Friedan has called an "age mystique," well before it becomes irrevocably embedded in our neurons.

We are all at risk of premature, degenerative aging because our culture abounds with a prejudice against "oldness." I recently overheard two youthful, vigorous men in their fifties. One, a new father who works out nearly every day, commented, "Since turning fifty, I don't know what's happening, but I'm training old." His friend responded, "You can't let that happen. Just don't think about it." "Yeah, I'll have to work on it," the first one said. "I just can't help but feel old when I train." Because I swim with him four days a week, I had not noticed any change in his appearance or his performance. What apparently has changed is his self-image, triggered by a milestone birthday interpreted with cultural prejudices. It seems his identity is subtly shifting into a mold driven by cultural stereotypes.

In applying mindful reflection to your personal identity, consider the cultural forces working against a vital, creative, and enriched midlife identity. On TV and in movies, cartoons, birthday cards, and advertisements, people over fifty appear unappealing and often slightly doltish. In addition to an idolatry of youth in the media, prejudice against maturity is expressed sometimes innocently in popular culture. Young adults imagine that life past fifty or sixty is only a half-life, as in the Beatles' song "When I'm Sixty-Four." The assumption is that at best sixty-year-olds can expect the muted excitement of fireside knitting, gardening, and a Sunday-morning ride. In pop culture being sixty seems equivalent to being one hundred. Are kernels of prejudiced pop culture notions perking in our brains?

Middle-aging stereotypes also ripple through modern literature. Even some of America's most talented writers express them. John Updike has chronicled his generation's development in four novels focusing on a character named Rabbit. For thirty years, Rabbit lives out several contemporary life scripts. He runs from a troubled marriage in his twenties, experiments with lifestyles in his thirties, settles down in business and marriage in his forties, and in his early fifties, retires. In the last novel both Updike and Rabbit are past fifty. At this age Rabbit is a tired, disappointed, and sad middle-aged man who prematurely gives up on life and then succumbs to a heart attack. The underlying message suggests that life after fifty has reached a dead end.

Women novelists tell a similar tale. Anne Tyler has described middle-aged persons with depressing sensitivity. Her portrait of a married couple who journey to a friend's funeral reveals a fifty-year-old husband who, like his wife, has a sadness caused not by an awareness of his mortality but by his sense of failure:

He was lonely and tired and lacking in hope and his son had not turned out well and his daughter didn't think much of him, and he still couldn't figure out where he had gone wrong.

This ordinary couple struggles to find meaning and contentment at an age they cannot quite comprehend. They are neither old nor young, but they are old enough to know that reality has not embodied earlier dreams. Whatever peaks they might have achieved seem to lie behind them. Their dreams envisage what might have been rather than what could be. In another novel Tyler tells the story of a repressed wife and mother who struggles for liberation from a family that takes her for granted only to end up right back where she started. In Tyler's "ladder of years" midlife is a step down. The message seems to be that we are foolish to try to break away from old patterns after forty or fifty. So much of even the best in our culture reflects a belief that after half a century, it is time for us to start packing it in.

Ironically, seniors often manifest this negative stereotype. Reports from Leisure World, a huge retirement complex in California, indicate a growing antagonism between those in their early sixties and those over seventy. Dr. Bernice Neugarten, a leading researcher of midlife and aging, has found that restrictive age standards become more powerful as people grow older, which might explain the Leisure World phenomenon. Professor Clausen also found that people in their sixties often do not want to identify with older people. I remember trying to persuade my father, suffering from too much empty time in his seventies, to join a senior-citizens club. "No way, they're too old," he kept saying, even though I pointed out that most were ten years younger than he. The stereotype of aging embedded in his neurons shaped his attitude and contributed to his decline and eventual placement in a nursing home, where he spent eight years of prolonged dying. It was not the years that undid him but the way he lived them after fifty, giving up a little bit of his strong, creative self with each step. As Dr. Bortz's title suggests, he lived too short and died too long, perhaps because he sensed no other option.

BUILDING A POST-INSTITUTIONAL IDENTITY

Helen: *I don't know how you're supposed to perceive yourself at midlife. At last I'm just enjoying it.*

A different generation has a new option. As one woman in my study said when she was in her midfifties, "In my mother's generation, to be fifty was to have one foot in the grave. For me this is the beginning of a very creative period in my life." One man said, "Being nearly sixty is surprising me. I don't think you have to walk around with a slipper in your hand when you're fifty-eight. In my thirties I imagined I'd become a potato by this age, but that hasn't happened. I wouldn't let it. I've been running, biking, and coaching rugby. In fact, my physical activity is on the rise. I feel great about myself." This man confided that he had struggled with a negative self-image as an addictive personality most of his life. Only in the past ten years did he proudly identify with the person he is becoming. On the other hand, Paul, whom we met in Chapter 1, was building a strong post-institutional identity at an early age. In his fifties he realized he wanted to redo what he had achieved. His corporate identity in particular was squeezing the life out of him. At sixty-five, Paul wrote that having broken free of past roles, he was "having the time of my life." Contrary to old beliefs, our direction and our identities are not set unless we choose them to be.

The adults in my study indicated in a variety of ways how they were critiquing age stereotypes. One question in the first interview I had with each of them was: Would you like to be twenty-five again? A salient difference between those who manifested second growth and others who did not could be found in their responses. The former invariably said, "No, because now is better." Even when they enjoyed being twenty-five, their attitude toward growing older was much more positive than we would generally expect to find. Many adults related stories of impressive courage, insight, experimentation, and determination in achieving a new positive identity that broke through old role boundaries.

Helen told of a tough battle with stereotypes in her middle years. For twenty-five years she had followed the conventional pattern of a working-class woman with only a high school education. She had married and stayed home to care for the house and raise her daughter. When I met her in her late forties, she was developing in ways she had never imagined. Several years earlier she had found a job as a school bookkeeper. More recently, she had begun a separation agreement and was becoming a single parent. She was beginning to experience renewal, but she had a hard time getting past forty:

In my twenties I wasn't sure what I was looking for. In my thirties I had many ups and downs. I had a lot of anger and felt out of control at times.

When I turned forty it was hard. It was like my youth was all gone. My parents kidded me about my age. My marriage was not working, and my daughter was very ill. I felt old.

It was then that Helen took a job as clerk in the business office of a small private school. She was fortunate to have a good boss, who mentored and encouraged her. At work she developed competence, self-confidence, and optimism; she became aware of hidden potential that had been buried in a repressive home environment. She also made friends who helped her appreciate her positive qualities and discover her good sense of humor. Eventually, she worked up to a more responsible position in which she was put in charge of accounts receivable. She did not define herself by this role. Success in work helped her discover qualities that she affirmed and then included in an emerging positive identity. After work hours she developed an appreciation of the outdoors and started to improve her physical fitness. She became an avid downhill skier in the winter and a regular walker during most of the year. Nearing fifty, she found herself becoming a vital, competent woman with new possibilities ahead of her. Her youth was not all gone after all.

In responding to my question about how she felt about being the age she was, she pointed to qualities important in a new post-institutional identity:

> I don't know how you're supposed to perceive yourself at midlife. At last I'm just enjoying it. I'm active and happier with myself now than I ever was. I have more confidence than I did in my twenties and thirties. I've discovered things about myself—a sense of humor, optimism, competence. I know I can do a lot that I never thought I could. I'm looking forward to whatever comes next. I have confidence that I can continue to grow and do whatever I set my mind to. . . . This is all so new for me.

Helen has dramatically changed both her lifestyle and her identity to become a self-actualizing person. Her emerging new self is characterized by growth traits and paradox. She is freer yet more connected. She accepts the fact that she is older, but she is also tapping youthful potential. She no longer measures her age by the calendar. She has thoughtfully battled age and gender stereotypes to become a new woman. Her new standard of success seems to be in continued growth and pursuing the goals she sets for herself.

A major task for Helen in shaping a healthier self-image and lifestyle was to become freer and more autonomous. For years she had tried to break out of a dead marriage and live on her own, but she was held back by fear and a sense of responsibility to her family. Helen received help from counseling and friends to become independent and to define herself in a much more positive light. "The old scene at home was not good for any of us. I knew I needed to be free," she said. After several years of struggling with separation, she finally got divorced. As she moved out of her marital role, which had defined her as subordinate to her husband, she became truly independent for the first time in her life. But she also embraced another paradoxical challenge. As she enlarged her personal freedom, she also strengthened special relationships. In addition to an enduring, close relationship with her daughter, who has now graduated from college, and several good friends, she became closer to her parents. Five years later she began a new relationship with a man. When I last talked with her, she was preparing to marry him. She was free to redefine the role of wife and integrate that into an expanding personal identity.

As I explored the subject of personal identity, I often asked questions about appearance. Some people I interviewed, as I mentioned, did not like their changing looks. I figured that if adults really are developing positive new identities, they must do more than just accept how they look. They should take pride in their appearance and not feel inferior to cultural idols. I found that those individuals manifesting second growth were not only consistently critical of our society's idolization of youthful beauty, but they also felt good about their changing appearance. That seems to be an important feature of self-recognition and acceptance. Helen's response to my question about the popular notion that beauty belongs to the young sets a new aesthetic standard for herself and the rest of us:

> The message of the media is not true. You think you're beautiful when you're young, but you're too worried about yourself, not relaxed nor deep. Beauty has more to do with emotions. Young is pretty. But as you get older, you can get much more beautiful. There's a greater depth.

Helen liked the face in the mirror. After fifty, beauty is not skin deep. Sitting on my desk as I write is the photo of an eighty-two-year-old man who was a dear friend and mentor; the character reflected in his glowing smile is beautiful. To me, in this picture he is more attractive than he was in photos taken forty years earlier. As we grow older, we take on the appearance of the person we are becoming. Depth of character adds quality to one's appearance, which is just not reflected in youth. With her growth and improving self-image, Helen believed herself to be more, not less, attractive.

LETTING YOUR YOUTH CATCH UP WITH YOUR AGE

Jim: *In running around, I failed to pay attention to the best thing that ever happened to me.*

In grappling with midlife identity issues, many people continue to focus on institutional commitments, identifying themselves by their roles in which success is often extrinsically measured. They hold on as long as possible to an established identity until retirement. Overidentification with roles makes adjustment to retirement much more difficult for them, because they find themselves with an impoverished identity. When you enter the roleless role of a retiree, who are you? Some people give in to cultural stereotypes and allow themselves to age prematurely. A small minority react to their age by denial and pretend to be what they are not. At least that is what I had observed until I began this study. It was then that I found another option of building a rejuvenated identity.

Jim's experience provides a vivid illustration of one aspect of this new option. However, he first had to overcome his initial denial of his age. A tall, angular sixty-three-year-old, Jim had had a long career as an engineer before he retired early. When we first met, he was eager to tell me about starting a new direction. The tempo of this interview was fast, as though he wanted to get through it quickly. I soon learned that the energy came from his anticipation of his forthcoming first marriage. After mentioning this great upcoming event, he then told me his story.

After graduating from MIT, he entered an engineering career immediately rather than going to graduate school. He loved his work and moved quickly up to more responsible positions. As he threw himself into his job, he became a workaholic. Meanwhile, his parents started to age and then became ill. They were dependent upon him and his sister. Jim agreed to provide for them and his sister as well, so that she could take care of their parents. During his thirties and early forties, his job and making a home for his parents and sister were his major concerns. His parents became weak, housebound, and eventually died.

Jim had planned to spend more time with his sister, getting out and enjoying life. They had plans to travel. But his sister became ill and moved to a warmer climate. Jim felt deserted. At about that time, he had also counted on receiving a promotion to an executive position. It did not come. Passed over for someone younger, he became resentful and decided to retire early. He found himself alone in his midfifties without prospects for a satisfying life. It was time, he thought, to make some significant changes.

The midlife he described seemed like a desert without an oasis: empty of close relationships, confined by obsession with a job, constrained by a few roles, and lacking in both growth and fun. In his midfifties Jim realized that his life had been too narrowly focused. He felt he needed more than ever to establish his own family and decided to concentrate on making the right connections.

> At first I started dating women twenty years younger than I. I met some very fine women, and I thought they were interested in me. But none was willing to make a commitment. After a few years I dated women nearly thirty years younger. I needed to have a young woman who was interested in having a family and bearing children. Since I was retired, I had time to take good care of myself. I thought, "I'm really a lot younger than my age. Why shouldn't these women be interested in me?" I felt I had sacrificed too much and left out something really important. I wanted to make up for lost time and start my own family. But it wasn't working.

His initiative had not taken him very far. His response to his age was basically to deny it and pretend to be much younger. Turning sixty, still in pursuit of a young bride, Jim received a letter from his high school sweetheart. When he went off to college, she had married someone else. She had had a good marriage, but her husband died early. At a high school reunion, she had learned Jim's address and decided to write him. Jim answered her letter and then returned to his hometown for a visit with his widowed former sweetheart. As they became reacquainted, they discovered that they still had much in common. He greatly enjoyed her company, but "she was too old for my plan. I still needed a much younger woman," he told me.

Denial of age was still going strong. Partly to prove to himself he was still youthful, he signed up for a twenty-eight-day Outward Bound course in the wilderness of northern Maine. It provided much more learning than he had anticipated. In fact, he experienced a self-awareness that was to change his life:

> Nearly everyone on that course was thirty to forty years younger than I. At first I was scared, thinking I wouldn't be able to keep up. But I soon learned I could stay with the best of them. I did everything. Sometimes I was really tired and ached. But I could do it. After a couple of weeks I started to wonder what I was doing. So I can keep up with younger fellows—so what?
>
> More important than the physical stuff, I started feeling like I hadn't for years. I guess I had just pushed a lot of feelings out of my life while I focused on work. One night looking at the sunset, I actually cried. On the course's solo, I had three days to do some deep thinking. I looked at years of chasing younger women and realized that was crazy. In running around, I failed to pay attention to the best thing that ever happened to me—my relationship with my old sweetheart. Right then and there, I made a decision.

When he got home, the first thing Jim did was to pay a visit to her and propose marriage. Shortly after my interview, they became husband and wife. In listening to Jim, I was impressed by the dramatic turnabout that led to the decision to marry a woman his own age. As we talked about this experience, I sensed that his interpretation of this process as overcoming denial was not fully accurate. He described himself as pretending to be younger than he really was and then waking up to his true age. I agreed, but I saw a more complex process at work as well. Jim's change illustrates how we can insert our life bonus in the middle of our lives rather than experience it at the end.

In his fifties Jim was dedicated to recovering a youth he had abandoned at an early age. His first, impulsive reaction was to shed the roles of work and family and then reassert his youth by denying his age. During his outdoor course something happened to allow him to change direction; but he did not give up on youth. "What you seem to have done," I observed, "is to allow your youth to catch up with you. The youth that you have gotten in touch with seems to have entered your experience of growing older without causing you to deny your age." Without being fully conscious of it, Jim was integrating his youthfulness into his development and evolving identity as a sixty-year-old man. His youthfulness was exhibited not only in his energy and physical activity; it showed in openness to feelings, sexual interest, spontaneity, delight in the present moment, and eagerness to make a long-term commitment. He was growing younger while growing older. The result has been a burst of new growth with a new personal identity.

The English novelist John Fowles wrote about the integration of youth and growing older in his novel *Daniel Martin*. The protagonist is a successful fifty-year-old English writer living in Hollywood with a woman more than twenty years his junior. They have a good life together and are in love. Yet he is not content. There is an incompatibility between their perspectives, which creates an incongruity in their lives that only he becomes aware of. While his young mate focuses on the present, he keeps returning to the past. When his best friend back home dies, Daniel returns to England, where he visits and subsequently falls in love with his friend's widow, who is his age. In thinking his way toward a decision about his future, he writes to Jane, the widow, about his Hollywood relationship and its impact on his sense of identity: "Jerry's very young, Jane. With her I have to live very much in the present. In today. The past becomes like an infidelity, something one has no right to remember or refer back to."

He realizes that to be faithful to himself, he must recover his past and integrate it into his contemporary self. While ignoring his age and his past, living with a much younger woman and running with a younger crowd, he was denying not only his age but also his real youth. To forge a satisfying life and form an acceptable identity, he has to bring into his present both his past experiences and his future possibilities.

After probing reflection, Daniel Martin declares that one must achieve "*whole sight*; or all the rest is desolation." His future and his past become the means to achieve his goal of a satisfying present. To form a new identity supportive of growth through the third age, we, too, need to integrate our youth and our maturity. Our vision of who we are becoming should expand to include our youthfulness along with our years. Rather than surrendering a little bit of our true selves with each step, we can instead let our youth catch up to us and thereby revive and rejuvenate our personal identities. That is the healthy alternative to denial, role playing, or succumbing to negative cultural stereotypes. Coming to terms with our age involves the paradox of flowing in two directions at once.

THE PARADOX OF GROWING OLDER/GROWING YOUNG

The idea of recovering one's youth can easily be misinterpreted. There is a huge difference between growing young and regressing or never growing up. I once interviewed a youthful sixty-year-old who seemed full of life and open to adventure. As I spent several days with him, he seemed more and more immature. His most animated conversations revolved around himself. He detested the idea of getting old and would not associate with "old people." Having left his "old" wife behind, he was interested in dating only women at least twenty years younger than himself. He was heavily invested in denial of his chronological age. His lifestyle was a romanticized version of late adolescence, footloose and fancy-free. In retirement he had the money to act out his twenty-year-old fantasies. In his longitudinal study Dr. Vaillant also found such immature adults, whom he labeled "perpetual boys." Those in denial of their age are among the worst-adapted adults in midlife. To grow young definitely does not mean to regress or to deny one's years.

Talk of "growing young" invariably raises a few eyebrows. Is this idea really trustworthy? Can we really experience rejuvenation in the second half of life? The possibility of genuine midlife rejuvenation has recently received strong support from the social sciences. The anthropologist Ashley Montagu has discovered a remarkable factor that helps explain human beings' successful adaptation and advance in the evolutionary process. Unlike other animals we humans are born as embryos, not fully enough developed to make it in the world on our own. We are helpless at birth and totally dependent on our mothers, unlike animals that can often maneuver independently shortly after birth. Furthermore, humans differ from other animals in that we hold some infantile and childlike characteristics for life. In contrast to apes, for example, humans retain recognizable childlike features such as shape of the head, body size, and relative hairlessness throughout our development. He calls this phenomenon neoteny. The term refers primarily to human physiology and is useful in providing an evolutionary explanation for several distinctive human features.

When he turns his attention to an individual's evolution in the adult years, Montagu sees an application of neoteny to healthy development. In addition to physiological traits, youthful behavioral traits have contributed to humans' successful adaptation, such as open-mindedness, curiosity, testing of new ideas, and inventiveness. Other important childlike characteristics include delight, excitement, laughter, and playfulness. By extending neoteny from physical to behavioral traits, Montagu argues that human beings can revolutionize adulthood, staying "youthful all the days of their lives." He believes that an appropriate aim is to apply the principle of neoteny to our adult development, to let youthful traits influence and guide our individual evolution. This means to grow young! From the perspective of neoteny, the goal of life is to grow young and "to die young—as late as possible." A delightful rendition of this upside-down idea was presented in the movie *Harold and Maude*, in which a seventy-nine-year-old woman liberates a highly repressed, morbid young man by teaching him to let childlike qualities into his adult life and be free.

C. G. Jung made a similar point. He believed that "in every adult there lurks a child—an eternal child, something that is always becoming, is never completed, and calls for unceasing care, attention, and education." Jung believed that the process of individuation, his term for self-actualization, constitutes "the only meaningful life." In his view reactivating one's inner child is the ultimate measure of success; it represents nothing less than a vocation.

The psychologist David Gutmann gave support to this view as he described a vital older woman admitted for clinical observation and treatment because of her strange behavior. Gutmann suggests that her bizarre antics could be explained by pent-up psychic energy that was trying to find a creative outlet. Her inner child was, as it were, pounding to be let out. The psychologist Emily Hancock has also found in a small study of adult women that their growth in later life was a result of rediscovering and reaffirming the girls they had been before reaching puberty. We need to respect the youthful, creative energy that has often been repressed in midlife. To move forward, we first must turn back.

Matthew: *I had this strange dream . . . a child looked at me with reproach. I realized I had to take care of the child within me.*

Matthew helped me see more clearly the paradox of growing young while simultaneously accepting age and one's own mortality. A fifty-four-year-old Canadian educator when I first interviewed him, Matthew told me that he was in the best period of his life: happily married with three talented children; in charge of a distinctive university program supported by grants; recognized for his leadership in his community; in good health and physically active in several sports. To my surprise I learned that if I had interviewed him several years earlier, I would have found him in dire straits:

> I think I've changed a lot in the past few years. About eight years ago I felt trapped. I could see that everything was going well. My marriage was good, the family was developing, my job was right, and I was in good health. But I started to feel like the floor had been taken away from underneath me. I was confronting the meaning of my life. What am I doing? What is the purpose of my life? For some reason I felt empty inside. I thought, "If I were to die tomorrow I wouldn't care." What had been so important, my career and my competence, just didn't seem to be enough. I went to a therapist for about a year. Through this process I discovered that I had been giving too much importance to professional activity and external achievements. I had been ignoring some very important aspects of myself.
>
> In particular, I had neglected my childhood qualities: playfulness, imagination, and creativity. At that time I had this strange dream that kept recurring. I saw a child who looked at me with reproach, as though it was my fault that he was dying. Sometimes the child would be lying in a coffin. I would reach out to embrace him, and then he would revive. Finally, I sensed that I was that child. I realized I had to take care of the child within me. I still have much to learn about this and to allow more time for play, imagination, and reflection.

Although very few of the individuals I interviewed experienced a midlife crisis of meaning, some, like Matthew, felt that something very important in themselves had been neglected in the process of adjustment and achievement. Matthew had become a puzzle to himself. At a peak in his life, he was falling into a depression.

As he talked about his problem with a therapist, he realized that he needed to listen carefully to the dream about his childhood. The child in him was criticizing his success, particularly in work, because he was allowing the role to stifle important childlike qualities. His mature identity was at odds with his growth. He had to reshape his identity and his lifestyle by developing a post-institutional self that was responsive to his inner child, who had been suffocating.

Matthew responded to the dream's message in practical ways. He made small adjustments. Instead of leaving his job, he changed his work situation, delegating more responsibilities to others, taking time for personal interaction and laughter, and putting more emphasis on people, less on tasks. He also modified his lifestyle to have more free time for reflection, relationships, and playful activities. One result of these changes was that he became clearer about his basic values and more self-actualized: "I feel centered, more in touch with what is real. I'm trying to integrate all this. It feels like a ripening within me." Ironically, by creating a fuller, more positive self-image he experienced even more success in his career.

In addition to lighthearted playfulness and openness to learning, another important quality in childhood is willingness to forgive failure and learn from mistakes. So often adults express regrets about mistakes made in the past. "If only I had known and done something differently"—in parenting, work, relationships, lifestyle. Brooding on regrets can certainly impede second growth. Young children do not take their efforts to learn and achieve so seriously. They do not expect to always get it right the first time. They learn from mistakes. A child knows that it is acceptable to "get it wrong" before getting it right.

Many of us strive to create an identity as the perfect spouse, perfect parent, perfect employee, exemplary professional. Our identities often become overstuffed with an inflated sense of importance because of all the serious roles we have. Matthew found it such a relief and so liberating to see himself again as a child, still making mistakes, doing some things well and others not so well, with plenty of room left for improvement, exploration, and discovery. Failure is part of learning. By recovering this capability of humility and self-forgiveness, we can restore a dimension of childhood in our adult worlds.

In his later years the psychologist Jerome Bruner became aware of a child within him ready to speak more lines than it seems had been allotted. In his autobiography I think he was suggesting that personal growth after fifty involves returning to one's childhood not to repeat the past but to recover and remake it into a later, better edition. Like other adults I studied, Matthew learned that his inner child had qualities that he needed to recognize and embrace in order to be more of a whole person—spontaneity and playfulness, openness to experience and curiosity, feeling and imagination. As the English poet William Wordsworth famously phrased it, "the child is father of the man." By listening to the child in us we can recover our individual roots and create a better edition—a more balanced, richer personal identity.

Now in his midsixties, Matthew has for over ten years been building that vital, richer personal identity. At sixty-four he decided to develop a new research project for a sabbatical, which would require him to learn a whole new set of skills. As he laid plans for this adventure, he wrote to me about his progress. "The next academic year will probably be one of the most exciting years of my life," he said. His youthfulness is more important in his outlook and unfolding identity today than it was when he was in his forties.

There is yet another side to Matthew's story of transformation that intensifies the challenge we face in applying the third principle of second growth to our lives. In his dream Matthew confronted not only his inner child but also the reality of his own mortality. The significant themes in his dream were lost childhood and dying. We need to address both. Coming to terms with the natural fact of one's death is also part of one's new identity. That need not be a traumatic experience, as a British psychoanalyst suggested when inventing the idea of midlife crisis. Matthew acknowledged a crisis, but that was not related to his awareness of growing older and dying. What seemed to prompt his crisis was stunted growth and the repression of his inner child. Matthew had to respond to his dream in two ways: by recovering his child and by accepting his aging and inevitable end.

Like others in this study, Matthew found that awareness of his mortality did not frighten him. "I'm aware of my death. I think about it. Death actually helps me grow. It forces me deeper into myself, and I try to be faithful to myself. I consciously reflect on what's important and take a direction that seems right," he said. There seems to be a correspondence between midlife renewal and a healthy acceptance of one's own death. The psychiatrist Irvin Yalom has observed that as a general rule, "the less one's sense of life fulfillment, the greater one's death anxiety." Several of the women in my study nearly died from cancer. "What did coming so close to dying mean to you?" I asked one of them. "It helped me cherish the life I have. You can emerge from this crisis frightened or grateful. At first I was terrified. But I came out grateful," she said. The greater one's sense of fulfillment, the less one's death anxiety.

Knowing he would die motivated Matthew to get on with his life, sort out his priorities, and commit to self-actualization. Like Jung, he saw this as a vocation. "We are a unique creation of God," he told me. "I think we have the responsibility to realize our potential as fully as possible." In becoming whole persons we move paradoxically in opposite directions. We need to recognize that we are growing older. Even a life bonus does not last forever. We shall die. Acceptance of death is part of our renewed identity process. Aging inevitably entails loss. With realistic optimism we can unite beginning anew with ending, growing young with growing older. This dual vision will enable us to achieve the "whole sight" needed for a ripening identity and a fulfilling lifestyle in the third age.

THE PARADOX OF GENDER

Barbara: *In my midlife I've become aware of my feminine side. . . . I have become a much more feeling person.*

Developing our own personal rendition of gender within our self-portrait was a crucial part of our youthful identity-formation process. We had to define ourselves in a way that made sense to us, given our assumptions of what it meant to be male or female. As we have matured, most of us have probably had to revisit this issue and do it all over again, not only because we get older but also because the first version was badly drawn. During the past twenty-five years, traditional assumptions about gender have been widely questioned as inappropriate. If we have realized that sexual roles were too narrowly cast, leaving us unbalanced, then we most likely have rethought and redesigned our individual self-portraits. Many of us have been trying to achieve a fuller rendition of what it means to be a man or woman. Women have increasingly learned to be strong, independent, assertive, even competitive, while they have continued to be nurturing and supportive. Men have enlarged their emotional repertoire to become tender, sensitive, and caring as well as assertive and autonomous. The sociologist Janet Zollinger Giele has described this phenomenon as a crossover of sex roles, which she views as one of the most significant factors in modern history. It is also an important factor in personal growth.

The adults I studied who manifested second growth had been rethinking gender for years. Perhaps it came as no surprise for them to realize that in midlife this task was still unfinished. How can a postmenopausal identity be genuinely feminine? How can a man be truly masculine with diminishing testosterone? Adding the adjective *old* to our self-definition as a man or a woman can decimate any residual sense of a meaningful sexual role. At least it will if we follow the usual scenario of adult development. In the second half of life, our personal definition of gender needs fresh attention, unless we want to drape ourselves with the mantle of androgyny.

In the newly recognized prime of life, we have a chance to achieve not only greater gender balance but also a fuller understanding of what it means to be a man or a woman. I mentioned earlier that as people grow older, men take on more feminine characteristics and women take on masculine ones. That was, perhaps, truer in the past when sex roles were more one-sidedly defined than it will be in the future. Second growth presents a slightly different picture than gender crossover. Jim, whom we met earlier in this chapter, was at first one-sidedly masculine: tough minded, assertive, and competitive, excluding feelings from his definition of self. Then he transcended this limited sense of male identity by becoming more sensitive, caring, and emotional. In his romantic involvement he developed not only his repressed youthfulness but also a side of his masculinity that had been buried. He was able to release the man he had never been in a deep relationship with the woman of his life. While integrating feminine and youthful traits into his makeup, he became more of a man. Similarly, Helen was also constricted by a narrow definition of gender. As she became more assertive and independent, she became more of a whole person. She also became more of a woman as she entered a romantic relationship in her fifties. Matthew had been influenced by the women's movement from the beginning and is no stranger to gender crossover. For over twenty years he has been creating personal balance by adding nurturing qualities to his identity and assuming some feminine roles, especially in the family. As he has integrated feminine qualities into his self-definition, his masculinity has become richer.

Barbara provided another clear example of this gender paradox in second growth. She was very autonomous as a young adult and went through several transformations before she uncovered a fuller femininity after turning fifty. She eloquently described her own process as one of continuing self-discovery and transformation:

> I'm changing and continually discovering things in myself that amaze me. One major thing I've discovered as a woman is a kind of balance of feminine and masculine elements within myself in a way I never knew possible. My journey has been to go to the edge, and as I do I find amazing dimensions to myself.

When we met, Barbara was a fifty-four-year-old physician who had recently begun to specialize in caring for elderly women. She was and remains a single woman with a number of good, close friends with whom she shares several keen interests. She described with great warmth some favorite activities: spending time outdoors with her friends, camping, and traveling. She displayed an unusual vitality and positive outlook. "I'm an optimist like my father—not like my mother, who was always upset about something," she said. However, like Matthew, she had experienced a down period in her late forties even though her career was at a peak.

After years of medical practice, she had begun to feel burned out, angry, bitter, and even resentful. Her career had been outwardly successful but increasingly dissatisfying:

> I felt terribly trapped in medical practice and couldn't see any way out. Clients were demanding more and more, and then they would turn on you. I would put in horrendous hours and feel I was really caring for them, and they would file malpractice and say I was deliberately trying to hurt them. It felt so unjust, and it seemed like people were trying to own me.
>
> I entered medicine in part because I wanted to be totally independent. In medical school I was nearly a stereotype of a male: aggressive and very competitive. In those days you had to be like that to succeed as a doctor and as a single woman in a nearly all-male society.

As a woman, she prided herself on her independence and being in control. To feel so overwhelmed and frustrated was new to her. "My situation seemed intolerable. I kept feeling trapped. I told myself I had to find a way out of this situation. When my dad, who had stuck at his job to the bitter end, died, I said to myself, 'You can't wait any longer. Do something.'" But being a doctor was her life. What was she to do?

While battling with mixed feelings, she discovered that she had a malignant melanoma. She believed that her body was sending her an important message. Feeling betrayed, stuck, and filled with doubts about the course of her life, she sensed that the cancer was a self-destructive way of reacting to her situation. Surgery eliminated the cancer. Reassessing her life and changing her medical practice and lifestyle addressed possible contributing factors.

Some vital props in a good personal identity had been falling in Barbara's life: good health, self-esteem, self-efficacy, and a meaningful sense of success. She felt scared, confused, and defeated. How did she manage to turn around? She first pulled back from her practice to allow time for mindful reflection and self-discovery. She developed a commitment to healing that was sustained by her optimism. She also uncovered and released a hidden part of her personality to achieve greater balance:

A major development in my midlife has been to become aware of my feminine side. Recovering a balance—between control and caring, being intellectual and emotional—is one way of viewing how I got out of the trap. I have become a much more feeling person. I've realized that feelings have a very important part in medicine. You start with knowledge, but in your interaction with patients you need compassion. An emotional level of interaction is perhaps most important in treatment. By discovering my feminine side and expressing it in medicine and with friends, I have been experiencing inner movement, an awareness of being feminine and vulnerable.

Barbara revealed that by becoming a doctor, she had deliberately undergone an identity transformation, repressing feminine qualities and adding masculine ones:

I used to be tougher than tough. I would never show emotions; I thought that would be a sign of weakness. Now I allow my emotions to show. The biggest risks for me are letting people see who I am. I wanted to be well-thought-of and would act to please people. I still want to be well-thought-of, but I am more concerned to express how I feel as openly and honestly as possible.

Barbara has been changing her identity and her behavior. She has also redesigned her medical practice so that it allows her to express her feminine qualities. She has shifted her focus to elderly women, combining her medical role with that of nurturing caregiver. She also has blocked out more free time to pay more attention to personal relationships and her own interests. Her growth illustrates a slow transition as she consciously worked on a post-institutional identity. In her fifties she began reshaping her identity as a competent woman, creatively balancing qualities that she had once thought incompatible. Through her adaptation to a very stressful situation, perhaps the most difficult in her life, she became more inwardly complex. In defining a new self, she has changed her definition of success, reaffirmed the girl within, and above all enlarged and revised her feminine self-image. She has become more of a woman than she ever had been.

The adults in this study show us how important it is to take an inventory of ourselves and to uncover aspects of our personalities that have been buried along the way. Untapped creative energy is working within us, pushing us against boundaries set by rigidly defined social roles and old scripts. If we harness that energy, it will help us break free from previous self-concepts that are inappropriate for the next phase of our lives. To develop a positive midlife identity you can

- listen to your inner energy and identify barriers to its expression
- consider the roles and life patterns that you may need to leave behind or modify
- critically assess and discard your age stereotypes
- break the myths of aging
- identify and recover your youthful qualities and integrate them within your self-image as you also recognize and accept the fact of growing older
- recognize and accept your mortality while affirming your continued growth and renewal
- redefine what it means for you to be a competent man or woman
- affirm your independence while also affirming your connectedness to others and to your larger reality
- redefine success and develop standards to measure it.

The third age beckons us to create an appropriate identity for the prime of our lives; by following these steps, we can move forward to become the person we aspire to be.

5

Principle Four: Redefining Our Work/ Balancing Work and Play

For the first time in the human experience, we have a chance to shape our work to suit the way we want to live instead of always living to fit in with our work. . . . We would be mad to miss the chance.

—Charles Handy, *The Age of Unreason*

COPING WITH PERMANENT WHITE WATER

We work in rough water. Bombarded by change, we face perils as well as promise. New knowledge and technology, the global economy's contribution to increased competition and uncertainty in the marketplace, and the increasing complexity within the work environment have put unprecedented pressure on workers at every level and in all sectors of the economy. The turbulence we experience in our work lives affects more than our personal economy. Changes at work also often have a marked impact on our efforts to renew our lives. Consider a few of them.

The emphasis on greater productivity and efficiency influences most of us. In both for-profit and nonprofit organizations we feel the pressure to beat the competition by working faster, harder, and smarter to pull ahead and stay there. The tempo of work and expectations concerning our performance has increased. A maxim at work everywhere today is "do more with less." This effort requires much more than the maxim suggests. The business writer Peter Vaill has likened working in this topsy-turvy environment to coping with permanent white water. Uncertainty, changing expectations, rapidity, and surprise increasingly invade our work lives and our personal worlds.

A result is that many of us are more stressed than we used to be. More than 30 percent of Americans complain of excessive daily stress on the job, and many more than that complain of stress once or twice a week. Job stress in turn spills into family and personal life. Health and the quality of life are endangered. One consequence of excessive stress is burnout, which is affecting more and more people. As we take the temperature of our working lives, do we feel fired up or burned out?

In addition to faster pace and greater uncertainty, we have been working longer and harder. Since the 1960s Americans have put in so much extra time at work that we have actually added a whole full month of work to each year. While Europeans have been adding leisure to their lifestyles, Americans have been losing it. We now work over 2,000 hours a year compared with about 1,550 for Germans; our workload exceeds that of every modernized country except Japan. Most women in the workforce put in at least another 1,000 hours at home. The cost of pursuing the American dream has risen for nearly everyone. The Harvard economist Juliet Schor argues that Americans must change this pattern and restore more leisure in their lifestyles. Her point is especially important for those of us interested in midlife renewal.

Another factor affecting many of us is widespread organizational change. One consequence of restructuring, downsizing, and reengineering is less job security and intensified competition for people at all levels, but especially for seasoned workers. When companies restructure, the people often pushed into unemployment are at least fifty. As we contemplate midlife renewal, many of us also fear uncertain futures and wasted potential in the second half of life.

With all these changes, ambivalence about work rises. We do not live easily with increasing ambivalence. One result is that more and more people are seeking alternatives to the rat race. Schor reports that some adults are "downshifting," trading in overwork for more free time. Downshifting increases leisure, but that does not necessarily add value to work. Some people are learning to do both. *Fortune* magazine devoted an issue to women in their forties who, having reached a pinnacle of career success, surprised everybody by leaving established careers and jobs to develop themselves in new lines of work that often afforded more leisure. I have seen a similar pattern in the lives I have followed.

Yet many people past age fifty, when they have the chance, look more seriously at retirement. They might engage in Hamletlike soliloquies:

> *To work or not to work,*
> *That is the question.*
> *Whether 'tis nobler after all*
> *To suffer the slings and arrows of outrageous fortune,*
> *Or by taking early retirement to end them.*

But what kind of deep meaning will retirement bring to a vital person with four or five more decades to live? There's the rub! I do not believe that retirement, at least as it is usually thought of, is the best answer to our work situations as we consider midlife renewal.

RECOVERING A SENSE OF MEANINGFUL WORK AND PLAY

As we design the second half of our lives, we are challenged to become more mindful of both our work and our play. The fourth principle addresses this challenge. In this chapter we shall meet adults who have transformed their lives by applying this principle in the midst of turbulence in the work place. Already we have met individuals who left their jobs to pursue more creative outlets, when they realized that their jobs did not meet their needs. Others have developed new careers and new forms of play, because they were searching for work that would add meaning to their lives and for play that would give them greater freedom, spontaneity, and fun. A few people in my study have retired from their jobs, but they said *retirement* was not an appropriate term to describe their situations. To follow them we might imagine how we can develop a more profound sense of work as a set of mindful, purposeful, self-expressive activities. That is a much healthier response to ambivalence, stress, and stagnation than the conventional model of retirement. As the adults in this study have searched for more meaningful work and play, they have also been developing another standard of success.

To begin developing a more profound sense of work, it helps to realize that our modern ideas about work are in fact artificial. Our notions of what "real work" means have evolved from the industrial revolution. Only in the past century did it become normal for men to leave home to go to work, which became defined as a paying job. The switch to a mechanized labor force altered everything, even our personal identities. Men became the "good providers," earning money for their labor; women often stayed behind to take care of the home and children. Jobs outside of the home became the employment norm. One result is that many highly valuable forms of work have been downgraded or neglected.

Except for the professional and entrepreneurial arenas, the meaning of work has often shrunk. Ironically, there has been a trend to fit our lives into the tight confines of our jobs. Job descriptions have a way of becoming part of our self-definitions. The idea of work as a job is much too narrow to support lifelong growth. People are expected to adapt their talents and personalities to jobs rather than the other way around. We need to outgrow this view of work, especially as we look ahead to the prospect of a vital third age. Midlife renewal does not call for checking out from work. We might retire from our current jobs, but we still need to recover a sense of more meaningful work as part of our evolving positive identity.

Kathy Kolbe, a consultant in career development, has an insight that can help us do this. Stress on the job often comes from blocked energy. Work that runs against our instinctual patterns produces an overload of stress and can lead to burnout. To flourish and be happy, she suggests that we discover and express our true instincts—our gut-level inclination to perform in a distinctive way. Her ideas as well as the research on flow both indicate that we need to identify and pursue what we really love to do. If we have not had that option earlier, we might give ourselves permission to do just that now. Many people in my study have learned to express their basic instincts in following their dreams.

In addition to following our basic instincts, the British business writer Charles Handy suggests that we use the freedom that often arises in midlife to build a lifestyle in which work is more personally fulfilling and morally satisfying. Handy recommends that we identify a variety of activities important to us and construct an enlarged work portfolio. This portfolio should include different types of work: paid work, volunteer work, home work, fun work, and learning. Above all it should include activities we love to perform. An expanded work portfolio enables us to shape our work to fit our lives and provides a larger framework for our new identities. Personal redefinition will inevitably include a redefinition of our work. At the same time, our personal redefinition of work will surely include a healthy balance of leisure time and a meaningful sense of play.

FINDING WORK NOT LISTED IN THE CLASSIFIED ADS

Woody: *I'm trying to make an interesting life.*

Many of us become so narrowly focused on our jobs and so wrapped up in our careers that we have little time left for family, friends, fun, or growth. That is the dark side of success. Men have tended to fall into this trap due in part to the male provider role, but women are increasingly stumbling into it as well. I interviewed a forty-eight-year-old executive who was married and the mother of three grown sons. She described her life as driven to achieve greater recognition, promotion, and more money so that her "retirement could be without financial worries." Already affluent, she nevertheless seemed obsessed with her job. She was a very successful, overworked woman who could not imagine a midlife opportunity to redesign her life. Regardless of the direction of my questions, most of her answers centered on her current occupation. "My father always wanted boys. He had three girls, and I was the oldest. I guess I'm proving that I can be as successful as any boy he might have had." She narrowly interpreted success in terms of achievement in her job and seemed unable to account for her unhappiness in life.

Woody exemplifies a creative alternative to this common pattern and another way of measuring success. A lawyer by profession, he was working for a small organization that provided labor relations services to hospitals and nursing homes in New York City when we first met. Married with two grown children, a member of several boards, he'd had a very full adult life. In his forties he experienced a turning point that led to rejuvenation, a major reorientation, and a pattern of new growth:

Forty was a rebirth. After my first Outward Bound course, which came at just the right time, I was on such a high. It has lasted into my fifties, though I am slowing down a little bit. Back then I was outdoors every weekend, backpacking, hiking, canoeing. I had never been athletic as a kid, but I found at forty that I had skills I could develop. I learned to love the outdoors, and just came alive. From forty to fifty was a period of tremendous change and growth, a period of happiness and excitement. I developed so much more self-confidence and new interests. Now that I'm in my fifties, I've calmed down a bit. But I am still learning, still open.

There is so much more to do than I have time for. I'm not seeking to climb the highest mountain or jog the longest trail. But I am definitely moving in different directions, finding new things that interest me. My wife and I love traveling, especially to exotic places. A couple of years ago I started learning Chinese. When we went to China, I spent time living with a Chinese family. I've also been learning scuba diving, which is a very different kind of challenge; I'm also learning about underwater life.

His story of a changing lifestyle suggested the beginning of an enlarged work portfolio balanced with increasing amounts of play. In his early fifties he was in fact experiencing a liberation from a boxed-in work life, which opened him up to new growth that has continued for over twenty years.

Woody was in an enviable position, riding a wave that he had largely created. He was the proud president of his small company, which had been recognized in city newspapers for outstanding services. As competition and complexity in his field intensified, he could have become narrowly focused on the job. He felt tugged in several directions. During his forties he had started to create a different life plan and began taking the risks needed to achieve it. For example, he cut down on his time on the job by managing the office more democratically, developing delegation and teamwork skills. Eventually, he succeeded in maintaining a forty-hour workweek and a nine-to-five daily schedule: "I work hard in this job, but I am less willing to hang around the office. There are so many other interesting things for me to do."

One of those things was volunteer work for nonprofit organizations. One project proved to be extremely important to him. A small group of volunteers designed and sponsored a unique program that linked disadvantaged urban youths with adults recruited from corporations and the professions in outdoor team-building programs to support the personal growth of all participants. His volunteer efforts increased the scope of his work and added fun to his life. He enjoyed using his talents in new ways and achieving a different kind of success. Like a boy proud of his performing pet, he pointed to newspaper clippings describing this adventuresome project.

While Woody was enlarging and redefining his work, he put more play into his lifestyle. He allowed one or two weekends each month for outdoor activities and time nearly every day for some physical activity. His play also included vacations and time spent with loved ones—his wife, children, and good friends. He also made time to continue learning. He reads a good deal, has done university adjunct teaching, and is constantly looking for new things to learn, such as the Chinese language and scuba diving. This pattern has become a fixed part of his life.

When Woody was fifty-four, he told me, "I like my life the way it is. I hope I continue to live the rest of my life the way I'm living it now. This is the best time of my life." He said he felt lucky, particularly because a number of his friends had lost their jobs and had been forced to start over. Slowly shaking his head, he commented, "I wouldn't want to go through what they have." As luck would have it, he couldn't avoid their fate. Just a year later, he, too, lost his position, because of decisions made by his company's board of directors. If anyone had to face a test of a personally defined sense of work, Woody did. But the process started in his forties enabled him to turn adversity into an opportunity. His story teaches an important lesson to those interested in second growth.

When his job came to a dead end when he was fifty-five, Woody searched for something else to do. It was not easy to find new work during an economic recession, especially at his age. Fortunately, he had a severance package that gave him a year to search for other employment. He considered the idea of reviving a law practice, but rejected it. During the previous fifteen years he had developed new skills and interests that he wanted to apply in his work. By coincidence he was invited to provide some consulting services to the outdoor program he had helped found. This went so well he was invited to consider becoming its associate director. Not seeing any other clear option, he jumped at the chance. Making this adjustment proved to be more difficult than he had anticipated, but after two years on the job, he told me, "I'm having the time of my life. I make less money, but the kids are grown so we don't need as much. Besides, I love my work. My wife now is excited by her career as a psychotherapist. When we get home after work, we often look at each other in near disbelief that this time in our lives could be so good."

Seven years later, he continues to serve in his position, which he describes as a wonderful accident. He still feels like he is riding the crest of a long wave, where he is "freer, no longer so driven by work needs, and at peace with who and what I am." In his early fifties he said he was in the best period of his life. He was mistaken. Later has been better. He recently wrote,

> I'm now sixty-three and about to celebrate my fortieth wedding anniversary. I am, thankfully, in good health and have two successful grown daughters and two grandchildren. I love being a grandfather and travel at least every two months to be with them.
>
> I still work hard and love every minute of it. The best thing is the variety. I never know what I'll be doing when I walk in the door. I may meet with corporate executives, conduct team-building training, work with teachers, participate in activities with kids, or help keep our computers working on-line. When I left my old job, part of the severance package included some outplacement support. In one session I was asked to describe a "dream job." In retrospect, it nearly defines what I'm doing now. The organization considers itself a learning organization, and I consider myself a learner. Most of the staff is young; I'm the oldest by ten years. I kid about losing my hair and how old I am. But I don't feel old and would like to think that I'm not considered old.
>
> I continue to love to travel. A year ago my wife and I spent a month in India. We still live in the first house we bought, with plenty of room when grandkids come. I have no plans to retire. Maybe in a few years I'll cut down to four days a week and use the extra days for extended vacations.

If we think of life as a series of investments, then Woody has continued to diversify his investments and is reaping returns beyond early expectations. He has shaped his work to support his growth and fit his ideal life.

A striking feature in Woody's growth has been how he has reinterpreted success. He once explained his life this way:

> I think—how can I put it?—I lead a life of contrasts. I'm a president of an organization, I'm publicly involved, I've started this new program for youth and adults, and outdoor activities, and so on. I play many different roles. What I would like people to say about me is that I lead an exciting life, that I'm venturesome, a man of many sides. I'm trying to make an interesting life.

As we start on careers, we usually of necessity focus on making a living. Woody did that well. But he realized that his life and his growth would not fit into that narrow concept. He shifted his perspective from making a living to making a life. In reassessing his priorities and reorienting his life around them, he has restructured his work to better suit the way he wants to live and grow. He has expanded his work portfolio to include learning and teaching, service to the community, and personal development as well as paid employment. In conventional terms he has moved down to a lower level in a smaller organization; but in terms of what really matters in a lifetime, he has created a position that more directly benefits the lives of others and is for him more challenging, more fulfilling, and more fun than being company president. He is proud of this success. He has been writing his own epitaph, daring to follow his passion, shaping work to express his interests and values, and contributing to others.

Making an interesting life did not happen all at once. Starting in his forties, Woody has worked on this design for over twenty years. A principle in the process has been to creatively balance work and play as well as self-care and care giving. In his fifties he told me, "I can now balance claims with little difficulty. I can be selfish in terms of doing what I really want. I'm living more in the moment than I used to. There are more things to do than my wife and I have time for. I'm pleasantly pressured in my life. And I love it." He feels the same in his midsixties.

Three qualities of Woody's character contribute to his success in life; they are qualities that I have found in various proportions in all who experience second growth. The first is his mindful openness to new possibilities and ideas and his accessibility to others. This keeps him flexible, he says, and brings him in touch with many new people and different areas of life. Second is a deep, realistic optimism. It gives him the resilience needed to cope with change and take risks. Third is his wonderful sense of humor. He stressed the importance of humor:

> I've learned that humor is very important to life and to work. In the last five or ten years, I have become incredibly irreverent in what I say. I can't believe some of the things I say to people now that shock them. But I say it humorously. I'm quick to be funny. Most of the time in the office we're laughing. This allows us to have fun at work. I even kid my adversaries.

In our interviews Woody kept me chuckling at his quiet jokes, often at his own expense. "For all my smarts, I still buy my suits at the wrong place. They keep shrinking," he joked. In other words, in spite of a lot of exercise, he was engaged in a "battle of the bulge" that he had not yet learned how to win.

Woody provides one illustration of how to break the narrow focus on a job as the measure of success. He has deliberately created a balance between work and play as he has set making a living within the larger context of making an interesting life. In the new scenario for the third age, making a life sets the framework for defining our success.

Judy: *I see myself now on a quest. . . . How do I take my talents and experiences and put them to work in a larger sphere?*

Like Woody, Judy been transforming her work on a broader canvas. When considering careers as a college student, she decided to follow her father and become a lawyer in his law firm. She married but was soon divorced. Her life became channeled toward success in a legal career. There was a major obstacle, however, because she was a woman in a male-dominated, aggressive environment. Back then a woman's place in a man's world was laced with restrictions. She told me,

> The women's movement has made a tremendous difference in opportunities, so if I were to begin today I might not have such a tough time of it. But when I started, things were different than they are today. I have a father who is a staunch conservative who taught me that women are not really valuable; they're really second-class citizens. I wanted to be first-rate, so I had to throw myself into his world and act as though I were not a woman. That was a drain on my life.

Wrapped up in her work, she was dedicated to success on men's terms. She recalled that time as a confusing, exciting, but sad learning experience. A major objective since then has been to outgrow the male concept of competitive success and to fashion a more personally meaningful path. She wanted to discover how to work successfully and affirm her womanhood.

By her early forties she had left the law firm and built a small company in real estate development. At forty-six she was remarried with a thriving real estate business. In life as well as in work, she felt more fulfilled than ever. She was becoming aware of her special talents for relating to and helping people, and she was learning to combine those talents with her skills in analysis and organization. In real estate she found an opportunity to affirm herself as a competent woman. As she reported then, "I have been making some very significant changes in the last eight years. I feel now that I am most creative. Finally, my talents and background have come together. I've reached the point where I can do almost anything I want to. That's a great way to feel."

The first thing I noticed in Judy's story was how she had transformed a single-focus, driven work life into a more creative, fulfilling lifestyle. As she rejected the role model set by her father, she sought a more original model that would include her distinctive traits. Over the years she has tried to shape work to fit her evolving personal identity in a quest for greater existential meaning:

> I see myself now on a quest. It's both spiritual and physical. A major change in my life has to do with work. I have achieved a lot of worldly goals, such as career, income, place to live. Now I see my quest in these terms: how do I take my talents and experiences and put them to work in a larger sphere? I am no longer modeling myself after my parents. My life is moving in a very different direction. I'm looking for a broader canvas in which to portray my life. Where I'm at right now in this quest is asking about the meaning of life. Why are we here? What should I be doing? It's just not enough to be something in life. I want to do something worthwhile, and that is how I'm beginning to view work.

Often work is framed by a competitive pursuit of income, status, and reputation, extrinsic factors that define success. Judy has struggled to get beyond those standards and achieve something more worthwhile. Her quest has moved her out of the conventional orbit of ambition; she, too, has been reinterpreting success in terms of her personal development and her service to others.

How did work provide her with "a broader canvas" in which to find meaning? First, she defined work goals primarily in terms of her values, talents, and interests. One value was to become more independent; this led her to start a company of her own. More independence supported another value, greater creativity. She then expanded her view of work even further. She sensed that previous work goals, especially in the firm, had contributed to a stultifying self-centeredness:

> I had spent my whole life wrapped up in myself. I'm much less so now, and I'm actually much more effective in work. I ask myself often about the kind of person I want to become instead of what my father wanted me to become. I have overcome some of the issues that were dragging me down. I don't have the internal competition anymore between acting like a man or woman. I've integrated those qualities. Now I want to perceive my work as doing something for others, not just serving myself.

Like Woody and others in this study, she has gradually come to see work as an opportunity for giving and sharing as well as for personal growth. In framing work as a form of service, Judy had unwittingly returned to an original sense of the Protestant work ethic by trying to integrate her religious values into her work. She expanded her work portfolio to include volunteer activity in an inner-city project, helping poor people of color take more control of their lives. She incorporated the value of service into both her career and her volunteer work. With a more diversified work portfolio, Judy became a more competent, complete, and nurturing woman. This expanded sense of work continued through the next ten years in spite of the fact that she later has had some very tough times to live through.

Four years later, I learned that Judy had experienced two severe setbacks as she entered her sixth decade. In the late 1980s the real-estate market was hard hit by a major economic recession; like Nancy in Chapter 3, she lost her company. Furthermore, her marriage did not become the partnership she had hoped for; she and her husband separated. When I spoke to her when she was fifty-six, I learned that she had suffered even more losses: divorce and the death of both parents. Was her second growth short-lived? Two of the most important props in a meaningful life, love and work, were knocked out from under her. What did she do? Like others I have studied, she showed creative resilience in responding to misfortune. But the resilience did not come easily or all at once. In fact, it took nearly a year before she mustered courage enough to call me back. Having previously told me of her success, she found it difficult to share her experience of frustration and loss. When I last spoke with her, she had just begun to see her change of direction in a truly positive light.

In searching for work after the collapse of her company, she was especially attentive to her evolving personal identity. A basic instinct was to be true to herself as a woman. Years in the women's movement had helped her recognize her feminine qualities, needs, talents, and interests. She did not at first imagine that her participation in local women's programs would lead to a new line of work. Yet in these programs she met women who were starting small businesses. They needed help. Judy sensed that she could retool her professional skills to develop marketing services for them. When I spoke to her then, she believed this new venture might be productive. This work lasted only a short time and was followed by another endeavor that also failed. I am sure that she had no idea, when she reached a peak in her forties, that her quest would lead her through such severe disappointments. However, from each setback she discovered positive traits that eventually liberated her to find a more satisfying lifestyle:

> My setbacks have actually freed me up. I've been discovering new, important areas in my life that are getting stronger, such as self-esteem and friendships. I appreciate my independence more. I'm also defining more clearly what I have to offer people. I'm feeling much more comfortable with the relationships that are developing with clients as well as with friends.

Our life's path rarely follows a smooth, straight line. In the past six years she has had a bumpy ride with what turned out to be a frustrating digression. When a challenging position opened up in a large real estate development company, she accepted the job because she had not found another way to earn her living. Once again she was caught up in a competitive corporate culture that went against the grain. When the company downsized two years later, recent hires, including Judy, were let go. Now what was she to do? This time she listened more carefully to her values. Reflecting on her need for independence, her feminine identity, and her priorities, she started a small law practice. "I have come to realize that people are primary in my life. I didn't see that as clearly as I do now. Since they are most important to me, I have designed my practice to serve people," she said. After a couple of difficult years, she is finally beginning to see signs of success on several levels.

What has the new shape of work meant to her? It is a way to find and express her special talents, to increase her sense of independence, to develop personal relationships with clients and members of the community, to make a worthwhile contribution, to have fun in what she does, and to make a living. In addition to paid work, she does volunteer work, devoting time regularly to her church and community. After several years involved with large groups in the inner city, she now serves on community boards, like those of the YWCA and a school for children with learning difficulties. She teaches Sunday school and so loves this experience she has begun work on a teaching credential, thinking she may want to teach fifth and sixth graders on a full-time basis in her seventh decade. She has also mentored adults in urban education and assisted individuals starting small businesses on a pro bono basis. In the ups and downs of the past decade, Judy has been learning to reshape and enlarge her work portfolio to better fit a growing self.

Ed: *I have poured myself into a new career pattern. . . . Now I am doing things because I want to.*

The next two individuals show a completely different way of following a midlife dream. In choosing jobs as young adults we hope to match our work with our interests and values. In midlife, interests and values often change, causing us to sense a conflict between what we do for a living and what we want to do. Going to work becomes harder when our adult needs are not being satisfied. In their late forties Ed and Dan realized that they needed to reshape their work.

I met Ed by accident. During my research a person in my study said to me, "You've got to interview my friend. I've known him most of his life, and he is going through some exciting changes." A long-distance phone call convinced me I should make a trip to visit him. Ed, a university tennis coach and physical education professor, looked and sounded younger than his years: "I'm fifty chronologically, but I feel like I'm thirty-five. My work with young people keeps me young; so does my family, because two of our children have not reached high school yet. I can't believe I'm so close to being a senior citizen." In addition to his energy and youthfulness, a striking trait was his probing, mindful reflection about who and what he was becoming: "About two years ago I started to reflect more and more about where I've been and where I'm going. I've had a very fruitful and interesting professional life. But all of a sudden I realized I needed to make some changes."

What happened to start him on a new path? Before turning fifty, he had a year's sabbatical and explored a growing interest in outdoor educational programs. He recalled one incident in particular: "We were climbing, and some of the kids were having trouble with the course. I found myself more attentive to those who were having trouble than to those who were excelling. Something happened in that group and in me that I had not experienced before. I felt such compassion for those who were struggling."

That experience led him to recast his competitive perspective. He now really cares more about people than winning. Previously, he would focus on athletes who showed promise of competitive excellence, ignoring those who did not measure up. On his sabbatical he developed an interest in helping people achieve whatever goals are appropriate to them. "I'm more interested in people, in giving them an opportunity to learn and achieve something that is important to them, and less interested in winning. I have a lot more compassion than I ever did," he said. The value of compassion began to surpass that of competition.

During that sabbatical, Ed engaged in mindful reflection, rethinking his life goals "from beginning to end." He became aware that there were several areas in his life that needed more attention. Personal relationships became more important. He started spending more time with his family, and his notion of close friendships deepened. He explained a change in everyday encounters: "When I say to a friend, 'How are you?' I really want to know. I really care." He was still committed to coaching, but began to relate to his athletes differently, more as a friend and mentor than as an authoritarian coach. Teaching in outdoor programs and directing summer camps for youth became as important to him as coaching.

His changing interests and values might not seem to match the job of a university coach who is expected to produce champions. His new insights and change of interest could have led him to consider changing his career. Instead, he chose to creatively redesign his position and enlarge his work portfolio in order to express his change of perspective:

I have poured myself into a new career pattern. I have cut way back on coaching, with fewer related activities. Others can do that just as well. I haven't cut back on the quality of team performance, but I am devoting myself much more to other activities. Cutting back on the university program would have been unthinkable just five years ago. I might have asked, Why am I doing this? and I would have answered, I have to. Now I am doing things because I want to.

In redesigning his work, Ed has been following his basic instinct. Years later he confirmed that he has remained on the course he set five years before. Where, I wondered, has this taken him? Not only has he remained a head coach, but he also does better in the job than ever:

> I have related to players better. I always related well, but now we have a much stronger personal relationship. We sometimes will skip a practice to do something as a group. That would have been unthinkable before. I emphasize quality performance during contests, but I also encourage them to develop beyond the boundaries of athletics. I want to see them graduate and to be involved in other aspects of campus life. I used to emphasize win, win, win. If a player did poorly, I would be very critical. Now my approach is to work through their performance with them and get their feedback.

How has Ed's more humanistic approach to coaching affected his team's performance? His team's record has remained respectable. When we last talked, the team had won its conference in each of the last five years. How does he feel about the changes he has made?

> The results personally are that I'm more content than I ever was. My life has so much more variety, and I have so much more compassion than I ever dreamed of. I'm youthful in my fifties and will be a youthful seventy-year-old. There is now so much more to do in my life than there was when I was younger. I'm growing and reaching in new directions.

Six years after his change of direction, Ed continues to spend more time with his family and friends and to express his playful interests in the outdoors. His work portfolio has diversified even further. He has added a new line of fun work raising bees, and he volunteers time to help young people. His enthusiasm for work has increased because he has redesigned it to express the values, instincts, and interests he discovered to be most important to him.

Dan: *I'm actively involved in developing a life plan that will answer questions about who I am and where I want to go in life.*

Dan is very different from Ed. Yet he, too, during his late forties began to rethink his goals and the direction of his life and concluded that his work was not allowing him to express some of his keenest interests and most important values. Dan manages a university center with a complex operation and a diverse staff. Several years before I met him, Dan had started a life review that led him to question who he was, what he wanted, and where he wanted to go with his life. When we met, he was well along in clarifying basic values and starting to make changes to better express them:

> I'm actively involved in developing a life plan that will answer questions about who I am and where I want to go in life. My plan should express my value priorities. Right now I have about fifteen top values, and I'm getting them into order. I think about these, write essays, and try to set a direction. But I'm also actively changing things. I'm exercising, losing weight, meditating, changing the ways things are done in the office, spending more time with my wife and close friends. I'm more interested in quality time and trying to reshape my life so that there's more quality and less crap.

While striving to be a competent manager, Dan had started second growth: reflecting, laying plans, organizing time and resources, and taking initiatives to realize personal goals. But in thinking about work and the meaning of his life, he discovered he had a problem. He sensed that he was falling into a rut and that if he did not change, he would waste his life. This led to some sharp insights and then some changes at work:

> Last year I realized I was carrying a lot of anger. That was a watershed. I hadn't realized I had it. I wondered if this was a midlife crisis, and then I said, I'm not going to become some guy with a midlife crisis. I realized that the anger had to do with my job. I was feeling conflict between what I wanted to do with my life and the pressures at work and what I had to get done in the office. The process never stops. No matter how much you put in, the job is never finished. As soon as something is completed, another thing pops up. My life is going into all these little holes that need to be plugged up. I realized, When Dan leaves, who will really notice or care a year later? No one. Then why am I doing all this? I was getting more and more frustrated.

Dan was experiencing more than turbulence and stress. He faced a conflict between what his job seemed to demand and his emerging interests and values. In midlife he had been developing a major new interest in culture, particularly art. The more he felt a strong interest in art, the more frustrating and tedious his routine managerial tasks appeared. "I found the little things to be more stressful and frustrating than the major things. What got to me was all the tiny, picky trivia," he said. He was going against his instincts. In planning his life, something had to give.

Dan responded creatively. He realized that the university center actually had as part of its mission the accumulation and exhibition of art. He had found that there was neither time nor personnel available to work on it. Then he thought, "Why not let cultural development become a major focus of my leadership?" In order to accomplish this, he started to delegate more responsibility and train people. Because their jobs were upgraded, his subordinates and assistants became more satisfied with their work. They could attend to the routine matters that had been driving him to distraction. With a clearer awareness of what was important, he could more quickly discriminate between what mattered and what could be put off or ignored, thus speeding up decision making. Most important, he incorporated his new interest in art into his job. This redesign of his work life has enabled him to integrate his personal growth and his dream into the work of the center. Both he and the university benefit.

Marty: *I'm reevaluating work and its place in my life as well as reassessing my job. I know now that the two are not the same.*

Even in a desirable career, after twenty or so years in one job, we may burn out. Some organizational structures and jobs do not permit transformation. If redefining work and balancing work with play constitute a challenge for second growth, how can we respond when suffering from burnout? Marty showed me that a creative response to burnout is to expand one's work to support the emerging complexity of one's mature life.

In his early fifties Marty suffered burnout and thought about early retirement. When he was fifty-six, Marty, an elementary public school teacher for most of his adult life, described his stagnation and told me about making a change:

I began to feel like my whole life was being covered up in sand. I'd been teaching in the public schools for a quarter of a century. At that point I wasn't getting anywhere emotionally, educationally, or professionally. I was looking [within] myself for another avenue; I just had to go down some other road. But I couldn't seem to budge. I was going through turmoil. Some friends suggested I get away one summer and try camping. At the age of fifty-four, I went off and spent some time in the woods. It was a bit scary to be without structure, all by myself with a lot of loose ends. When I got back home I realized that I needed to give myself a lot more time to look at myself, to consider changes occurring within me and changes which could take place.

We might expect that someone unhappy at work would concentrate on what was wrong with the job. Marty developed a different focus. Instead of complaining about the job, he started reflecting on himself, his values, talents, interests, and the possibilities in his personal world. He reported that even in his midfifties, "I had not yet found the ultimate me." So his first task was to work on his personal identity.

He decided to take some risks to "try out new me's." At work people noticed that he was more assertive, more outgoing, and more experimental. He had never been one to lead a movement, but he decided he wanted to uphold the no-smoking rule at school. "At first I was afraid of public ridicule and being shunned for taking a stand," he said. "But I did it, and it worked. I was standing up for myself and other people's rights. I was willing to share in taking that risk. Since then I've been much more comfortable at being outspoken and shooting for what I want." He started by taking small but decisive steps to be more assertive and gradually developed more control of his work situation.

His self-discovery provided insights into new possibilities for his work. As he told me, there are many more things he can do: "I learned I could make changes in my life. That is the basis for the optimism I have now. Now that the children have grown and left home, I'm freer to do what I want. I'm learning to enjoy this freedom, to be more outgoing and positive. This is all a revelation to me. I wasn't like that before."

He used his freedom both to enlarge the range of activities that he considers work and to follow his instincts. Marty discovered that he likes to cook. One summer he took a job as a gourmet chef, something he had never before considered. He learned on the job and was pleased to find out that his new employer was highly satisfied with his performance. He also did some catering on the side. He returned to teach in the fall, but has continued cooking at home and on special occasions. Years later friends still ask him to cook for events.

While experimenting, Marty kept reflecting about his work and its meaning. A major breakthrough for him was to define his work more broadly than by his job as an art teacher. When he was fifty-eight, he told me, "My attitude toward my job has been changing. I'm less interested in it than I used to be—not that I care less for the children, but I'm cynical of the bureaucracy." He realized that work was actually as important as ever, but he had given it a novel interpretation: "Work includes what I do with my life, my relationships, what I'm working on, and not just what I get paid for. I'm reevaluating work and its place in my life as well as reassessing my job. I know now that the two are not the same."

Marty's comments surprised me. Because of his experience of burnout, I had anticipated that work would become less important to him. In fact, I expected him to take on an attitude that devalued work, downgrading its importance for the second half of life. With Marty and others in this study, the opposite seems to be true. With a whole new slant on it, his work now means "what he is working on" at a particular point in his life. It includes diverse meaningful activities that allow him to express his talents and values. For example, as an educator he has always loved to learn. Now he recognizes that learning is an important element in work. However, what he has been studying in the past ten years is not related to teaching. He has become a student of American history. At fifty-eight he was immersed in a study of the Civil War. Three years later he was studying Native Americans.

Marty has also explored various art forms, including stained glass and computer graphics. Increasingly, he sees work in terms of developing his artistic potential and increasing his artistic production. Having ended his employment in the public schools after thirty years, he can now work regularly at his art, producing sketches, paintings, and computer graphics for local companies. Sometimes he receives a commission or contract, which gives him a job. But job or no job, he works regularly. He thinks of himself not as retired but as moving in a different direction. "I refuse to fit the stereotype of the retired man. I'm exploring and expanding myself, involved in different activities and the community. I wake up looking forward to what I can learn from the day. My life is more fulfilling than ever," he said. That extraordinary self-assessment comes from a man who ten years before felt as though he was being buried in sand.

In developing the artistic side of his personality, he has also learned to creatively balance play and work. He told me, "Play is important. For me it's not competition. If I compete, it's only against myself—like sailing or skiing, when I'm trying to get better. But art is play for me, even if I get paid for it. So is cooking." Play for him, as for most of us, is an activity that he takes pleasure in. But it means more than just having fun. We stand a better chance of doing more of it if we appreciate its fuller meaning.

Play is important to growth at all ages. It is the source of our creativity. It is also important to health, not only as a form of therapy but as a form of healthy adult adaptation. Dr. Vaillant discovered that those best adapted to life in their fifties allowed more time for vacations than did the least-successfully adapted, who often found little or no vacation time.

Similarly, the reporter Peter Chew found that "leisure was the key to men's eventual successful passage through the most critical years of their middle life." Play is no less important to adults than to children. Human beings are not only *Homo sapiens* and *Homo faber*, but also *Homo ludens*—beings who are thinkers and workers and, preeminently, players. Play has fundamental importance to individual development; it is even a foundation of human culture. Play frees the human spirit and provides the basis for the highest forms of human expression. If we are to become more open and creative, as well as happier and more fulfilled, we need to increase the element of play in our lives. We also need to infuse more of it into our work. That is a sure way to activate the child within us so that we can grow young.

Marty's redefinition of work to include play helped him overcome burnout, and seeing himself as player and artist freed up his creativity. Ten years after experiencing burnout, Marty was enjoying the most fulfilling period in his life: "I'm doing well now. I'm expanding in many ways and am happy. I look forward to challenges. I'm just sorry that no one brought up the question about how to manage your life at this time." Marty's story of working one's way through burnout by trial and error provides a model to others trying to set a more fulfilling life course.

STRIKING A BALANCE BETWEEN WORK AND PLAY

Stu: *I'm changing in my attitude toward work. If I am to become more of a whole person, I need more time away.*

At age fifty-three Stu was at the peak of his career as a cardiologist. He found his work challenging and rewarding but was questioning its place in his life, especially once he realized that he often put in eighty hours a week. Stu loved his work and was proud of his achievements but nevertheless felt some ambivalence. He made this clear as he described his search to find greater satisfaction through a more balanced life:

> I have enormous numbers of patients who are very grateful to me for what I have been able to do. Sometimes things don't go the way you hope, and that's devastating. Two days ago I operated thirteen hours on a child who didn't make it through the night. I was really shaken by that, but I had to be up early the next day for a similar kind of surgery that has worked out just fine. I'm really happy with what I am doing as a surgeon.
>
> But I'm changing in my attitude toward work. I'm finding that it is more important to have more leisure time. I have surgeon friends who are just plugging along, good at what they do but with their noses to the grindstone. I want to be as good a surgeon as I can be, but if I am to become more of a whole person, I need more time away.

A major reason Stu sought greater freedom from his professional role was to spend more time with his second wife, whom he married in his late forties. They had been building a strong partnership, and their marriage provided him great satisfaction. He was trying to organize his life so that he could continue to experience the challenge of his career while finding more time for his marriage and for play. Stu's major goal for the second half of life has been to become a whole person. That has become a new standard of success.

As he has become older, he has had difficulty fitting that latter goal into his ambitious work life as a physician. Following his residency, Stu flung himself into his role as surgeon. Having once considered becoming a missionary, he dedicated himself to serving others by becoming the best surgeon he could be. During the Vietnam War he even volunteered for special assignment, but returned after a year because of heart trouble. At forty-five he was successful in his career, but his first marriage was disintegrating. Through a tortuous divorce he kept his focus riveted on work. When he remarried he began giving more attention to personal expectations. Probing reflection about life's transience and meaning pushed him to think hard about both work and leisure.

As he addressed the paradox of work and play, he saw that it was related to the paradox of freedom and responsibility. When we explored the issue of personal freedom, Stu commented,

> Your questions about freedom are particularly important for physicians. The claims on us are very legitimate. When someone calls me to see a child who needs surgery, it's hard to turn down. That child's needs have top priority. I have not yet done very well with the question about freedom and balancing claims. My wife knew that when she married me. We're working on that issue. There was a time when I didn't try to do much else but work. I even thought for a while surgeons shouldn't be married, just devote themselves to their practice. I certainly don't feel that way now.

Stu had to clarify several of the legitimate concerns in his world that were in tension: serving patients, his wife and their marriage, good friends, community service, and personal growth. He saw many other physicians, indeed many people his age, "just plugging along," stuck in a rut and not reflecting on priorities and possibilities. He felt fortunate that he was beginning to find ways to break out of his "rut," which by society's standards was viewed as a great success.

He was trying to put work in a new perspective. Work had not become less important or less worthwhile. Rather, he found it less important to work all of the time as a doctor. Instead of stuffing most of his life into his career, he attempted to fit his work into the way he wanted to live, which called for more service activities and more leisure time. Now in his mid-sixties, he continues as chief surgeon, but he volunteers his services regularly to the community and recently received a prestigious award for his contributions. In addressing the issue of leisure, he has been trying to develop and apply a new principle. In his midfifties he told me,

> My major objective now is to organize my life so that I have more time away from work. I'm in the hospital by seven and often don't get home until after nine at night. So I tend to take long weekends whenever possible. I also am taking long vacations. Next month, we'll spend three weeks in Maine. I did-

n't do this five years ago. I would have felt guilty. Vacations are becoming much more important. Of course, this may have something to do with the fact that I greatly enjoy being with my wife. She is helping me to be more open with my feelings and to see more clearly what is important to us.

Stu's efforts to get away from work were part of a plan to establish a balance of one week of leisure for every three weeks of work, though not always in that format. Ten years later he told me that he is still trying to find that balance, but apparently with more success. He and his wife have purchased a second home on the coast of Maine, where they now spend up to twelve weeks each year.

By creating more free time within a very demanding schedule, Stu has affirmed his priorities of professional excellence, personal freedom, love, service, friendship, and his own growth. He has also become more playful in improvising a lifestyle that has no recognized models. Like many I interviewed, Stu sees himself as being very different from his parents. He does not have a role model, but finds bits and pieces in others' lives and weaves them into his own. In becoming more playful, he finds fun in "designing" his life. "I'm making it up as I go along," he said. Like others in this study, he has been composing an interesting, more complex life.

Norman: *Work is becoming more important to me than ever. . . . But my wife and I realized we had to get a break.*

Norman provides another example of creatively balancing the opposing tendencies of work and play. A research scientist who had had a stable life marked by many successes, Norman had worked for the same institution for nearly forty-five years when we met. I thought that because he was nearly seventy, he might at last be anticipating retirement. In fact, that was the farthest thing from his mind:

Some people say that at this point in my life, I should be slowing down. But I'm not slowing down, because I'm doing what I want. I have no interest in retiring. I hope to be actively productive for at least another twenty years. I want to keep moving. It's not that I need to, but I want to take advantage of opportunities. I still look forward to doing the work I do. And I'm getting better at it.

This was an incredible statement: almost seventy and expecting a productive career for at least another twenty years! I learned that Norman's father had been active until age ninety, so his expectation did not seem so unreasonable. But what was this work of his that he was getting better at?

People are problem-solving animals. That's what we do and that's what I do in my work. In fact, I'm doing this all the time. It's hard to distinguish between my personal life and my life as a scientist, because I'm always thinking and working on a problem. That's my work.

You asked if my attitude toward work had been changing. Yes. In a way work is becoming more important to me than ever because now that our children have grown, it provides the most challenge in my life. I'm willing to take more risks with work now, too—like moving to another institution, so that my project can develop more fully.

This sixty-nine-year-old man talked like a vibrant fifty-year-old. He had experienced the successes in his career that he had hoped for, but he was ready to keep on developing. He had just won a federal grant for a research project and was named its director. Years of research work lay ahead.

One might think Norman an incorrigible workaholic. In his own words, he was working all the time solving problems. I had trouble matching this vibrant person with his workaholic self-description. Then I discovered two important elements in his life: personal relationships and the time he devoted to play when he was not thinking about work. Norman acknowledged that the biggest change in his life lay in his relationships with his family and on the job. He and his wife were close to their two grown children and three grandchildren. They found that grandparenting demanded special attention: "Grandchildren need more time and devotion than other relationships, especially since ours represent two different cultures. Our family has always been important to us; this requires extra special devotion. We are constantly working on adjusting to this complex family."

In addition to time spent caring for family, Norman said that he had become much more accessible to younger people: "I am more accessible to friends, most of whom are at work. And I'm open to younger scientists to a fault. If one walks by with a question, I'll stop what I'm doing. Even if I'm in the middle of something, I'll stop. I feel I have to respond."

In his caring attention to family and his increasing accessibility to younger colleagues, even an outsider like myself, Norman exceeded the boundaries of a workaholic. He did so even more dramatically in play. When I first asked him about play, he said he did not engage in it much. Like many people, he at first interpreted play as sports, which he had never done. He then mentioned playfulness in work. It was only when I asked him about his weekends that I discovered an entirely unsuspected dimension in his life. He and his wife were both busy professionals during the week, sometimes barely seeing each other for several days. But on weekends, every chance they got, they drove off to their cabin in the woods.

> Years ago my wife and I realized we had to get a break. We were climbing the walls with all the family and work responsibilities. So we bought a little house up in the mountains, and we go there as often as possible. I built a stone fence around our property, work in the garden, and take care of the house. We often hike through the woods. This is totally divorced from our lives here in the city. When we go to this house, we recharge our batteries. After four days of seeing no one, spending all our time outside, we are refreshed. You could say this is my play.

As it turns out, this scientist who said at first that he worked all the time actually has spent an increasingly large part of his middle years in extended, regular periods of play. Norman's time at his mountain home has introduced a healthy balance of play into his dedication to work. Through this balancing, Norman created a more complex world than he had previously expected he might: "Some people say that one should live simply. I see my life as more complicated. I enjoy the excitement of constant change. This is a great time for me."

Second growth involves giving ourselves permission to become more complicated. Complexity emerges not only from change, but from the paradoxical balance of opposites, like work and play. With his interesting lifestyle Norman has not had time for retirement.

TRADING IN RETIREMENT
FOR A BETTER OPTION

For many people, retirement is not appealing, especially with a much longer life expectancy. The term literally means "withdrawal"; it suggests being out of circulation. Who wants to be out of circulation for a large portion of one's life? The sociology of aging has shown that retirement often signifies the desocialization of the elderly, who lose meaningful social roles. Retirement often becomes a roleless role. Our conventional sense of retirement fits with a worn-out theory, which described aging as a process of disengagement and decline. If we trash this theory and focus on creatively growing older, then we might well ask, How appropriate is retirement for a vital person with forty or fifty more years to live? If we can reasonably expect to live ninety or one hundred years, then the loss of meaningful work when we are as young as fifty or seventy is a tragic waste of human resources. Retirement can turn productive lives into casualties. Withdrawal from work can deprive a person of a major activity, a sense of social responsibility, and important relationships. I see another option.

Midlife careers that sustain the paradox of work and play through a long third age can provide a meaningful alternative to retirement. The uninterrupted leisure that is often associated with retirement is not an ideal. Charles Handy suggests that leisure only makes sense "when it is the other side of work, when it is re-creation for more work. Work is what we will want to do, work rediscovered, work redefined to mean more than selling your time to someone else, work that is more in tune with the rest of life, work that is more personal, more creative, more fun than most jobs can ever be." Toward the end of my research project, I interviewed a dynamic eighty-year-old who has been actively developing his work portfolio for decades. He only quit his job at seventy-eight, because he was too busy with other interesting things. For many people in my study building a new career in midlife has provided an unexpected challenge and sense of fulfillment. It has been a way to make a life.

John: *This is life as I want to live it. The parts come together in a satisfying whole.*

Some people have become experts in transition management. John Coleman, formerly an economics professor, is one. He attracted national attention in the 1970s when, as president of Haverford College, he took a four-month sabbatical to work incognito as a garbage collector in New York City "to learn what it was like at the bottom of the ladder." He continued to experience alternative forms of employment each year until he "retired" from higher education. At fifty-seven he headed a foundation;

but he also worked as a member of the New York City auxiliary police force. He has modeled the idea of constructing a diverse work portfolio. At sixty-five he abruptly changed this career to fulfill an old dream: he wanted to be an innkeeper in Vermont. After he bought a bankrupt old place, he turned it into a successful business. To express his satisfaction, he named it The Inn at Long Last.

Five years into his new career as innkeeper, he felt more fulfilled than ever. At seventy he wrote, "This is life as I want to live it. The parts come together in a satisfying whole." John achieved a richly satisfying midlife career not only because he was doing what he really wanted to do at this point in his life, but because he was able to weave together various important themes and skills from previous careers into a coherent pattern. This pattern signifies personal integrity, where "the parts come together in a satisfying whole."

When I spoke with him two years later, he told me that he would move on from being an innkeeper when he reached seventy-five to work on yet another career. He thought it might be in the theater. He wanted to move into an entirely different line of work, because "we have sides to our personality that are just waiting to be let out." As it turns out, at seventy-five he sold his inn and bought a small newspaper. His new career as publisher/editor allows him to be more fully involved in community life. Work redefined to suit how he wants to live provides the challenge and the opportunity to sustain his second growth, which has been unfolding for three decades.

Louise: *My job was one of the most important things in my life. But I realized my true love is the theater.*

Louise, at fifty-five, also illustrates how a dramatic career change can enable one to integrate the talents one most values into a satisfying work-play pattern. Married for over thirty years and the mother of two grown children, she began a career that was radically different from her previous one just before turning fifty. She had finished graduate school when she was thirty-nine and became a social worker. She found her work surprisingly fulfilling. Her comments about work when she was in her late forties were very positive:

Work is a very important part of my life. I find validation by doing what I want to do and doing it well. Through work I have found new things about myself. I've discovered that I'm competent. That was a big discovery. When I started work at forty, I asked for a salary that was way below what they were prepared to pay me. I wondered if they would hire me. I had no idea what I was worth. I have found out that I am one of the best workers I know. I take what I do to heart and do the best I can. I have also discovered that I'm a lot smarter than I thought. I have also learned that I can deal effectively with people. I used to be uncomfortable with authority. I've learned to challenge my boss, to assume authority, and make decisions. I guess I learn more about myself at work than anywhere else. So I see work as a great opportunity.

Work was one of Louise's most important investments, providing her with a great opportunity for self-discovery and growth. With her attitude and competence, it did not surprise me to learn that she had soon experienced success in her job. Eventually, she became head of a department in an urban hospital. In less than ten years, she had reached her first career peak.

As a supervisor Louise found opportunities to be creative in program design and problem solving. Her work was satisfying in many ways. Like Woody she learned to be very efficient and was able to limit her work to about forty hours a week so that she could spend time with her family and devote herself to her avocation, acting. As an actress she played key roles in local plays, receiving laudatory reviews in both local and city newspapers. During her forties a major issue for her was learning to develop a balanced work portfolio, responding to the competing claims of work, family, church, self, and theater. She seemed happy.

However, I learned later that she had become disenchanted with her job. After several years as an administrator, she had grown frustrated. She had begun to feel squeezed by a powerful bureaucracy that stifled initiative, consumed much of her time in red tape, and led her into what she perceived as unnecessary political entanglements. As she had started feeling boxed in, ambivalence toward work had surfaced.

Then her daughter suffered a prolonged serious illness that required Louise to take a leave of absence to care for her. During that time her father died, requiring an extension of the leave to assist her mother in adjusting to living alone. After several months away from her job, she felt not only ambivalence but also a deep resistance. Her work, once key to her growth, now seemed a hindrance rather than an opportunity. What she felt she wanted most was to devote herself to her "true love," the theater. She talked it over with her husband: "Do you think I could make a career in the theater? If so, I don't think I'll make much money, at least not at first. Can we afford this?" He responded, "You'll never know if you don't try. I think we can live on my income, if we're careful. Why don't you give it a try!" With that, Louise notified her boss that she would not be returning. Following her passion, she started to lay plans for a full-time acting career. But at fifty she found it difficult to break in. Eventually, she located an agent, found parts in several off-Broadway plays, and began a new midlife career.

By the time she was in her midfifties, Louise had acted in a variety of plays, had directed her own shows, and was active in summer theater. After several years she looked back and reported:

> I'm very glad I made this move. I have a good agent now, and I'm finally making some money. It's not a lot, not really much to live off, but I'm happy. This is what I've always wanted to do. I've been in several plays this year, and I have directed three that have all received good reviews. I audition often, but it's tough. There is so much competition. I'm not totally satisfied with my career so far, because there's not enough of it. But I must say, my reviews have been very good. I'm hopeful. I'm happy because I have finally tried doing what I want. I love the challenge, and I'm moving in the direction I want to be in.

Louise's midlife career change turned an avocation into her chosen vocation. She continues to work in the theater as both an actress and a director. Although the roles for actors her age are not as plentiful as she would like, she has chances for work in a variety of plays, from Shakespeare to modern. She also entered and completed a graduate program in theater, which qualifies her to teach at the college level. As she told me, "I have been acting and directing in various capacities for eighteen years. I know this area very well. I'm exploring other ways of expressing my talents and increasing my involvement, such as teaching." Her work portfolio has continued to expand. In addition to her new career in the theater and in teaching, she has done volunteer work in the community. In redesigning her life, Louise not only enlarged and personally redefined her work, she transformed much of it by setting it within the context of play.

FINDING MEANING IN THE PARADOX OF WORK AND PLAY

Second growth leads us to develop a fresh, positive attitude toward work and to redefine it as a personally meaningful set of activities for the third age. We have to shift from a modern, high-pressured, constricting model of work to one that is richer and better balanced. Perhaps focusing on a single-track career is appropriate for young adults. But when we are ready to address the second half of life, it is time to trade in a single-track model for one more versatile and more appropriate for a fulfilling third age. Perhaps now more than at any other time in our lives, we can make a difference while making a living. By developing a complex work portfolio we will both support our personal growth and add value to our world. A broader scope invites us to volunteer our services and to share our talents. If we downshift from frenetic overwork and driving ambition in our jobs, we can find time to become more engaged in the social sector and contribute to the enrichment of others' lives. Each of us has an opportunity to better care for, sustain, and promote the well-being of our society and the earth. While affirming the importance of our work we need also to enlarge and promote play. As we do so we will add fun, as well as meaning, to our lives.

In this chapter we have seen several ways to redefine and balance work and play for a meaningful third age. To apply the fourth principle in midlife renewal you can

- determine your priorities and clarify what you love to do; follow your basic instincts
- enlarge the scope of your work beyond a job/career to build a portfolio that includes paid work, fun work, home work, volunteer work, and learning
- risk doing something new that will develop another side of your personality and add new value to your life
- restructure your job to express key interests and values

- balance your work with play in which you feel free to express your talents, spirit, creativity, and values
- design your work and play to shape an interesting life, one that adds value to others' lives and supports your evolving personal identity.

There may be other initiatives to consider. What is most important is to nurture and respond to the creative energy emerging from deep within us, to clarify what we really want to work on, and to develop the full range of our talents through new forms of work and play. It would be a shame to waste this opportunity. Don't let someone else write your epitaph.

6

Principle Five:
Balancing Personal
Freedom and Intimacy

You shall be together . . .
But let there be spaces in your togetherness,
And let the winds of the heavens dance between you.
—Kahlil Gibran, *The Prophet*

LIBERATION ONE MORE TIME—
GREATER FREEDOM AFTER FIFTY

Liberation has been a defining force of the twentieth century. New forms of freedom have burst forth all over—in countries, cultures, and customs, in ideas, arts, fashions, work, families, gender, generations, lifestyles, and life stages. The third age sets the stage for another personal liberation, one that can be disturbingly exhilarating. As new freedom offers new options, it can also stir up fears and evoke resistance. While it disrupts the status quo, it raises unsettling questions and leads to surprising discoveries. Liberation always requires fresh thinking. What is this new freedom in the middle of our lives all about? Freedom from what? To go where? To do what—and with what consequences?

The freedom that can emerge in midlife has not had good press. Some writers and the media have contributed to a misleading idea that confuses midlife freedom with midlife crises. We often hear that turning forty or fifty triggers angst about our mortality and inner turmoil, leading to an inevitable crisis that in turn prompts behavioral change. Victims of midlife crises can surpass adolescents in acting out. Midlife crises are now supposedly as common as a winter cold. In fact, they belong to the myths about middle age, along with menopausal blues and marital blahs. We need to demythologize these beliefs. Some people have midlife crises, but most do not. Crises do occur in midlife, but they are usually caused by a variety of factors, certainly not by chronology alone.

I contend that confusing midlife liberation with a midlife crisis points us in the wrong direction. It suggests that increasing personal freedom occurs at the expense of loyalty, relationships, and community. That is not what I have found in the experience of adults I have studied. I have seen in their lives a tremendous expansion of personal freedom along with a deepening of intimate connection. The fifth principle in midlife renewal involves balancing these supposedly opposing qualities.

A personal experience might clarify this challenge. I often take solitary walks in the wooded hills near my home. These walks give me a chance to reconnect with nature and to reflect on what I have been experiencing. Hiking at twilight, I once felt a powerful longing as I looked up to follow the smooth flight of a large plane moving away from the sun high above me. Bright golden rays reflected off its silver body as it headed for a distant destination. Something in me wanted to leap up, to go on its journey to some place I have never been, to leave my space, which seems well known, bounded, and predictable. The high-flying plane symbolized greater freedom, a release from familiar boundaries. It pulled at me to move in a new direction, go beyond known limits, live differently, and discover potential and possibilities as yet undetected. I wanted to cry out, "Take me with you!" The only flight I took on that walk, however, was in fantasy, an imagined trip on a plane fast fading at the edge of twilight. An inclination towards greater freedom has been a catalyst for reflection and change.

On another evening walk, I felt a different longing, which came as I saw in the distance lights coming on inside a house set back from the road, lights broadcasting to the cold, approaching darkness that people were at home. As I watched the lights sparkling through the windows, I imagined warmth in that house and the pleasure of individuals intimately connected within their own space. I felt a pull deep within me, as powerful as the one inspired by the plane, to enter that home, to share in the talk and quietness, the work and play and companionship that filled that space and made it alive. The pull from that idealized unknown home symbolizes for me an intention toward new depths of intimacy and stronger connection. Just as an unexpected need for greater freedom has arisen, I have also recognized a growing need to become more intimately connected with significant others. This longing for connection has also been a catalyst.

Home—flight; bound—free; rooted—unrestrained; familiar closeness— the mysterious unknown. What am I to make of this inner energy aimed at apparently opposite intentions? Which should I follow? What happens if I heed one and not another? If I were to choose freedom at the expense of intimacy, I know that I would pursue loneliness. Even when I have mindfully responded to an inclination for greater freedom, I have occasionally put tension in my marriage and risked creating distance between me and the one person with whom I feel most at home. Yet if I were to cling to intimate connection at the expense of freedom, I believe I would foreclose on growth and begin to stagnate. Boundaries of familiar love can sometimes seem like confining enclosures. It is very difficult to grasp these two different value trajectories; like distant galaxies, they seem at times to be moving away from each other. How do I hold on to both at the same time? This dilemma, experienced in twilight walks, reveals another paradox in second growth. It points to a step that is perhaps the most difficult, disturbing, perilous, yet exhilarating and graceful of them all.

Liberation is as important to our growth at fifty or seventy as it is at fifteen or twenty-five. Significant growth entails an increase in freedom on several levels: freedom from arrogance and ignorance, from blind faith and stereotypes, from repressive constraints and paralyzing psychological barriers, from mindless habits, worn-out commitments, and frustrating entanglements. Meaningful freedom from leads to the exhilaration of freedom to. In midlife we have opportunities to free ourselves from constraining factors, an emancipation that in turn frees us to discover new ideas, develop latent talents, reshape faulty traits, follow our own interests and values, encounter new situations, meet new people, pursue new goals, increase our creativity, and contribute to others.

Intimate connection in the second half of life is also as important as ever, perhaps even more so than in the first half. A long second half without love seems a dreadful fate. But to hold love, we do not have to give up our freedom. Greater freedom after fifty can lead us to deeper levels of intimate connection. Whereas liberation may involve cutting some ties, it can also open the way to richer relationships. In marriages and friendships I have seen both more freedom *and* new patterns of intimacy. One

man in particular has helped me appreciate and clarify what this principle
can mean.

Ken: *I've come to realize that the most important thing I can have is freedom.*

When we met, Ken was fifty, very successfully employed, and happily
married with two grown children. He had been a university administrator
for over twenty years. A tall, quiet man, he exuded competence, confidence, and a deep sense of caring about people. In talking with his colleagues, I discovered that Ken was one of the best-liked and most
respected leaders in his university. At first glance, I thought Ken would be
someone quite content with the status quo. He did not seem the type to
advocate liberation, nor did his situation seem to call for it. So comments
he made at the beginning of an early interview surprised me:

> During the past five years I've come to realize that the most important thing
> I can have is freedom. The importance of freedom goes along with becom-
> ing more interested in learning about myself and the world. There's an awful
> lot I wish to do, and I'm just trying to get my priorities straight. There are
> many things I can just now appreciate that I didn't give enough attention to
> before.

Because the concept of freedom is notoriously slippery, I used our interviews to explore his sense of it more fully in order to clarify my own
understanding. Ken began by explaining how his quest for freedom had
led him to question some of the values and assumptions that had guided
his life. Like many other people, Ken had focused on external achievements to define his success. He had been a superachiever who really liked
to be first. His outlook had been competitive both in work and in leisure.
A former regional tennis champion, he had more recently been recognized for his prowess in biking. Learning about himself led him to question goals and values that had been driving forces in his development up
to that point. He began to devalue a competitive outlook as he became
more reflective and committed to getting his priorities straight.

The first dimension of Ken's freedom resembles mindful reflection. His
liberation began as a learning process about himself and the world. He
had started by raising questions about things he had taken for granted,

such as his assumptions about success and the value of a competitive lifestyle. He said that his questioning and learning were part of an exploration about the meaning of his life as a whole. His philosophical thinking led him to question not only his own priorities but also what his university and our country could be doing to be more socially responsible:

> I'm asking more questions about what our ideals really are. For example, what is this institution doing and what should it really be doing? Are we being true to our mission or being caught up in political games? What should we be doing with the natural environment that needs our attention? What should I be doing with my life?

Ken struck me as an independent thinker with a tendency toward idealism. I wondered if he had always been like that. His reply indicated that he had actually undergone a rather radical change of orientation recently: "No, I started as a realist, not an idealist. My skills are in finance and management. As a younger man coming into an organization, I was much more likely to . . . do what was expected of me." His liberation opened up several dimensions of himself and his world. Greater clarity of perception increased his independence. It freed him to set his own expectations about what he should be doing with his life rather than trying to live up to expectations he felt were imposed by his organization and his career.

Ken's reflections have led him to imagine what he wants to do for the second half of his life. As a young man he developed a career that has been rewarding on many levels. With no ambition to become a college president, he had reached a satisfying career peak. At fifty his aspiration for more freedom was not prompted by midlife crisis, disappointment, lack of control, or unhappiness; rather it came from soul searching about what he most wanted in the next fifty years. At this point, I saw him tentatively exploring a variety of possibilities, often moving towards goals that seemed difficult to reconcile. For example, more freedom sometimes seemed like just a chance to get away from responsibilities; but then he would express a desire for freedom to become more engaged in environmental work. It took him several years before he was able to reconcile the complexities in his thinking and develop a lifestyle that enabled him to express his deepest values.

Ken's liberation has also included a keener recognition of cultural obstacles to freedom. He became more aware of familiar pressures that could distract him from his chosen course. For example, social roles and our country's materialistic values can send us down predictable paths toward external goals. In midlife, Ken awakened to a need to reexamine customs and preferences, to stand more independently, to become more inwardly directed. With greater awareness, he began to distance himself from previous pursuits. As he put it,

> I'd like to be free from all the silly and superfluous things people get wrapped up in to enhance their own egos. I've been questioning the meaning of our lives. Material things and status aren't as important as they were, like getting the latest model car. In my generation we tend to set up a system of goals to have the best of this or that. We collect status symbols like badges, trying to get as many as possible to show off to others. I've had enough of this. I don't need to be in front of a lot of people. Instead, I want as much freedom and independence as possible to pick and choose the kinds of activities that I think are really important.

Henry David Thoreau, one of Ken's heroes, once said that if a man does not stride with his companions, he may hear a different drummer. Ken was inspired by Thoreau to differentiate among the propelling forces in his life. To realize freedom, follow the beat of your own drum!

The psychologist Mihaly Csikszentmihalyi has said that the pursuit of happiness requires us to distance ourselves from external rewards so as to become freer to shape our experiences. As he entered his fifties, Ken was doing that. He felt freer from American society's materialism, consumerism, and status symbols. By distancing himself from popular external rewards, he was defining a more appropriate sense of success, which is an important element in renewed self-definition. He was also setting more clearly his own standards of conduct and satisfaction and trying hard to follow them, especially when it meant going against the popular stream. In one dimension, freedom means giving ourselves permission to do what we really want, to follow what we deeply believe in. As Ken put it, he is working at being free to chose more regularly those activities that are really important to him.

Often, liberation requires us to question previous role models as well as old roles. For example, Ken has come to see himself in midlife as being quite different from the way his father was at the same age. "My father was a step short of taking advantage of an opportunity, whereas I take chances. My father was too concerned about having money in the bank. He wanted security, and that held him back. I take risks to make something happen," he said.

Ken's father symbolized a very common adult concern. As people become older, they often want to avoid risks. Fear of uncertainty and the unknown can curtail renewal. Security can easily become an obsession; to minimize risks and play it safe is the opposite of freedom. Security might decrease tension, but the appeal of a stress-free life is a deadly trap. The cost of playing it safe is huge. The psychologist Jane Loevinger suggested that many of us foreclose on growth because we turn away from the uncertainty necessary for significant learning. If we are to learn to be free, then we must learn to work with the fears that we will encounter as we face significant risks. The quest for greater personal freedom requires accepting uncertainty and not giving in to fear.

So far Ken's midlife liberation has operated mostly on a psychological plane, where he has learned more about himself, engaged in values clarification, become more critical of social values and institutional behavior, and redefined himself and his notion of success. For growth to occur, freeing of the mind must also be translated into activity and lifestyle. As we saw in the last chapter, a major area for us to reexamine is our work. As Ken's life unfolded during his fifties, he expressed his freedom by making some significant changes in both the form and substance of his work.

Ken was very proud of his work, but increasingly he felt a need to get distance from his job and its obligations. He became frustrated with aspects of his position that interfered with his experience of renewal. For a quarter of a century, he had looked forward to going to work. But at fifty he felt torn between "paying his dues" on the job and marching to the beat of his own drum:

> I sometimes feel a great need to get away to the mountains or the forests, a place of solitude where I can escape the feeling of being boxed in. I prefer to be in the wilderness, watching cranes sitting in the marsh or beavers crunching branches. The freedom to do those kinds of things and to be without obligations—that represents to me one of the highest forms of attainment.

For Ken being outdoors symbolized freedom: "Thirty days on the Appalachian Trail was freedom!" But to increase this sense of freedom he could not just walk away from work responsibilities. During his early fifties he came to realize that his real task was to find a balance. He was trying to put more freedom into his lifestyle by following "Thoreau's comment about living between civilization and nature, with one foot in each." Finding balance has required putting more weight on the foot in nature and allowing more time for play. He has become freer as he has clarified his values and interests, redefined his work, and increased the scope of his play in the outdoors.

When I first listened to Ken talk about increasing his freedom, I was uncomfortable. We are all familiar with reports about exaggerated individualism in modern American society. Our era has been described as a "me generation" of self-centered individuals intent on doing their own thing. A search for greater freedom often appears as a selfish pursuit. I do not see that happening with Ken, and I do not think that is what freedom in second growth is all about. Ken's search for freedom has directed him toward meaningful goals in his own growth *and* toward more socially responsible activity and deeper levels of sharing. Freedom is not doing whatever we want regardless of the consequences. Ultimately, Ken's quest for greater freedom has been part of his attempt to define his own unique meaning in the context of the world around him. As he has developed his vision of freedom, he understands that a meaningful life also includes significant relationships—with family, friends, community, and nature. As I have followed his course of personal liberation, I saw more clearly this paradox in which greater freedom reaches into closer connections. Freedom *from* and freedom *to* can lead to a greater degree of freedom *with*.

This dual aspect of freedom—freedom to and freedom with—became clearer several years after my initial interview with Ken. When I spoke with him at age fifty-five, freedom still was a high priority for him. At that time he was considering early retirement from the university, which was possible because of his many years of service. Retirement represented one way to achieve even more freedom. But, he said, retirement for him would not really mean an end of work. Freedom from his current job would enable him to devote himself to working with others more systematically outdoors. He had come to realize that this was what he really wanted to do. In fact, he had already started down this path and had begun to learn how to integrate his passion into a larger work portfolio. He eventually decided not to take early retirement, but instead changed careers to more adequately express his values.

I have been impressed by how creative he has been in linking his desire for more freedom to his desire to serve his community and the environment. Although not part of his administrative duties at the university, he started to work closely with students in various outdoor programs. He designed an outdoor orientation program for students and taught university courses about the wilderness. He enjoyed teaching so much that in his late fifties he left his administrative position to teach on a regular basis. His new career gives him more time to learn and to strengthen his connection to nature. Although he sometimes seeks solitude outdoors, he usually ventures out with friends and students. During a recent spring vacation, he organized a four-hundred-mile bike ride through the Smokey Mountains with students and colleagues. A few years ago he formed a community project to develop public land for victory gardens like those he knew as a child during World War II. His urban garden project brings people together outdoors to enjoy and preserve nature, and to promote the sustainable development of his small city. During his fifties he has pursued his dream, merging his quest for freedom in the outdoors with public service aimed at protecting and restoring the environment. His increasing personal freedom has led him to greatly enlarge his work, expand play, enrich his lifestyle, invent new forms of service, and enjoy and care for the earth.

An interpersonal dimension of his midlife liberation became apparent as he talked about his wife, Valery, and their long marriage. After their two children left home and embarked on their own careers, he and Valery found that they had much more free time. She used the opportunity to return to her career as a professor, which she had left over twenty years before to raise their children. She shares with Ken a love of learning and outdoor experiences. But in their togetherness they also pursue some individual interests separately. Their new freedom at home could have set them drifting apart. However, Ken and Valery have found that their individual growth actually improves their relationship:

> My wife and I have always had a great relationship. We've understood how we can give each other space. I've felt that our relationship is better because we affirm each other's freedom. She does things in a different way than I do. We keep learning from each other, and we have learned that supporting each other's freedom is essential, because it allows growth, which is so important.

In describing his marriage, Ken was pointing to a central paradox at the core of his life. He feels both freer and closer to wife, family, friends, and his community. Like other men of his generation, as Ken has struggled to become free from myths, images, and ideas that stifle growth, he has realized that his new freedom should be directed toward significant others, not away from them. In freedom emerging from love, Ken finds the strength to merge with others in greater intimacy. The communications specialist Deborah Tannen has observed that men often want freedom from, whereas women want freedom to, especially the freedom to express themselves in relationships. Perhaps what we see in Ken's second growth is an androgynous model of liberation that embraces both types of freedom, which in turn enables him to develop a freedom to be with. This principle of balancing freedom with deepening relationships is a source of creative tension, joy, and challenge. "Midlife lib," as I have been learning, is producing new patterns of marriages and friendships.

A NEW KIND OF MARRIAGE— INTIMATE INTERDEPENDENCE

Actually, this tension is not entirely new. Arlene Skolnick, an authority on American families, has suggested that trying to resolve the tension between freedom and connection is a central theme in American history. It has recently become more pronounced, especially in family life. Many people today find that this dramatic issue is a practical everyday matter in their marriages. Women in particular have addressed the competing claims between freedom to grow, especially in their careers, and love for husbands and children. Their accomplishment suggests that an adolescent goal of autonomy is superseded in adulthood by the more complex goal of balancing deeper attachments with an enriched individuality. One outcome of recognizing the fruitful tension between love and freedom is a changed understanding of how marriages can work.

According to Judith Wallerstein, coauthor of *The Good Marriage*, the phenomenon of balancing liberation and intimate connection has recently led to a new model of marriage, which she calls a "companionate marriage." This model takes on special significance for couples in midlife after their children have left home. She argues that at this time, we need to let go of our marriage as defined by procreating and raising children. We can redefine it so that the focus is on the needs of the partners and the needs of the marriage.

The historian Francesca Cancian, when tracing changing patterns of love in America, has also found this new type of marriage emerging. She calls it an "interdependent marriage." In these marriages there is an emphasis on equality in all important aspects of the relationship, balanced with dedication to both self-development and building intimacy. This type of marriage does not just happen all at once. It takes years to develop and requires a bundle of virtues, including courage, patience, humility, forgiveness, and tolerance for ambiguity. Maggie Scarf, in her book *Intimate Partners*, has suggested that a good marriage reaches an ideal stage, when "autonomy and intimacy are experienced as integrated aspects of each partner's personhood and of the relationship that the two of them share."

I have found this new type of interdependent marriage emerging in the lives of those who manifest second growth. The conventional imbalance between dependence and independence is replaced in these marriages by intimate interdependence. These partners' marriages in midlife become more balanced, more symmetrical, and more open to ongoing transformation. One man in describing the changes he and his wife recently experienced illustrated how this model might emerge:

> When we were first married, it was all "we." After twenty years we are perceiving our relationship more in terms of "the two of us." We have both been influenced somewhat by the women's movement. I do much more around the house than I used to; she assumes some responsibilities I used to consider mine. We share parenting. What's new is that there is more of an emphasis upon our independence. We're both changing, and we're learning to respect and support our differences.

As their children began to leave the nest, he and his wife seemed to be on a track similar to that of Ken and Valery's. They were trying to shape a marriage with greater freedom and interdependence, one that stretched their bond without breaking it. He was realistic enough to realize this transformative process was disruptive of previous assumptions and arrangements and that it would take many years to work out.

Another clear illustration of an evolving interdependent marriage came from El and his wife, Stephanie, whom we met in Chapter 3. When they decided to change course so that he could pursue a career in woodcarving while she opened the antique business she had been dreaming about, they also changed the nature of their traditional marriage. No longer did he go to work while she stayed home. They built a dual career and moved into a new home in which there was complete equality. In planning a new life, they affirmed not only his goals, but hers and theirs as well. In their interdependent marriage, El and Stephanie found new ways of sharing while supporting each other's growth. When I visited them seven years after they had first laid plans for a new life, I was impressed both by the freedom in their lives and by the depth of their connection.

For all their differences the interdependent marriages among those who manifested second growth seem to have three characteristic features. First, couples are committed to and cherish their relationships. When I have had the chance to see them together, the partners are relaxed and free with each other. Building a common space between them is a high priority. They are truly at home with each other. They have been creative in finding ways to promote and celebrate their union. Some have designed their homes to express their relationship, as we shall see shortly in Sharon's story. A few have renewed marriage vows or had festive anniversaries or changed their lifestyles to support their togetherness. Most of them put great emphasis on vacations, allowing free time to enjoy each other and play together. A priority for them is spending more free time together.

Second, while nurturing their union, the partners are independent and affirm each other's individuality. They address the competing claims of freedom and attachment and are less competitive. They recognize and appreciate their differences and support each other's individual growth. As Ken put it, they "affirm each other's freedom." Ironically, although they plan special times together, many also take vacations or trips alone or with friends. Most have described special interests and activities they pursue apart from their spouses. Some people discover that their individual aims and endeavors have created rifts between them, which had to be recognized and healed. Having increased their independence, they also return to their partners to build stronger bonds of interdependence.

Third, in building their marriages, these partners maintain open, genuine communication. Most speak of their spouses as best friends who listen with understanding and encourage their interests. Their conversational style is often a dialogue in which they talk through an issue to discover its ramifications. They are not afraid to argue, which they sometimes do to clarify and define individual and joint responsibilities. Several men told me that they and their wives are learning to talk on a much deeper level than they used to. As they tap their emotional reservoires, these couples rethink and rework life together. They share not only what is on their minds but also what lies in their hearts. They risk greater emotional candor, which can produce tension but which eventually builds greater trust. In their togetherness the winds of heaven dance between them.

Sharon: *Our new home expresses our needs to be separate and to be together.*

Sharon presented another example of this principle. When I met her, she was fifty-three, a school administrator who had been married for thirty-four years. She left college to marry at nineteen and then had four children in rapid succession. With young children at home, she finished her college degree and then entered a graduate program that enabled her to develop a career as a school librarian. Those were exhausting years, with too much to do and too little money. Life after forty saw improvement. "After forty we were both successful in our careers and more financially comfortable. We saw that we had done all right as parents, and our marriage jelled. We became more supportive of each other. This was a good time for us," she said.

Her good times nearly ended at forty-nine, when she developed breast cancer. Four years later, she had fully recovered; she had also changed significantly. Overcoming this terrifying illness actually had a beneficial effect on her. She explained:

> The best period of my life is right now, especially after having a life-threatening illness. Knowing in my gut that I will die makes life sweeter now. When you have this kind of illness, knowing you will die isn't a gradual possibility. The effect has been to make me treasure what is now. I'm also frightened. I look at my grandchildren and wonder how much of their growing up I'll share. But I'm healthy, and I work very hard to stay that way. There's a heightened awareness of life.
>
> I have dealt with this crisis and come through it in better shape. When everything looks black and you come out on the other side, you are either bitter or grateful. I'm grateful. And with the changes we've made, I feel freer—not much more in control, just freer.

Sharon has learned to express her new freedom in a number of ways—psychologically, practically, and in relationships. She has become more mindful about her priorities and how she lives. She has redefined her identity, going beyond role definitions to become more distinctively individual. She has asserted more control over her time, developing her career as an administrator so that she is able to engage in things she values, such as physical activities, cultural events, and time with her husband and her expanding family. Her father, she told me, was very successful in his work but never allowed himself the luxury of enjoying his life. She has learned not to follow his example. Spending time alone has also become increasingly important; so has exercise. She was always physically active, but in recovering from cancer and staying healthy, she has devoted more time daily to physical activities that include swimming, biking, walking, and running. She uses her freedom to nourish a healthy, growing self.

Within this dramatic change Sharon had also experienced greater freedom with her husband. She described her marriage as an intimate partnership. She and her husband have developed great mutual respect for each other as individuals. Each is committed to individual activities and separate times; but each makes time for shared activities. With their children gone, they decided to build a new home, which expresses their new concept of their marriage. There are offices on each side of the house. They do their individual work in them separately. In between is the space they share. As Sharon put it, "Our house reflects the balance we have been working out in our marriage. We have to leave our separate offices to get together."

In addition to activities around their home, they plan and organize their play, which has become an important part of their life together. Their play is the creative use of their free time and includes cultural events, time with family and friends, walks with their dogs, and laughter. Sharon told me, "One reason I married my husband was because he is so funny. He has the best sense of humor and has kept me laughing even through my illness." Sharon and her husband became more independent as they entered their third age, moving on different tracks yet paradoxically becoming more closely connected.

As Sharon's marriage has evolved, the shape of her family has changed from what it was when she and her husband were concentrating on raising their children. She has been using her freedom to extend intimate interdependence within their expanding family. She remains close to her four grown children and has developed good relationships with their spouses and her grandchildren. Sharon also began building a closer relationship with her aging parents, who live far away from her but nevertheless need her attention and occasional assistance. Because of the longevity revolution, modern families like Sharon's have become multigenerational, with a complex network of relationships. Like many other adults at this time of life, she realizes the need to rethink what being a family means. As families become more defined by adults, we have an opportunity to free ourselves for new kinds of intimacy. Sharon's love spreads to four generations. Within this complexity she finds opportunities to expand her freedom to be with significant others in new ways and on deeper levels.

Jacob: *We've made a real partnership.*

Another couple, married nearly fifty years, has worked creatively on a new model of marriage during the past twenty-five years. When I first interviewed Jacob, he had recently turned sixty. He had met his wife, Ruth, when they were in college. After graduating, they married and agreed that Jacob would go into teaching. He soon completed a doctorate that prepared him for a career specializing in educational research. Ruth's role was that of a traditional wife, staying home to raise their two children. According to Jacob, they had a very good life. After he turned forty, his professional life started to blossom:

> I had a number of good things going for me, but it was after I entered my forties that I began to find the person I was. By my midforties I was launched into activities and the personality that I had always wanted. A new department sprang up, and I was in on the ground floor.
>
> This was a very creative period. I was also starting to develop new traits. I had been shy but was learning to enjoy being in social gatherings. I learned to develop a sense of humor and a conversational style that enabled me to relate easily to people. At forty-nine I then left this creative position to become a college president.

As president of a small college, Jacob continued to develop personally and professionally. At this time Jacob and Ruth's marriage began to change. With the children gone away to school, Ruth began a career outside the home and started commuting to a job in a nearby city. Their changing situation at home pushed them to redefine their roles and responsibilities in their marriage. The traditional gender roles they had followed when raising their children were no longer viable. Situations like this can severely test a marriage. Jacob and Ruth entered a critical period in which they were challenged to establish more equality and a better balance in their marriage. After considerable reflection and dialogue, Jacob assumed responsibilities of homemaker. Taking on that role required not only gender crossover but also a critical rethinking of his presidential role. One does not usually picture a college president cleaning house, shopping, and preparing meals. Jacob creatively reshaped the president's role by stepping beyond it and remodeling his self-image. He and Ruth learned to revalue and share the work that once was solely hers. They also started a new form of collaboration as researchers and writers, which has led to joint projects and publications.

What prompted Jacob to make these changes? He explained that he had learned from his wife how to be more perceptive of what their relationship needed to flourish. They realized that with an increasingly complex life, they had to come up with a new definition of their roles and to create more equality. As they faced their new situation, women's liberation burst on the scene, prompting soul searching about previous assumptions regarding gender and responsibility. Ruth and Jacob were open to critically examining gender stereotypes and to overcoming them. This freed them to explore a different pattern in their relationship.

Their changing marriage in turn played a crucial role in Jacob's personal development. As he and Ruth shaped a more symmetrical partnership, Jacob began to discover aspects of his personality that had not received the attention they deserved. As I mentioned before, the adults in my study have become aware of hidden potential.

One layer within us that plays a pivotal role in second growth, especially in terms of interpersonal relationships, is emotional intelligence. This represents a capacity to be aware of our emotions, to allow them to be positive motivating factors, and to enable us to relate more authentically to other people. Like many men in this study, Jacob was learning to become smarter emotionally, an achievement that was facilitated by the close, open relationship he had with his wife. After several years as a college president, he discovered another obscured aspect of his personality, a dream of becoming a scholar/writer. He realized that he needed more freedom to pursue this dream. Their marriage supported both his growth and his quest for greater freedom. In his midfifties Jacob mustered the courage to leave his presidency in order to become an independent scholar.

Jacob later told me how his marriage has continued to liberate and change him. When Ruth turned sixty, Jacob said, "Ruth to me is still eighteen. For all these years she has been a partner and more than that." In addition to being a partner in work and marriage, Ruth has acted as a mentor, helping Jacob enrich his understanding of essential qualities in an ongoing intimate relationship. She is more finely tuned to the dynamics of such a relationship than he has been:

> Ruth has a great capacity for analyzing our relationship. She's been teaching me how to do that. In the last ten years I have come much closer to understanding the needs of our relationship. So we are much closer—we've been growing especially close during the past five years. Now that we're free from the college, we can spend more time together, and we work together. We've made a real partnership—working, traveling, and living together. This partnership is not an accident of time. I have been learning from her the ways of relationship that will make things better for us.

Jacob sees his growth as bringing him to new peaks and increasing the complexity of his personal world. Another part of this complexity includes his work, which is more varied than it was in the past, taking him to many different areas and countries. He and Ruth continue to maintain their home outside London, but they often take trips that combine business with pleasure.

It was in this latter aspect that I found another significant change in Jacob's lifestyle and marriage. I asked him where play fit into his busy life. He replied,

> I'm not sure what play is. My wife might say that I am working every moment. I am very systematic and well organized in my work, and I do think about it a lot. But actually I'm expanding my idea of work to include play. I never really took the time to listen to music, for example. Ruth loves music, and I'm systematically learning more about it and growing to love it, too. We go to concerts now, much more than we ever did.
>
> In spite of some of the work that takes me away, I am spending more time with Ruth, both at home and traveling. We go for walks nearly every day.

Time with her is becoming play for me. Going to a concert is play. I enjoy shopping and love cooking. We do those things together, too. I love to find a good restaurant and spend an evening with a good meal and bottle of wine. This combination of time with her and things I love to do constitute play for me.

Now seventy, Jacob has a consulting relationship with an oceanside college, which provides him the opportunity to combine work and play. He and Ruth regularly spend hours together walking along the beach near the college and enjoying the seasons of the sea. "I find it hard to believe, but I'm actually getting paid for spending time in this beautiful spot. We have the time to really enjoy being here," he wrote me. These two, experiencing another peak in their interesting lives, are not average. Though not wealthy by executive or professional standards, they have enjoyed many of the privileges associated with higher education and professional recognition. But they have in common with others I have studied a commitment to grow, both together and individually, through their interdependent marriage. Integrating the paradox of greater freedom and intimacy, they are fast approaching the anniversary that for them is appropriately called "golden."

FREEDOM AND FRIENDSHIPS

The principle of freedom and intimacy also appeared when I looked at close friendships. Classical Greek philosophy saw this connection long ago. When addressing young males' aspirations to happiness, Aristotle advised them that the virtuous use of freedom could lead to good friendships, without which happiness is inconceivable. Because of the gender inequality of his time, he did not apparently consider it possible for husband and wife to become truly good friends. For Aristotle truly good friendship was a male prerogative. How times have changed! Most of the men I interviewed named their wives as their best friends.

I found that many men were hesitant to use the category "best" or "close" for current male friends. Jacob's comments reflect the experience of many men with whom I talked: "I regret that I have not maintained close male friends. I'm not sure why this has happened. But it's an area in my life I think about a lot and wonder what I can do to improve."

Perhaps the nature of Western societies makes it difficult for men to be open enough with other men to become intimate. From an early age males are competitive and assert their independence to achieve status. Deborah Tannen has observed that American men are more competitive than women even when communicating. Men often provide information that makes them seem superior, while women communicate to develop rapport. Competition can certainly impede intimacy. One is not inclined to be very open with people who might win something that one has coveted. Business, mobility, a competitive ethos, and homophobia work against enduring close friendships for adult males, no matter how virtuous they might have become. Even Aristotle might have found this perplexing.

All of the women in the study who exhibited second growth—single, widowed, and married—reported that both their continuing liberation and friendships have become top priorities. Most described one or two close friendships in particular. They were careful to distinguish friends from close friends. Close friendships move on a deeper level. Intimacy emerges from a profound level of sharing and trust. This intimacy in turn generates greater freedom. In moments of intimacy close friends feel freer. Women often said that with a close friend they could be relaxed, open, and free to be themselves. The intimacy of sharing also contributes to a high degree of truthfulness. They feel free to tell a close friend anything, the women told me.

Irene, the remarkable widow we met in chapter one, described the intimacy of close friendships that other women alluded to:

> Since my husband died, I have become even closer to my friends. A good friend is someone with whom you can have intimate conversations. When you're raising a family and working, there isn't enough time for friends. Gradually, I realized I needed to devote more time to them, and I do. My best friend has a husband who is ill now. We talk and really understand each other. We've become so close. She says she can talk to me in a way that she cannot talk with anyone else. We try to have enough time for long, intimate conversations. I think this is the basis for friendship.

These women organize their lives in order to spend quality time with close friends. No matter how busy they are with careers and family, they set aside time to be together. Each will schedule a luncheon, shopping, a trip to an event or a museum, an outing, a long phone call, or a casual get-together for herself and her close friend, just the two of them. Married and single women alike take vacations with best friends. Some have best friends living far away from them, so an annual rendezvous becomes a priority. Nancy, whom we met in Chapter 3, had this to say about her friendships:

> A top priority for me is taking time off to be with really good friends. I organize my life to make sure that I can be with my closest friends. Sometimes that means taking a vacation together. But on a regular basis, we try to talk, do some shopping, see a show, or play tennis. I sense I am growing a lot now, and good friends are a big part of this. They give me a sense of who I am. I'm learning to give more of myself. That's what friendships are all about.

Friends are also crucial in forming positive personal identities. As we re-define ourselves, we will almost certainly recognize that our new positive identity is both our individual achievement and a gift from someone who loves us. Barbara, the physician we met in Chapter 4, was particularly articulate about what she felt she owed to close friends:

> During the past ten years I have become much closer to a few friends. I was raised to be independent and keep a distance. That's no longer what I choose to do, though I am in some ways more independent than ever. One of the biggest differences in my life is that I am more open. I let my friends see who I am. My best friends especially are helping me open up and get in touch with my deepest feelings—fears, anger, compassion, playfulness. I take risks with them I'd never have done earlier. They're part of my growth.

Barbara and other women spoke of their friendships with a sense of profound gratitude. They also told me of the gaiety and laughter they experience with close friends. The closeness they feel with friends frees them up for new growth.

If building really good friendships is important to midlife renewal, are we destined to impoverished living if at fifty we lack close friends? What happens when friends die or move so far away that a close relationship is not possible or is at least difficult? A seventy-year-old retired business executive told me, "After fifty you don't make new friends. You rely on your family and a few old friends for meaningful companionship." If he is correct, we might face the prospect of a third age bereft of intimate friend-ships.

Nearly every woman I interviewed, however, contradicted his view. They commented on their surprise and delight at making really good friends in their adult years. Irene met her best friend at the age of sixty-six. Women in their fifties, sixties, and seventies are still developing good, close friendships, as are some of the men in this study, indicating, I be-lieve, that most men could learn to cultivate deeper connections and inti-macy with friends. It is never too late to make new friends. A meaningful liberation should free us to build good friendships as well as good mar-riages. As the path of freedom reaches toward fuller self-actualization, paradoxically it also leads us into more intimate connections with our spouses, our families, and friends, both new and old.

Increasing the quality of love and freedom, then balancing them within our unfolding lives, is a major task for both men and women in third-age renewal. Some see these concepts as antithetical. If love were simply a bond, then it would curtail freedom. But as the stories in this chapter show, the bond of love can also liberate people and promote individuality. Mindful reflection begins the liberating process. Probing questions open up broad new terrain, which in turn often raises fears; but love can instill the confidence we need to confront and overcome our fears. Love can teach us to see our partners, our friends, and ourselves with new clarity. Only love truly sees and appreciates another person's distinctive individu-ality. As we move in new directions, we should realize that love and free-dom are complementary. Human beings are not born free; we become free through personal growth and through being loved. Bound by love, we are also bound to be free.

7
Principle Six: Building a More Caring Life

I'm thinking more about what I want; but I'm trying hard to balance that with giving to others—here at work, in my family, and to solving some of the problems we face in this world.

—Mimi

INCREASING OUR CAPACITY TO CARE

The psychologist Erik Erikson suggested that in middle age, individuals confront the distinctive task of caring for future generations. He called the development of this special form of caring generativity, the penultimate virtue in personal development. Recent research supports Erikson's suggestion. Interpersonal and social caring is now recognized to be an important ingredient of healthy adult adaptation. Many people who report midlife satisfaction also say that in their forties and fifties they experience more compassion, altruism, and generosity than ever. People manifesting second growth have definitely manifested an increase in caring. Yet as I followed the lives of the people in this book, I discovered that this virtue includes more than Erikson and other psychologists have suggested. Developing our capacity for several different forms of caring is the sixth paradoxical principle and challenge in midlife renewal.

As we reflect on our lives, we need to examine the structure of our caring. What we most deeply care about shapes our values, beliefs, direction, personal identity, and our relationship to whatever we consider to be ultimate reality. The structure of our caring also provides meaning in our lives. Caring is always important; in the third age it becomes more so. A major challenge for us at this time is not only to become more caring toward others, but to rethink and restructure what we care about.

Like the other themes in third-age renewal, clarifying our deepest cares can be both liberating and confusing. In addition to developing our own individual patterns of caring, most of us have been influenced by narrow individualism and consumerism. Modern Western culture has been drifting toward a competitive, materialistic, and self-regarding type of caring. This self-regard is reflected in a variety of ways: how we relate to others, what we strive for and invest in, and even our patterns of consumption. The economist Jeremy Rifkin has reported that on average, Americans in the 1990s consume twice what they did forty years ago. Without realizing it, we often become status-conscious consumers. The cares that swirl around and through us are often selfish, shortsighted, and superficial. Some people are pulled along by this cultural current; they become wrapped up in themselves and increasingly focused on material concerns. The longer we are exposed to it, the more powerful its effects on us can be. Most of us have known adults who seem to have succumbed to this current, more wrapped up in their own needs and less caring about other people as they age. As we learned in the last chapter, one aspect of midlife liberation is to free ourselves from cultural norms that impede our growth.

Renewing our lives calls for a countercultural alternative to this materialistic, self-regarding current. *Generativity* is not quite the right word for what I see happening as people grow by restructuring their capacity to care. The care I have witnessed is more complex and paradoxical, moving along several trajectories at once. For example in the first steps of second growth we learn to listen carefully to our hearts and dreams. Our caring is appropriately focused on creative self-actualization. But in this process we also learn to listen to our connectedness. Our caring is attentive to what others want and need, and to what is needed to support the future. Mimi, a woman who has grown prodigiously during her fifties and sixties, described this paradox as a struggle to achieve balance in what she cares about:

> I think it's important to enjoy life—I mean really enjoy it. I probably still
> don't do that enough. But I can't understand how people can devote them-

selves only to their own enjoyment. That to me seems selfish. I have been in-volved in many issues—education, environment, and especially women's is-sues. I see improvements, but we have a long way to go. I'm devoted to addressing those issues. I see myself as someone who gives. I'm thinking more about what I want; but I'm trying hard to balance that with giving to others—here at work, in my family, and to solving some of the problems we face in this world.

The dynamics of her caring evolve kaleidoscopically, pointing toward her own health, growth, and enjoyment, but also toward family and friends, colleagues and neighbors, environmental issues, the needs of soci-ety, the present, and the future. "The problem I have with all this complex-ity," she told me, "is that I always seem to overbook." Perhaps "overbooking" her commitments in a daily schedule is another indication of the growth of her caring. For over twenty years she has been learning to balance the diversity of legitimate claims within her expanding structure of caring.

FINDING MEANING THROUGH AN EXPANSION OF CARING

Dorothy: *A major objective in my life is to feel that I've made a difference, that the world is better because I have been here.*

Most stories presented so far reflect an increase in a person's capacity to care for others as well as for his or her own self-actualization. Dorothy's story vividly illustrates one aspect of this paradoxical caring in second growth, a challenge with which many of us are already familiar. Like most of the adults in my study, Dorothy was not even aware that she had been doing anything special. Now in her sixties, married for over forty years to a man she appreciates and enjoys, and the mother of three grown daugh-ters, Dorothy describes herself as a fairly traditional woman who devel-oped a career as a university teacher while filling the roles of wife and mother.

She was in her midfifties when we met. When I entered her apartment on the upper West Side of New York City, the dining room table was lit-tered with papers and books she was using to put together a lecture. Apol-ogizing for the mess, she told me it would soon be cleared up so that she could set the table for dinner with her husband:

I've been a conventional housewife. My daughters tease me because I really like puttering around the house, cleaning, sewing, cooking. That's who I am. I'm teaching full time now, but the hardest work I ever did was raising kids. I've had a traditional role, and I've enjoyed it. My daughters are turning out well and I am pleased with my role as a parent. Becoming a professor is important, but I'm happy being a housewife.

As it turns out, Dorothy broke the conventional housewife mold. As I learned more about her, I was amazed at how she underestimated the accomplishments of her complex lifestyle. A significant change in her life pattern occurred when she started to take care of her own potential by pursuing a career while tending hearth and home. With three young daughters and a husband to care for, she enrolled in a graduate program that eventually took eighteen years to complete. While a graduate student, she also taught part time. Once, when her youngest daughter was still in junior high school, she commuted two hundred miles each week to teach full time at a state university. Some might think she short-changed generativity. On the contrary, like many modern parents, she transformed a traditional woman's role by juggling her commitments to self, work, and family. She grew as her capacity to care became more complex.

Now that her daughters have left home and she has her Ph.D., she has been freer to concentrate on building a professional career. But her generativity remains strong both in the family and in her transference of caring to women around the world. In addition to teaching, during her fifties she was actively involved in the international women's movement and linked this involvement with a research project. While dedicating herself to women's issues, she also expanded her caring in other directions. Six years after our first interviews, she was so concerned about environmental degradation that at age sixty she was considering a new career focused on environmental causes. Her caring extends into multiple commitments— to herself and her career, her community, her family, women's issues, and more recently, our planet. Why does she do all this? Because caring provides her with a framework of meaning.

When I asked about meaning in her life, she at first quipped, "The meaning of my life? The meaning is in the living of it." That abrupt answer so jarred me that our interview lapsed momentarily into silence. She then added,

Well, there's more to it than that. There are times when I think about the suffering in this world. When I walk past a person on the street who is down and out, I think, my God, how can we let people live that way? I want to make a difference. I think I have, as a parent. But I also want to contribute to the world, to alleviate some of the suffering. A major objective in my life is to feel that I've made a difference, that the world is better because I have been here. That is how I see meaning for my life.

She proceeded to tell me how she has tried to alleviate the suffering of street people in her city neighborhood. With several friends, she organized a soup kitchen in her local parish. At first this effort was seen as an informal gesture for a limited duration. To nearly everyone's surprise it became an established organization. "So many street people have been coming daily to the church for meals, conversation, and other forms of assistance. They make some members of the parish, especially the rector, uneasy; but it's being accepted," Dorothy said. After five years, the soup kitchen was thriving, serving 150 people a week. Her caring has made a big difference.

Dorothy told me how her caring has also expanded within her family to reach through three generations. In her thirties and forties her generativity was directed mostly towards her children and their future. But in her fifties, like many other adults, her focus shifted to a generation that preceded her. She became closer to her aging father, whom she cared for regularly until he died at age ninety-one. In addition, she became more conscious of needs among her siblings. She became closer to her three brothers and their wives. Like Sharon, whom we met in Chapter 6, Dorothy described how she tries to be attentive and supportive to several generations within her family simultaneously. She also told me of new friendships with people outside the family "who have something to share, who care about me." A reciprocity of sharing and caring mark her friendships as well.

Over the past twenty years, Dorothy has clearly developed a more caring lifestyle. This has been an integral part of her growth. Yet I found an unresolved problem when I asked her, "How do you take care of yourself?"

I'm not doing too well on this one. I've had trouble budgeting time for myself. I'm trying to enjoy life more, but I'm still pretty much focused on my responsibilities. Like I want to spend more time outdoors with my husband, to have a better balance of work and play, to enjoy the garden we're making at our country home. I hope I'll be able to work this in.

Dorothy has done unusually well in creating balance between caring for career development and caring for others, but she has had difficulty allowing time to play and take good care of herself. In her midfifties she was struggling to be more attentive to this aspect of her life. She and her husband both enrolled in psychotherapy to help them clear away inhibitions to growth and express emotions more freely. She had also begun to do moderate exercise and to explore ways to manage stress more effectively. As the complexity of her care has increased and deepened during the past two decades, she has experienced greater emotional richness, closer relationships, more compassion, and a more profound sense of meaning. She once told me that she feels "much more alive today, younger by far than my mother did at this age." But to sustain her growth she also realized that she needed to balance her expanded caring for others with better self-care. Many caring people are "not doing too well on this one." One person in particular was very helpful in showing me how we can do better in addressing this task.

A CAREGIVER LEARNS SELF-CARE

Chuck: *We preach "love your neighbor as yourself," but just don't get around to the second half. . . . You need to care for yourself. . . . I'm learning to care for the person I can be.*

Most of the adults I interviewed have been swimming against the cultural current of consumerism and self-regard. They have seen meaning not in accumulating things, status, or power but in their growth and in extending care toward others. Yet they have often found it hard to fit committed self-care as an element of growth into their framework of meaning. To them it seems selfish or unimportant. John, who cared deeply about his work and his family, jokingly commented, "I do absolutely nothing to take care of myself." Old assumptions and values make self-care difficult. Many adults have told me, "I never took care of my own needs. I always felt that I had to do what others expected of me." It has been difficult to accept self-care as a legitimate value because we confuse it with selfishness.

Chuck's struggle vividly illustrates how individuals committed to midlife renewal can learn both to value self-care and balance it with caring for others. When we met, Chuck was fifty-one, had been happily married for twenty-three years, and was a proud father of two sons. He had been an Episcopal priest for twenty-five years. Walking up the stairs to the rectory next to Chuck's church on a bright, warm summer day in Maine, I was greeted by a cheerful man dressed casually in jeans and a colorful T-shirt. Chuck welcomed me into his home and into his confidence.

One of the first things I learned from Chuck was that he was a recovering alcoholic. The hardest thing he had done, he told me, was to announce to his parish the previous year that he was entering a treatment facility to overcome his addiction once and for all. Because he came from an alcoholic family, Chuck had become especially attentive to internalized forces that inclined him toward addiction. He made a commitment to an intensive counseling program so that he could reach a fuller, deeper understanding of himself. In his recovery program he became more reflective, which yielded insights into his addictive lifestyle and promoted new growth. He admitted that he was also a workaholic. In recovery he was searching for a new understanding of himself and ways to lead a healthier life. His casual attire and relaxed manner suggested his search was successful.

Entering his fifties was apparently a turning point for Chuck. Like many of us, he realized that time had become a scarce resource: "I have less time to live. When we're young we think we'll live forever. Now I know my time is limited, and there's a lot more I want to do and to learn," he said. One obstacle to genuine satisfaction, he discovered, was that throughout his life he had kept a lid on his emotions. He had been reared to think first of his family, to contribute to its tranquillity and not to express emotions that might be disturbing: "Not passion and, above all, not anger." In his parental family and in the church "it was not acceptable to emote." But powerful inhibitions had serious consequences in his life.

He had avoided self-knowledge by adopting a professional caregiving role:

I know a lot more about myself today than I did a year ago. Sometimes what I learn is painful; other things are pleasant. I'm engaged in a process of self-discovery that's new for me, and I'm not about to stop. I've also realized that this profession gives me lots of opportunities not to know myself, to concentrate on others and put off attending to my own needs. We preach "love your neighbor as yourself," but just don't get around to the second half.

Caring only for others can become a defense mechanism, diverting one's attention from unresolved issues and unmet needs. By devoting his life to others, Chuck had avoided the unsettling process of clarifying what he really wanted from life. Powerful emotions and needs were pushed aside and buried in his unconscious. But repressed feelings have a way of returning in disguises. We might confuse what we really want with what a significant other once preferred us to want. Or worse, we might choose as a value the opposite of what we truly desire. In Chuck's case, ignoring his own wants led to the self-destructive behavior of alcoholism.

Then one day he came to a transforming realization:

> I was beginning to hear something from within. This was a watershed. Something within me was beginning to say, "You need to care for yourself." Up until this point in my life, others always won out. In my parish and in my family, I had minimized myself. Perhaps because I had this orientation I went into the profession I did, where everyone else's interests and concerns are more important than my own.

This discovery of a repressed self waiting to be affirmed and realized came to him as a surprise, and he had difficulty finding the right words to describe the change:

> I'm having trouble putting into words what I need to do. My AA sponsor calls each day and asks, "Chuck, what are you doing for yourself today?" I used to answer. "I don't know. I don't know what to do for me. I only know how to do things for other people. That makes me feel good. I don't want to be selfish."
>
> I've started to change. I've done some things that I really wanted to do and taken an attitude that says they are as important as doing things for others. This is an aberration in the pattern of my life. I realize I have a lot of choices, and some of the important ones I would never have considered before. I'm beginning to accept doing things because I want to, and this feels as good as doing for others. I realize that if it feels good, it's not bad. I don't think it's bad to be selfish anymore.

Many of us are mindless about what is in our best interests. We have not reflected mindfully on the relationship between what we care about and our chances for becoming an authentic self. This mindlessness may even be a consequence of a limited focus on generativity, as it was for Chuck. Growth for many has also been overshadowed by an inappropriate sense of guilt. Self-consciousness has often been more of original sin than of original blessing. At this time in his life Chuck began to listen to a healthy inner voice, which called him to find and affirm the person he could become. He developed a more accepting, self-caring attitude as he learned to counsel himself:

> I've been working for the past year on learning to love myself. In the hospital, I kept asking, Self, who are you? All I could come up with was this smiling person who did things for others. But what's behind that? I'm learning now to care for the person I can be.

Chuck's orientation to others, his eagerness to think of their needs and to provide service, is exemplary. He has led a caring life. But his caring has been unbalanced. When he began to question the purpose of life, he found that his own existence was getting left out of the answer. He could not frame an alternative perspective without using a term that suggested sinfulness: selfishness. He had trouble thinking and talking about this important aspect of his life. Our culture has not provided us with the appropriate terms and a suitable frame of reference. Self-care becomes confused with selfishness, pursuit of self-fulfillment with narcissism, self-actualization with self-indulgence. Chuck struggled to accept the paradox that caring for himself was as important as caring for others.

Each of us has the responsibility of caring for and becoming the "person I can be." That is our basic calling, which no one else can assume. There is a saying of Jesus recorded in the apocryphal Gospel According to Thomas that could have been helpful to Chuck as he struggled with this paradox. Jesus is reported to have said: "When you bring forth what is within you, then what is within you will save you. If you do not bring forth what is within you, then what is within you will destroy you." That which is within us is our inner truth. Some might call it our spirituality or it might be our growth potential. This saying suggests that if you nourish the person you can be, then your life will express your inner truth. If you repress your potential, then it will turn against you. Our growth must affirm both directions in the law of love: toward our neighbors and toward ourselves. I believe that is what Chuck was learning.

As Chuck counseled himself to set a new direction, he decided he needed to do something about overcoming emotional inhibitions to bring forth what was within him. One emotion he needed to learn to let out was anger:

> I experience more anger now than before, because I used to just stuff it inside me. I'm not doing that anymore. I'm quicker to recognize now how I feel and let it out simply and directly, to get it out and over with. I realized that much of the anger I had stuffed deep inside was actually directed at myself.

Repressed anger had eaten away his self-esteem and optimism, pushing him further into addiction. Failure to nourish his inner truth was destroying him. By releasing anger he was able to be more aggressively committed to healthy becoming. His inhibitions had buried more than just anger. In the twelve-step program he learned to own up to and express other emotions, like affection and humor. Like many others we have met, he was, in fact, developing his emotional intelligence, an essential component of his full self.

As he generated a more nurturing approach to himself, Chuck also realized that he had neglected the playful side of his personality, especially his sense of humor. Typically, the clergy's role is a serious one. Yet Chuck found a way to lighten it up a bit. When organizing a summer vacation Bible school, he realized that he could legitimately spend more time with children. He used the Bible school as an opportunity to be playful and funny. "I need this time with kids. I'll spend all morning with them. I play the guitar and sing them songs. We just have a ball," he reported. This summer experience gave him confidence to infuse humor into his ministry. Giving freer rein to his playful side helped him redefine his role to better fit his growing self.

Another area he loved but had neglected was music. He had sung in church services and with children, but that did not satisfy his deep desire to tap his musical potential. In caring for others, there was little time for that. When he was in seminary, he had started playing the guitar but later dropped it. With the children he had taken it up again, strumming and singing songs with them. In his midfifties he finally made a commitment to learn to play the guitar really well. He treated himself to regular lessons and began to play every day. His story shows how self-care has fostered not only health but also greater emotional richness, playfulness, and creativity.

Learning to express self-care led Chuck to restructure his everyday activities to achieve a better balance. He described how he deliberately set more time aside for himself. Usually in the morning, he would allow himself an hour to think, read, pray, and keep a journal. This was time to be quietly with himself. He also spent more time with his family. In the afternoon or evening, he and his wife would walk a couple of miles. He also told me about morning ventures with his younger son on a paper route. At first he went along because he felt his son needed support. In the cold, New England winter mornings, he drove the car while his son delivered. This experience was a complete break from his routines. Later, after his son learned to drive and had his own license, Chuck continued to accompany him "because I really want to."

As he was assessing his life, Chuck sensed another casualty—a decline of friendship. He and his wife had left behind some close friends when they moved to his new parish. In his ministry he had been too busy to develop new friendships. He realized two things about his midlife friendships. First, most people he named as friends were simply acquaintances; second, true friendships could and should run at a deep level. He and his wife agreed that there were several couples they would like to get to know better. They changed their schedules so that once or twice a month, they could spend an afternoon or evening with another couple: "There are a few people that I really love and with whom I can be completely open. We've decided we need to strengthen these relationships. We make a point of getting together with these people at least once a month. We've never done this before." In this instance self-care has prompted him to balance larger freedom with greater intimacy.

Two years after we met, Chuck made another previously unthinkable decision. He agreed to take a four-month sabbatical. He had been offered one before but had refused on the grounds that he did not need it. Finally, he could accept something that was just good for him; he was learning to give himself permission to respond to opportunities that offered growth and enjoyment. Two of those months he devoted to reading and reflection to develop an intellectual side that had been neglected because of parish duties. He also "selfishly" decided to leave home and spend time living in a theological seminary so that he could brush up on his education and engage in challenging conversations. He spent the other part of his sabbatical doing something even more egregiously pleasurable. He took a six-week trip to England and Scotland with his wife. There they explored their family roots and celebrated their twenty-fifth wedding anniversary in Canterbury, the mecca of their religious tradition.

Self-care led Chuck to be more attentive to his wants and needs, to emotions and learning, to love and friendships, to creativity and play, and to his physical health. To develop a healthful lifestyle, Chuck made more changes in his life. In addition to regular brisk walking, he and his wife decided to spend more time outdoors, especially in the summer, working around their cabin and canoeing on a nearby lake. He also changed his diet. Like many Americans, he had long indulged in junk food. Now much more careful about what he eats, he cut down on red meat, fat, salt, and sugar. He lost some weight and decided to keep it off. He was more careful to get "the right amount of sleep," about seven hours per night for him. To manage stress better, he developed the discipline of listening to his feelings and responding to himself caringly. Daily meditation, his music, a more relaxed, self-accepting attitude, and brisk walking were part of his stress reduction regimen. He had given up smoking several years earlier and at fifty became sober. At fifty-five he celebrated five years of sobriety and a healthy, active lifestyle.

Chuck's growth has moved him into greater complexity, which has prompted him to redesign the whole fabric of his life. A crucial element in this redesign has been the increasing care he has given himself. He has learned to listen to what he most wants and sets time aside to make it happen. By focusing on the structure of his care, he began to apply other paradoxical principles of renewal. For example, we saw how he was working to redefine his personal identity to become the person he has the potential to be. More attentive to his emerging interests, he also enlarged his freedom: he is now free from his addictive patterns, freer toward the self he wants to become, and freer with others he truly cares about. He was also redefining his work and putting more play into his life through music, humor, and outdoor activities with his wife.

As he approached sixty, Chuck and his wife decided that they needed to make another significant change. "Thirty-one years as a parish priest were enough," he told me. So that he could resign from his position, which would require them to move from the rectory, they winterized their lakeside cabin. They now live in their ideal environment, with more time to be close to nature, to enjoy each other, and to explore new ways of caring for others. Chuck also started to build a new career in elder care, working in hospices. His story illustrates how a caring person engaged in midlife renewal can integrate the paradoxical qualities of generativity and self-care, and bring forth the best that is within. Perhaps "love your neighbor as yourself" means that when we learn to genuinely love ourselves, we will have a greater capacity to love others. One of the ironies in Chuck's healthy transformation is that he enjoys caring for others as much as ever. Being committed to his own good has not diminished his commitment to others. The secret is in the balance.

LUST FOR LIFE:
CARING FOR OPTIMAL PHYSICAL HEALTH

So far we have seen how taking good care of ourselves calls for critical reflection, values clarification, risk taking, creative experimentation, and daily discipline. It includes becoming more open to our emotions and creative potential, more nurturing of ourselves and our relationships. With the chance to live a whole century, it is also more important than ever for us to maintain healthy bodies and optimal health. Achieving this desired state through the second half of life requires much more discipline and exercise than we ever imagined appropriate for people over fifty. Yet many adults resist regular, sustained physical activity. One woman in this study told me, "I would rather care for my soul than my body." How, in this day and age, can she separate the two? Mind, spirit, and body are complementary aspects of the entity we call a self. If we aspire to a long, caring life that stretches for a century, then our life style must include the discipline that nurtures our physical well-being.

Cultural values work against this insight, because we so prize comfort and convenience. Modern lifestyles do not usually provide the physical challenges needed for good health. We have to build them into our daily schedules. For example, on the whole our modern lives are unnaturally sedentary. We have grown accustomed to inactivity. Many of us drive everywhere and walk as little as possible. That is not good for either our minds or our bodies. Research and experience show that if we care well for our bodies, we can improve our intellectual and emotional functioning. If we truly lust for a longer, fuller life, then two old sayings are more applicable than ever: "A healthy body promotes a healthy mind" and "Use it or lose it."

We should care mindfully about our physical fitness for several reasons. With the possibility of living longer, we need to change the "normal" process of aging that until now has been the dominant feature of the second half of life. Much of what we have considered aging is in reality disease and degeneration from inactivity, bodily abuse, and neglect. We will dramatically change the way we age if we take much better care of our physical condition. A fit, healthy body provides a foundation for continued growth and improvement in the quality of our lives. Remaining active and physically fit will also help us maintain self-confidence and self-esteem, two ingredients needed to create a positive personal identity and to grow young while growing older.

We should also aim for optimal health for social reasons. An aging society needs seniors who are vital, healthy, and independent citizens. Our nation cannot afford aging in the conventional way with heavy reliance on treatment for degenerative ailments. Spiraling health care costs could impoverish the nation. If we really care about the future of our country, we need to care about our physical well-being so that we do not add to the drain on increasingly scarce resources.

As we look to the future, our aim is not merely to live longer. We want to serve and enjoy the present and lay the foundation for a vigorous, generative old age. We have within our grasp the chance to live the gift of life fully and completely up to the moment of death at a ripe old age. That ideal happens too infrequently. The deaths of most adults in our society are premature. They are brought about neither by old age nor by diseases that previously ravaged societies. The leading causes of death now are the consequences of our lifestyles: diseases of the heart, cerebrovascular disease, cancer, cirrhosis, and accidents. Treatment of these diseases are often painful and expensive. Many of these conditions are preventable.

There are reliable medical guides to help us live more fully by developing more healthy, vital lifestyles. For example, Dr. Kenneth Cooper, known for his programs of fitness and aerobic exercises, has produced a variety of sound, practical suggestions for incorporating exercise into a mature lifestyle. More recently, medical researchers like Dr. Walter Frontera of the Harvard Medical School have discovered significant improvements in strength, dexterity, and functioning among people in their eighties and nineties after systematic exercising that includes weight lifting. Such discoveries provide powerful inducement to midlife exercise. All kinds of exercise that we used to think appropriate only for young athletes are in fact beneficial for adults over fifty. Regular, vigorous exercise is the closest thing to an anti-aging pill now available. Self-caring adults use it.

The benefit of exercise depends on its quality and regularity. Medical studies have found that for both men and women brisk walking several miles a day over a long period of time is very beneficial. Irregular and moderate exercise isn't enough. To achieve the level of exercise needed to promote well-being and longevity, people must walk briskly or jog about fifteen miles per week. Many Americans in my study committed themselves to a regular exercise program as they learned to take better care of themselves. None of those I interviewed from European, Asian, or African countries engaged in formal exercise, but they all frequently walk much greater distances and more briskly than Americans are accustomed to. One need not become a "health nut" to achieve optimal health.

The adults in my study who take care of themselves by exercising have testified to a variety of benefits through the third age. They are able to enjoy many activities they had thought they would have outgrown. Their exercise builds tissue and muscle mass, increasing their strength and agility. They feel better, work hard, are actively involved in organizations and communities, can do more than even they dreamed of, and continue to enjoy outdoor adventures, physically active play, and sex. Some adults are more vital at sixty than they were at forty. Even those now in their sixties and seventies have described a rich variety of activities that includes running, hiking, wilderness camping, fly casting, biking, tennis, sailing, kayaking, canoeing, cross-country and downhill skiing, swimming, weight lifting, aerobic exercise, and dancing. Burns, still robust and vitally engaged in his eighties, told me how he started to jog at sixty, because he wanted to be fit enough to continue playing tennis and squash. He jogged with younger friends into his seventies, until his knees gave out, and did not retire from his architectural practice until he was seventy-eight. At eighty he looked and acted like healthy individuals fifteen years his junior. Individuals in this study have the energy and strength to sustain lifestyles that provide pleasure to them and benefits to others.

CARING FOR OUR MATERIAL WELL-BEING

As we expand our caring for the future, we should also pay attention to managing our personal finances. This concern belongs in midlife renewal, though it has often been ignored in the literature of adult growth. With an extra thirty years, personal long-range planning to sustain both our physical and material independence is a must. Attending to our future well-being is not necessarily materialistic or selfish. There are social as well as personal reasons for caring about responsible self-care and financial management.

Just as physicians have warned us against unhealthy lifestyles, so economists warn us that many Americans are not planning ahead and saving for the future. As the baby boomers crash into the ranks of the elderly, society will be put at risk if they have been careless about health care, savings, and personal finances. Society can only afford a limited amount of dependency. If the number of physically and financially dependent elders increases while the number of young productive workers declines, our families, our economy, and our social structure will be seriously endangered. An alternative is to have independent elders. If the future generation of elders ages the way past generations have, only longer, our nation could go bankrupt paying for elder care. In developing healthy and prudent self-care, our caring should extend way beyond ourselves and immediate families to future generations—even to seven generations beyond us, as a Native American saying puts it. If we are to be responsible trustees of the future, then part of our responsibility is to plan our lives so as to continue to be independent, socially productive adults.

CARING FOR THE EARTH:
AN ECOLOGICAL SPIRITUALITY

The graying of America is often especially visible in churches. Many people who drifted away from religion in youth return when they are older. Is this another indication of increased caring? Few of those I studied would say so. I have not seen that an increase in the capacity to care necessarily leads to religious practice or affiliation. Some of the adults attend church regularly, but only 15 percent told me that their religious faith was stronger than it had been. Some said they had been more religious when they were young; others have always been indifferent. I am not sure why. I suspect that they have not found traditional faith providing them with reliable information and insight consistent with modern views influenced by science and practical experience. Even some who have faced life-threatening illnesses remain reluctant agnostics. Many have expressed a grateful caring for life that includes an openness to the mystery of the cosmos. A deeply felt awareness of the miracle of life within the immensity of the universe might put us near the doorstep of religion. Whether this form of caring moves into religion depends on the individual.

When I asked the adults in this study about spirituality, I received a totally different and much more definite response. Most felt they were becoming more spiritual. As I questioned them, I learned that their spirituality often falls outside the framework of traditional Western religion. At least, it is not tied to prayers, sacraments, and scriptures. And in some respects it runs counter to accepted beliefs. Most, even those who attend church, said their growing adult spirituality is linked to their outdoor experiences. These individuals reported that they feel a deepening relationship with the natural environment, a sadness at civilization's devastation of the planet, and a growing sense of caring for the earth. The physicist Albert Einstein suggested that modern spirituality should include breaking out of the prison of traditional categories so that we can move beyond them to greater caring for nature. "Our task," he said, "must be to free ourselves from this prison by widening our circle of compassion to embrace all living creatures and the whole of nature in its beauty." The spirituality mentioned by many in this study seems to be moving in that direction. It does not imply a realm outside the framework of time and space. It is often a deeply felt perception of our inherent connection to the earth, all life, and the cosmos.

When nature becomes a presence, we might sense a power that confirms us as an integral part of the mysterious universe. Such moments inspire a larger sense of self and provide a much larger framework of meaning. Caring for ourselves and the future points logically to deeper, more systematic caring for our common home, the earth. That may at first seem a strange orientation to modern people because we have often assumed that the earth is here for us to use for our own purposes. We have forgotten that our planet does not belong to us; we belong to it. The long-term meaning of our individual lives and our generation is inseparable from the earth's well-being. If we care for ourselves but waste the earth, we are spoilers. The careless and destructive treatment of the earth that is characteristic of modern civilization jeopardizes life, the future, and our own meaning. As the richness and beauty of this fragile ecosystem is depleted and wasted by human beings, the potential meaning for our personal lives is diminished. Awareness of our place in the natural order challenges us to care more reverentially and practically for the earth. We can develop a spiritual ecology that affirms the interconnectedness of everything, that celebrates life and earth as sacred, and that protects the environment from degradation and exploitation. That is another important lesson I have learned from this study.

I have discovered a growing movement, known as creation spirituality, which has promoted this kind of caring. This orientation is critical of traditional Western religious thinking, which has portrayed humans as having a dominant position over nature. Creation spirituality emphasizes a caring relationship of harmony with nature rather than domination over it. Thomas Berry, a leading spokesman for this spirituality, has described it as a life in which we practice "befriending the earth," a phrase that captures a significant aspect of the lifestyles of those in this chapter.

Many growing adults are increasing their capacity to care for nature and for their relation to the natural world. Their evolving spirituality is expressed in awareness and celebration, and in concrete, practical ways such as conservation, environmental restoration, the arts, and special projects. As I reviewed interview transcripts, I discovered that all of those mentioned in this chapter have been serving environmental causes even while they worked at improving their self-care. Their environmental caring has extended into the wilderness and into gardens, organizations, and practical activities; it has touched the present and reaches toward a universal future. This form of caring expands the boundaries of our selves. It also enriches personal lives, complementing self-care by adding awe of life and the cosmos, communion with nature, and a larger sense of responsibility, meaning, and purpose.

LEADING TO A MORE CARING SOCIETY

We have seen how second growth through the third age evolves through expanded, deeper caring on many levels. Our notion of caring has been too narrowly conceived. Certainly, it includes generativity, altruism, and compassion for others. But a truly caring life extends in so many different directions. As we care for others we need also to care for ourselves. But self-care should aim beyond oneself to our connectedness with both future generations and our planet. Our midlife challenge is not only to become more caring, but also to restructure and learn to balance different types of care. Focusing on just one dimension of caring distorts our vision of who we are and restricts our meaning.

As I have reflected on the contributions of caring adults, I see the emergence of a counterculture of caring that can help us shape a hopeful scenario for the future. Some forecasts of our future in an aging society are frightening. They depict an uneven battle for scarce resources between rich and poor, and between growing ranks of seniors and other groups, especially young people and the poor. Already the social security system is being protected as welfare shrinks. Calls for more family and child support, for better education and youth counseling, and for stronger health and recreation programs often go unheeded. An increase in elder dependency points to even greater impoverishment of children. Poverty now touches only a tiny portion of the country's elders, yet more than 50 percent of minority children live in poverty. The historical trend toward worsening conditions for increasing numbers of poor, disadvantaged, and young people will accelerate unless there is a change in the way Americans age. As those of us in the third age think about and express greater caring, we have the capacity to change this trend.

Second growth points to a scenario of great promise. Citizens engaged in midlife renewal will be committed not only to genuine caring for loved ones and themselves, but also to greater caring for community, for learning and truth, and for the earth. They will care about addressing the needs of society. Citizens over fifty have a chance to provide our communities with leadership that draws upon rich inner resources and a half century or more of experience. Our hope lies in the growing number of adults who learn to rethink, restructure, and expand their capacity to care.

The time is fast approaching when the United States population of adults over sixty will be double that of schoolchildren. Healthy, vital, independent, active adults will have the freedom to explore limitless opportunities for volunteer service to express greater caring. We might form a huge elder corps, on the model of a domestic Peace Corps. We might build informal networks within our communities to improve education, advise enterprising new businesses, start new institutions, lend a hand to poor regions and inner cities, promote better neighborhoods, improve child and elder care, and contribute to the enhancement of life for generations to follow. We can become leaders of sustainable development, strengthening movements to conserve and enhance natural resources. We can help monitor parks and wild lands, and model new ways to appreciate and care for the earth in cities and in the wilderness. We can fight a culture of over-consumption, narrow self-regard, and environmental exploitation to build healthy cities and equitable economies. We can help businesses develop a sense of purpose and meaning beyond the bottom line. We can provide a great dispersion of renewed, caring, moral leadership to a world that so desperately needs it.

Our society in turn needs to radically rethink its perception and expectations of the growing ranks of adults in the third age. Competition among self-centered interest groups, which often disturbs communal interdependence and a natural harmony with our environment, can be transformed by new forms of cooperation and sharing expressed by caring adults. Healthy, independent, caring adults will not drain the economy with health-care demands. Those who are entering the new terrain of an expanded, enriched, caring lifestyle have the opportunity to lead the world into a future that will keep hope alive. If a majority of adults in the third age learn to sustain second growth and balance creatively the multiple dimensions of caring, they can lead the way to a more caring society. Just think of how much new meaning that could add to all our lives.

8

It's Your Life After All: Stepping into More Purposeful Living

DESIGNING YOUR OWN LIVING MOSAIC

When we got under way, I promised to show you a life course that deviates from the conventional pattern of adult development and aging. Until now our vision of what we can experience in the second half of life has been veiled by a shroud of disempowering notions about becoming older. We know that *older* need not mean aging in the conventional sense. As we add years, we can also transform aging with the principles of renewal. Who can possibly foretell how our stories will play out? Not long ago, people assumed they could. Aging was thought to be predictable. Once on its trail, you go downhill.

I hope you can now see that we are not bound to spend our life bonus aging in the usual way. An emerging new life structure with a long third age—in fact, the longest period in our lives—offers us an opportunity to redesign the second half of our lives. We can take advantage of this opportunity by injecting into our third age a new growth process, just when convention holds that we should begin degeneration and decline. This second growth will transform our middle years and postpone aging, as it has for the people you have met in this book. What we call this process does not matter; but I like the term *second growth* because it suggests a new direction with distinctive qualities and tasks unlike those of earlier growth. Second growth evolves by applying the paradoxical principles explored in the preceding chapters; and it promotes midlife renewal. We can now review the whole process and see more clearly what a difference it can make in a person's life.

The six principles of third-age growth and renewal are not a series of separate, individual activities. We do not address one and then another and another, as though passing through an obstacle course. Instead of a linear process of development, I see an unfolding mosaic. What has fascinated me throughout this research is the design I see in the lives of these adults. It has been like appreciating a great work of art, which becomes even more impressive when you notice the design the artist put into the creation of it. Though not conscious of this metaphor, individuals I have studied have been creating living mosaics. The patterns of their lives constantly change, moving first in one direction and then in another, with fuzzy areas crystallizing into impressive contours, dark corners providing contrasts to new brightness, and all essential aspects contributing to unique composite forms. None of us can predict how the mosaic of our lives will appear from year to year, what shape or direction it will take. Perhaps our primary task in the third age is to become life artists who bring design to the often elusive vision of who we are becoming.

Like a work of art, a living mosaic increases in value as one keeps working on it. The creative process of second growth enriches the lives of those who nurture it as well as those whose lives they touch. As one prodigious "grower" in her midsixties remarked with a raucous laugh that amused us both, "I am improving with age!" That insight tickled her, but she meant it. Already an accomplished executive and prominent social leader, she was realizing that with her new growth she had redefined what she meant by success. The idea of improving with age provides us with a distinctive sense of meaning and purpose, particularly when our improvement benefits others.

I will never forget El's story about asking himself the question of purpose for the first time in his late forties. As we learned in Chapter 3, he gradually articulated his aim. "My purpose is to become the person I truly am and to share," he said. This purpose wonderfully characterizes midlife renewal. His purpose, like other second growth ingredients, is paradoxical. To become your true self puts the focus on you; sharing puts the focus on others. A purposeful life in the third age involves what Charles Handy has called a proper selfishness, which in part is shaped by a dominant ethic of "support and encouragement of others." Not only can we have it both ways, but also we *must* have it both ways if we are to experience second growth.

In the preceding chapters, we have met over three dozen people who have addressed midlife challenges. By focusing on a distinctive aspect of their growth, we have examined each paradoxical principle one step at a time. In this final chapter we shall meet two very different individuals who, at around age fifty, initiated this process with concentrated, critical self-reflection. The man has sustained new growth for fifteen years, the woman for nearly thirty years. By tracing the course of their lives after age fifty, we will have a full, clear view of the living mosaic of second growth unfolding as a vital, purposeful process.

CREATING A BALANCE AMONG MULTIPLE COMMITMENTS

Ted: *I saw that I had to have a set of four goals. . . . One of my issues is how to fit it all in.*

As he was finishing his architectural degree program in his midtwenties, Ted was invited by a professor to join a new firm in a Boston suburb. Ted would bring his specialty in landscape architecture to round out the firm's portfolio. With a new marriage and his degree in hand, he was off to a fast start. I met him thirty years later, when he was fifty-four and at a high point in his life. He told me there had been many ups along the way, but also some downs. Although he was doing well financially when we met, there had been times when he was nearly broke.

Early in our interview, he told me a very personal story about radical change. Several years earlier, he had realized that his life was not as healthy as it might have seemed on the surface: "My life's good now, but for many years it was essentially all business. I paid little attention to my family or even myself. I put in one-hundred-hour weeks, traveled fifty times a year, worked on Christmas and weekends. I lost sight of important personal goals."

He had also lost his first marriage to divorce after twelve years. Soon thereafter Ted married a woman he met at work and with whom he had much in common. They developed a close marriage but had no children of their own. Within ten years, however, they were in danger of splitting up. "The marriage was going sour—you could smell it," Ted said. In spite

of impressive professional success, Ted began to reflect deeply and critically about himself and his life.

Shortly before he turned fifty, a friend invited him to go on an eight-day
Outward Bound course off the coast of Maine. Separated from his routine, Ted made some personal discoveries that were to change the way he
lived:

> I realized that my life was out of whack. During a two-day course solo, when
> I had the time to reflect, I saw that I had to have a set of four goals: family,
> community, personal, and professional. In my career I had neglected the first
> three. I told myself that if I didn't learn to balance these four, I would have
> an impoverished life and become more and more unhappy. I would lose my
> health, my family, my sense of meaning.
>
> This insight dawned on me during that course, but it crystallized during
> the year, especially as I became involved in volunteer work, serving on a
> board. For the first time I did something significant outside my firm. That
> experience helped me become more committed to quality time with my
> community and my family, and to spend quality personal time taking better
> care of myself.

At fifty Ted consciously put himself on a different trajectory by diversi-
fying his commitments. With his four-point life plan, he started a process
of transformation that has included all the ingredients of second growth.
Probing self-reflection was and is a driving force in his development. It
leads him to reassess his values, activities, and commitments, and to control how his energies are channeled. His experience demonstrates how the
principles of midlife renewal will help you integrate what you have
learned about second growth so that you might better apply its principles
to your third age.

Realizing he had been overly invested in his career, Ted cut down on his
professional work time to concentrate on other important areas. He made
a series of gradual changes at work that increased his freedom to shift his
priorities; he learned to delegate more of his responsibilities and to keep
commitments to family and community. When his architectural firm was
young, he had acquired bad habits, thinking he had to do everything and
control every situation. With his change of plan, he worked to break those
habits. Eventually, he had to rethink and redefine both what success and
work meant to him.

As he redefined his work, Ted reassessed his risk taking. For years his risk taking was structured by his professional work. To develop his four-point plan he needed to take different kinds of risks:

I've always been a risk taker. For years my risks have been in business. They still are, but they're very different. Now I'm not hesitant to tell a client that I can't do something because I have a family reunion. That's a big shift. I would never have done anything like that—like turning down an important meeting to have an anniversary with my wife. I used to shuffle three clients at once, but no longer. I'm learning to say, "I'm sorry, but I'm booked." Now that I have established my priorities, I make a commitment and stick with it.

This kind of risk taking freed up personal space to concentrate on other values, particularly his marriage. When I first met with him at his home in a Boston suburb late on a Friday afternoon, he was waiting to go off for the weekend with his wife, Ellen. By this point in his life, he had finally reduced his professional life to a forty-hour week. Ironically, in spite of putting in less time on the job, he maintained both an esteemed reputation and a comfortable income. And he seemed to be having a lot more fun.

Perhaps the most significant result of his change of direction was the improvement he experienced in his marriage. Just six years earlier he and Ellen were having frequent fights. As Ted began to free himself from old habits and shift his priorities toward a more balanced life, they developed a vibrant, "incredibly close" marriage. At fifty-four he told me,

We have an absolutely wonderful relationship. I don't think there is a better marriage. We're equals, we do everything together, she's my buddy. We're now building a second home on a Maine island. That's kind of a metaphor of our marriage now—a partnership with lots of sharing and compromise. We worked on the design and are building it together. I like modern; my wife wants traditional. It's mostly traditional, but modern enough to suit me. This home is for us to grow in.

It also helps me focus on a personal goal of staying healthy. I want to stand on this island for at least another forty years, to be like Scott Nearing, who was so creative and vital until he died after his hundredth birthday in his home on the Maine coast.

Ted and his wife had become partners in more than just building a house. They were working on a new life plan, carving out more free time to be together and to engage in healthy, playful activities.

Their marriage has continued to develop into a real partnership of equality, interdependence, mutual love, and play. Since the completion of their island home, they have jealously guarded their weekends so that they can spend quality time together there. Weekends provide time for the continuing re-creation of their lives. They have been developing the discipline needed to take breaks from work commitments. Within this new lifestyle they both expand their freedom and focus on their common life. Ted has devoted himself to this crucial relationship. When I asked him six years later what scared him at sixty, he replied without hesitation, "The thought of losing my wife. That's the most traumatic thing I can imagine." The second most traumatic thing would be to lose his work. Twelve years earlier the work might have come first.

Another goal in Ted's four-point plan involved community service. Over the years this intention branched out in several directions. He volunteered to serve on a couple of nonprofit boards and several community projects. Much of his volunteer service has focused on helping young people. He also became involved in environmental projects. His appreciation of nature has grown; in fact, appreciating nature's beauty is the equivalent of religion for him: "I had too much formal religion growing up. Now the experience of changing seasons and spectacular days move me like my mother would say religion should. My wife and I both get a lot of fulfillment from experiencing nature." The expansion of his caring to serve his community and the environment marks another step in Ted's continuing growth.

His final major goal was to take better care of himself. At fifty he started a regimen of exercising at least three times a week. At first this involved vigorous exercise, such as weight lifting, swimming, and tennis. He later dropped tennis because it was too expensive and instead took up biking. He also changed his diet, reducing calories and fatty foods. He was never a smoker, but he had a drinking problem that he felt had to be resolved:

> In my forties I probably worked harder and drank harder than my colleagues. I wasn't an alcoholic, but I drank a lot more than I should have. Several drinks in the evening made me feel great and calmed my fears. I was never away from restaurants, airplanes, bars where I could easily get some-

thing. Then, on Outward Bound, there was no booze. I discovered I didn't need to have a martini to have a good time. One of my goals when I returned was to cut down. Now I limit myself to a couple of drinks a day.

He has adhered to his resolution to remain a moderate drinker. He learned, he told me, to satisfy his thirst with copious amounts of mineral water. He has been taking good care of himself not only by dieting and exercising but also by allowing himself the time to do the quiet things he loves, such as drawing, working in his shop, reading, and talking with his wife.

Creative personal growth enriches our lives and adds considerable satisfaction; but it does not transport us into perpetual sunlight. As we learn to open more readily to the outer limits of experience, we are bound to recognize darkness, loss, and pain in our lives. The more appreciative we become of life's exquisite fragility and graceful opportunities, the more sadness we may feel when we encounter wasted potential and lost benefits. I wondered what regrets and sorrows Ted might have. He shared two of them. The first had to do with his estrangement from his daughters from his first marriage:

> For quite a while after the divorce, my two daughters did not forgive me for leaving. They were ten and twelve when I left. Now that they are in their thirties, we get along, but there is not the closeness there was before. My son, who was only eight when I divorced, eventually moved in with us, and we had a good relationship. He's twenty-eight now, and we're good friends. If I have any sadness—the only thing that gets me down—is thinking about my daughters, wondering, When will I ever get close to them? That's a gap I wish I could fill.

The long pause in the tape, which I noticed when I was transcribing this interview, reminded me of how deeply this revelation had touched both of us. After making significant changes, we cannot escape the consequences of behaviors that we have learned to regret, even if we alter those behaviors in our third age. We are all challenged in growth to carry our painful burdens without sinking. Twenty years after his divorce, Ted's burdens concerning his daughters did not seem to have grown lighter.

Another difficult challenge and loss Ted had to address involved his personal identity. The small architectural firm he joined out of grad school had grown in size and reputation, eventually adding a workforce of three hundred employees. Ted's name was included in the firm's name, which provided him with a reassuring sense of status and achievement. Ironically, however, continued corporate growth produced a personal loss. As more partners were added, they decided that the firm's name needed to be simplified; his name, along with all but the founder's, had to go:

> It hurt to take my name off the letterhead. I felt I needed it then, because I was searching for that reputation. I came to realize eventually that it's not the name on the letterhead that counts, it's you. I don't need my name there. That was a good thing to discover; but honestly, I missed it and sometimes still do.
>
> I have a friend who is being forced to step down from being a president. He's feeling terrible. He shouldn't. I'm trying to help him realize that he isn't losing stature. I have learned that losing a title doesn't mean you're losing your worth or influence or ability to make a difference. This is an identity problem. Actually, I find more meaning in who I am now. When I see the open spaces that I have designed, and think of the enjoyment people get, I feel satisfied.

Like so many of us in professional roles or structured institutional settings, Ted had identified himself with his job and the esteem that it provided him. When his name was dropped from the firm's name, he understandably felt a loss of both identity and status.

Much of our adult identity is linked to status symbols. Titles and public recognition become like diplomas, signifying achievement. As students mistakenly may doubt their intelligence unless they see A's on their report cards, adults often doubt their worth unless they possess conventional marks of success. How can we be sure we are really successful without them? Even if we drop them voluntarily, we fear that others may not understand. We might also feel humiliated. In forming an identity, we select our own set of status symbols, tangible markers that become personal measures of our success. However, these externals can do more than reflect success; they can easily become equated with it. They often become the goal rather than the sign. It is painful and scary to see them go, even when we know that signs of success are just that—representations, not the reality.

Hunting for status symbols as signs of our adult identity sets us on the wrong track, away from genuine growth. The struggle to overcome our dependency on status symbols can be a wrenching experience, especially after we have invested so much of our identities in them. But we have to let go of these externals if we are to release our inner potential, shape a post-institutional identity, and improve with age. Eventually, Ted discovered, as we all can, that his intangible inner resources, his values and experiences, his improved health and sense of youthfulness, the quality of his relationships, and all that he contributes to others were what really counted in forging an identity to be proud of.

To become the person that we can be, to realize our inner truth, we have to step beyond the roles that have defined us or we shall not realize our unique potential, which transcends them. Creating a positive identity without relying on institutional roles and reputation becomes a high-risk challenge for many of us in the second half of life. Since our society does not particularly value maturity as some other societies do, we have to move against the cultural stream and forge strong new identities with little social support. This process does not happen overnight. There were times, Ted said, when his confidence was shaken. Without an impressive title, he sometimes felt uneasy and uncertain, especially in meetings with "big shots." Eventually, he felt more comfortable with such people as he learned to see beyond status symbols to recognize them as just other human beings.

As I interviewed him in his midfifties, I sensed that he really liked the person he was becoming. He felt full of energy, still youthful, more confident, smarter and wiser, appreciative of what he could do and what his future offered him. Midlife renewal was a label he could wear comfortably. He had achieved a very positive personal identity, extending beyond the boundaries of his career. After four years of effort, his balanced four-point life plan was obviously working for him. "I'm more optimistic—realistically optimistic—and have more sense of control. I'm keeping the balance," he said.

I was curious to see how this improved sense of self would fare in the years ahead and planned to check in with him again. Five years after our initial interview, I tried several times to reconnect with Ted and learn how his life and growth were progressing. It was hard to reach him. He was so often out of town that I wondered if the old compulsive work pattern had reemerged in his life. I was tempted to ask his wife if I could interview her instead. After a year of trying, I succeeded in making an appointment to visit him for another interview. As we shook hands, I noticed that at sixty he had retained his tall, athletic build and confident manner. When I asked him how he felt about himself, he responded, "Great! I'm active, have lots of energy, but I'm even more reflective than I was."

I replied, "You know, six years ago you told me that you were in the best time of your life."

"Well, I was wrong," he said, a smile spreading across his face. "This is the best time!"

Then he told me a story of unexpected challenges to his growth plan: "But if you had come just two or three years ago, you would have found me down in the dumps. I was miserable." What had I expected, a smooth ride uphill? Where did we ever get the notion of a linear progression in healthy development? Here again, I encountered a pattern of reversal and progression, ups and downs within the spiral of second growth. Keeping this process alive during the down times can be very hard work. Sometimes our forward motion seems to slip into reverse. We can become discouraged by detours. That is why we need realistic optimism to keep growing, because this new terrain is so uneven and dauntingly unpredictable.

Ted nearly lost his balance and had to struggle to keep his new growth alive. His story, with its setbacks and recoveries, resembles those we have heard from others:

> When we first met, you caught me on the crest of a wave, just before we crashed. After the 1988 recession, our company got hit hard. We eventually had to let half our staff go. That was so hard to do. Then partners had to work even harder, doing everything. For three to four years we had such pressure.
>
> I lost my balance. You know, I was down to forty hours a week but went back to sixty- and seventy-hour weeks. A lot of companies went belly up, but we survived. Letting so many people go was awful. But it's getting better. We just hired two new architects, and the signs are positive. I'm freer now to get my life back in order.

Ted's ordeal this time was unrelated to his own behavior. Just as he was personally flourishing in his midfifties, an economic crash pounded him and his firm. In an architectural practice, months can be invested in a project that later has to be scrapped because the contract could not get sufficient funding. Clients become scarce, plans change, and projects are put on hold. Many colleagues, including some of those he had been mentoring, were dismissed, and that hurt. In addition, he experienced personal financial pressures. I could imagine how his personal growth got neglected when survival became a primary objective.

The dynamic balance faltered but did not disappear; Ted did not entirely lose his life plan. I learned that he still took care of himself, had a good self-image, and was very much in love with his wife. Throughout these tough years he and Ellen kept their commitment to each other, which supported their individual growth and helped both of them maintain a sense of youthful vitality. Earlier efforts to shape a positive personal identity, support derived from his marriage, and his realistic optimism helped Ted endure this storm. As the recession waned, he began restoring the balance in his life so that his four major goals were better served. While he let his community service decline and did not devote as much time to exercise and creative pursuits as he once had, he found that through this trial his marriage and family life actually improved. Growth was not aborted; it just took a tack that for a while seemed to move him away from his destination.

He was eager to tell me about the long weekend just passed, which he had spent with his family at their island home. All three children had since married. Ted was eventually reconciled with his daughters, who had come to accept his wife and their marriage. So he was at last experiencing a large, complex family in the home that love built, sharing the house for the weekend with the families of his three children, including seven grandchildren. With delight in his eyes, he told me about his family's time together and about becoming good friends with his sons-in-law. The island home, once a metaphor for the life he wanted to create, had, in fact, become the special place where important personal dreams were realized. Before the end of that full weekend, he and his wife sailed their sloop "down east" on a reach as far as they could before heading back. They enjoy what he calls "a perfect marriage": "We have real camaraderie. I'm proud of her, respect her. We're equal intellectually and physically. We plan our lives together and balance our activities. Through all the turmoil in work, we kept our weekends together sacred."

While regretfully acknowledging his loss and sadness years ago, the winds of optimism and the support of love did not fail him. As we build a perspective for second growth, we cannot let short-term consequences overshadow long-term possibilities.

In addition to a stronger, more vibrant marriage, Ted has found his professional work to be more meaningful as he has restructured it. Despite the strain and difficulty of the recent past, he expressed an appreciation of the results of his work. He had achieved a deeper sense of meaning than I had sensed previously:

> In those five years, we had to work a lot harder, and I lost some of the balance. But we did some good things. When I go into a city and see a beautiful park or garden, the open space that I designed being enjoyed by people, that makes me feel good. My purpose, if I were to define it now, is to build wonderful places for people to enjoy.
>
> There's another side to this work that is of critical importance. We're working to rebuild inner cities, like Cleveland. We feel that we've got to address what has been happening in these cities. We've got to make improvements there. And part of our work includes restoring and improving the natural environment.

Whereas previously his descriptions of professional challenge reverberated with a sense of competition and status accomplishment, he now proudly saw his work as making social and environmental contributions. In his professional work as well as in volunteer service, and in his family, he has been developing a more caring lifestyle.

In his eyes, his firm had evolved into a socially responsible business. As he showed me around his office, he was noticeably proud of the elegant, imaginative, productive outcomes reflected in the large, artistic photos that graced the firm's office walls. He said that he saw greater importance in his contribution to urban environmental restoration. He described several recent projects and how he derived personal meaning from the value his open spaces added to the lives of those who used them. As I observed evidence of his contributions, I thought that if we are to recover from urban blight and develop sustainable cities, then our society needs designers like Ted who create healthy, habitable, aesthetically attractive open spaces. Ted has been enlarging the meaning of his work by contributing to urban renewal through environmental restoration. By redefining his work to include social and environmental responsibility, he finds greater purpose in it.

Ted has redefined his professional work in other ways as well, which became apparent when he described his relationship with his younger colleagues:

> A lot of my work now is teaching and mentoring. I have to help the younger people along. Some of them have looked at the way partners work, and left. I know I'm kind of a role model. I now see myself helping the young develop. That's a concern we have to work on here.

Ted's work gives him an opportunity to expand and express his capacity to care through mentoring. For him, satisfaction and meaning come from what he contributes to others in the workplace and to society and the environment.

In this evolving framework of work he is also exercising more leadership. The advice he once gave a friend seems right. By losing a title you are not diminished in stature, nor do you lose your influence. Ted's name may not be included in the firm's name, but he has nonetheless become a leader. His vision and values shape the direction the firm's work takes.

As his work evolves, Ted looks at retirement differently. In his midfifties he said that he would start to reduce his activities and prepare for retirement when he reached sixty. Having passed sixty, he has changed his mind:

> Retirement's not for me. I want to do more. I love my work—not all of it—but I'm finding it more rewarding. I love to draw and have more time for that now. Work adds a lot of meaning to my life. So does my marriage. One of my issues is how to fit it all in—how to give really important areas more space in the flow of my life.

The four goals he articulated when we first met, although modified slightly through the years, have remained his major challenges. He does not want to leave work behind; rather, he wants to create better balance among his important interests. While some men dream of retirement, Ted dreams of re-creation. He drew a diagram to show me how he sees his life flowing through his sixties. Work is an important tributary joined by several others. At sixty-three he was still redesigning his work, trying to cut down time on the job so that he can be freer to give more to other interests. "There's still too much traveling to do," he told me. In his last report his plan is to allow more room in his life for other activities, including drawing, volunteer work, play, friendships, outdoor physical activity, and time with his wife.

During the transition period during his firm's reversals in the late 1980s, Ted neglected several areas. For example, he did not fully keep up his previous commitment to self-care. Now back on track, he exercises more regularly and appears to be in excellent health. He told me that he had lost a little weight and that his muscles seemed firmer than they had been when he was in his forties. He is also allowing more time for play. As with many men, much of his play includes sports. He is an avid golfer, carrying his clubs to combine exercise with his game. He also bikes. More of his play now is done with his wife. They ride horses, sail, and occasionally take challenging expeditions. Several years ago, they went with friends on an African safari to observe wildlife. Their play often involves strenuous activity and adventure. Recently, they began learning how to train and run sled dogs. Their play is both fun and a way to stay in touch with their youthfulness.

In addition to more play time, Ted has renewed his commitment to volunteer time for his community. During the recession he had to let his volunteer work go. He has recently identified several projects that he wants to support. He showed me charts of the Maine coast and pointed to several areas where he was involved in environmental projects to preserve and protect Maine islands. I sensed that with less involvement in his firm, he would be looking for other projects to support.

At the close of our last interview, I asked Ted if he had identified a purpose in his life—that is, in addition to what he had found in his marriage and his work. "I haven't gotten there yet," he replied. "If you mean by purpose that I believe God has some plan for me to discover, the answer is no." His answer at first surprised me, because his description of his development radiated purposeful living. He lives as though he has a purpose. After a brief pause I said, "Perhaps our purpose lies in the creative process of our own growth." "I like that," he said.

Many people, however, especially men, have trouble with this view. In a workshop exploring midlife growth, a man once confessed, "I'm having difficulty with process. My wife is a journey person; she can go with the flow. But I'm a destination person. I need to have a clear, specific goal to keep me directed." As another goal person, I could identify with his orientation and our common challenge. "Perhaps," I said, "your next destination should be your journey." Goals are appropriate to circumscribed situations and roles. While setting goals is a proven way to move us in a new direction, we can become so fixed on them as to lose sight of the process that is our underlying objective. Increasing freedom sometimes calls for letting go of goals. When creating a living mosaic we cannot know exactly what will evolve. We have to stay open to surprises. In another workshop that explored the challenges we face in the third age, a participant observed, "This is not the road less traveled—it's the road never traveled, up until now." Our journey is packed with ambiguity and surprises. A major part of our purpose now lies in nurturing the inherently mysterious creative process of second growth *and* to bring fourth what is within us. We cannot predict the future. We can only strive to hold our vision, keep exploring new options, and continue with hope. Our purpose—some have named it a "calling"—lies in our journey, in which we discover the rich diamond of our true selves in the rough potential of our lives and then develop its true worth. The woman we meet next provides another illustration of this creative journey.

Daphne: *My life just took off as I turned fifty. . . . In my fifties I zoomed.*

Daphne, who is now nearly eighty, is one of the most vital and active adults I have met. Her story is one of new beginnings throughout her third age. We met in her comfortable home in Berkeley when she was seventy and about to embark on a new career. In her full life she had already had a variety of careers: as a Wave in World War II, a homemaker and mother, an interior designer, a volunteer worker with community projects and environmental groups, a board member, and now an independent scholar. In addition to her work, she has raised three children and has several grandchildren. Divorced in her forties, she later "experienced romance" and now lives with her "sweetheart." They have developed an intimate, interdependent partnership with many common interests. They share an enthusiasm for friendships, travel, and outdoor activities, all of which help keep her more vibrant than some forty-year-olds I have interviewed.

In one interview she described how she changed direction twenty years earlier:

My life just took off as I turned fifty. I had been doing a lot of exploration in my late forties. I was asking many questions about myself but also about my world and what opportunities I might find. I started to learn some exciting things. But then I realized I had to do something with these ideas. I had to dare things I would never have dreamed of doing earlier.

Discovery, dreaming, learning, and daring appear to be characteristic elements of her new life after fifty, as we shall see.

Daphne today seems to thrive on challenge. It was not always so. She explained how early middle age for her marked a nadir, not a peak.

My forties were terrible, the worst period in my life. I had been married twenty years and raised three children. In the midsixties I read Betty Friedan's *The Feminine Mystique*, and there I was. She described me to a T. I was the wife, homemaker, and entertainer. Wherever I'd go, I'd be introduced as Mr. —'s wife. I had no identity of my own. Even though I had completed college, worked, and done interesting things on my own prior to marriage, somehow I had lost my own identity. I was in a rut. Later, I got a divorce and became a single parent. Then I felt out of place. That was a bad time. But in my fifties I zoomed.

Liberated from confining traditional gender roles, she gradually felt her life taking off. That liberation, I believe, set her on a course of expanding freedom that led to second growth throughout a long third age.

She has continued to "zoom," though she admitted at seventy-five that she was slowing down. But only a little. When I spoke with her at age seventy-seven, she had just returned from a week of backpacking with friends in Idaho and was preparing for an international conference in Australia, to be followed by globe-trotting on a long route back home. Slower perhaps, but zooming past conventional limits nevertheless! Her creative transformation marked a major change in her development. Was her late growth really so new and different from what she had previously experienced? "Haven't you always been like this?" I asked her. "Oh no!" she replied. "I am very different from the way I was in my thirties and forties."

In setting a new direction at age fifty, she not only broke out of a gender box, she moved ahead of her time by initiating second growth. As she went through her divorce, she did considerable soul searching, which she followed by taking risks, developing skills, and learning the discipline of self-care:

> I started asking a lot of questions. I entered Jungian analysis to learn more about myself. I also explored the world, to see what was happening and where I might fit in. You might say I went on a journey—a journey within but also a journey outside.
>
> And I literally trekked on my own. I became physically active again. During marriage I had been reduced to tennis, maybe once a week. I started running and hiking and taking much better care of myself. I also learned to meditate. I'm still learning how to care for myself. I just finished a ten-day silent retreat. My friends tell me I look like I've just had a face-lift, but I tell them that I've just had ten days of quiet. It's wonderful.

Daphne's self-care now includes regular exercise, meditation, new learning, and time with good friends. Disciplined self-care has been a constant factor in her personal transformation. Here is how she described her daily life at age seventy-five:

> I always get up at seven. I do my thinking work at home, before going out to meetings or speaking projects. I spend my evenings alone with my partner. I give myself at least an hour a day for exercise. I go to aerobics class or walk in the hills or sometimes swim. I've started to lift weights to build upper-body strength, because I couldn't open jars. Twice a week a friend comes over and we walk—we've done that for twelve years. Every so often I go off on a ten-day silence retreat, where I practice meditation. And every year I get together with old women friends for wilderness camping.

Taking good care of herself has been a very important element in her growth; it has meant daily discipline to maintain the physical condition needed to realize one's dream and support a vital life.

At fifty, in addition to her increased self-awareness and change to a more active lifestyle, she thought critically about work and what she wanted to do with the rest of her life. She developed a successful career as an interior designer, a career that lasted many years. But not long after it was launched and as her children were becoming independent, she decided to take another risk, a really huge one that would mean living out what she had thought to be an impossible dream. Her eyes sparkled as she began telling me another story about what happened shortly after she turned fifty.

She had always dreamed of going to India and living there. By chance an opportunity emerged in the form of a grant to study traditional Indian village crafts, which were almost extinct. Her career skills and interest qualified her to undertake this study, so she applied for the grant and won it. It was the chance of a lifetime. She set her decorator work aside temporarily and lived in rural India for over a year, traveling to remote villages and becoming friends with Indians, who taught her about their crafts. What she had not counted on was that they would also influence her values and notion of success. The experience pushed her into deeper reflection, which led to a continuing process of transformation.

Her decision to go to India as a single woman in her fifties reflects key qualities that have sustained her growth and are common to the others I have studied: internal searching, risk taking, openness to paradox, courage, optimism, and self-confidence. In daring to realize a powerful dream, she was continuing on the second curve of a new beginning. Like Ginny, the factory worker we met in Chapter 2, she consciously developed an optimistic philosophy that said in the face of an unknown possibility: Why not? For nearly thirty years Daphne has searched and dreamed and dared herself into a series of adventures. Her daring is linked to another key characteristic, which is her strong commitment to discovery and learning.

In her late fifties, after her mother died, Daphne struggled to come to terms with her loss. Among other things, she realized that she missed having her mother to talk with about the experience of aging. She wanted to learn more about the next stage in her life. What would it be like? How could she prepare for it? At that time she did not have older friends in whom to confide. She decided that the best way for her to obtain answers to her questions would be to study women in their seventies and eighties who seemed to be enjoying their senior years. She decided to go back to school to learn a completely new field: adult development and aging. At sixty she completed a master's degree based on interviews with a select group of women who were aging successfully. She was so intrigued by what she learned from these women, that she continued her conversations with them. In her late sixties, she decided again to return to school. This time she went for a Ph.D. in psychology, studying the art of successful aging as a dissertation topic based on the qualities she identified in her sample of elderly women. At the age of seventy, Daphne received her Ph.D. and with her partner hosted a large, lively party to celebrate her achievement and to launch a new career.

Having finished a career as an interior decorator, in her seventies she has become a scholar and speaker on aging. Her work has become increasingly important, not less so. Retirement does not describe her situation at all. She is so engaged in her work that making an appointment to see her, I found, can be an ordeal. Yet her definition of work differs from what we have seen in most of the men's stories. For men, work, narrowly defined, has been a barrier rather than an avenue to second growth. Like Ted, they first had had to cut down on professional work to focus on other areas. In this process they have also redefined their work so that it supports growth and can be better balanced with play. Daphne, on the other hand, has seen her challenge in the third age as enlarging the scope of meaningful work, not reducing it. Her work now is not primarily defined by income-producing activity or an organizational role. It is broader and much more personal than a job.

In developing this later life career, Daphne has built a complex portfolio of work, most of which is volunteer. She gives speeches, writes articles, and has become an international leader in the advancement of vital, successful aging. She has often been invited to significant public events in Washington, D.C. and around the world as a speaker and conference participant. She is also active in the environmental movement, serving on several boards, engaging in environmental restoration projects, and hosting events for environmental causes such as the Sierra Club and Yosemite National Park. Her work has been an important way for her to develop a more caring life, as it has been for others in this study.

Throughout her personal unfolding during the past twenty-five years, Daphne has rethought and reshaped her personal identity. While creating a positive identity, she has nevertheless been confused by issues related to age. On several occasions we have talked about how she sees herself in terms of her age. I suggested once that she seemed to have extended her middle age. Her response surprised me. She disagreed at first and said that in reality she had reached the age category of "old":

> I consider myself well past midlife. I'm in the later years. But I'm still young in some ways. I can do things almost as well now as I could twenty or thirty years ago, except I'm a little slower in some physical activities. In many ways

I'm better because I have had more experience and I think I have more wisdom. I know a lot of women my age are withdrawing, but I'm not. I don't
consider myself old, though I know I am old.

She is old but not old, young but not young. Like other adults in my
study, she is aware of being older but does not experience herself as old.
Like others in this study, she has recovered youthful traits and integrated
them into her life. Given the complexity of her experience, she is understandably unsure how to define her age. Perhaps her confusion has pre-
vented her from buying into the conventional meaning of a given age and
helped her shape an identity that combines growing older with growing
young.

I have found that many individuals in this study have been unsure of
the meaning of their chronological age. What does being a particular age
mean? According to some measures used in the social sciences, fifty-five is
considered the beginning of "old age." That standard is often publicly acknowledged; fifty-five can get you a senior's discount and sometimes early
retirement. Tom, whom we met in Chapter 2, accepted this standard,
which I think triggered his premature aging. If we let the numbers rule
our awareness, we will think our way into being old way before our time.
People like Daphne go a different route. One vibrant eighty-year-old told
me, "I don't think of myself as aging or older—except after long hours
working in the garden when my back hurts. I'm slowing down, but my
mind is alert as ever. My wife and I lead a wonderful, active life together."
Daphne and men like this are puzzled by this paradox of growing
older/growing young. Now that we recognize the paradox, we might learn
to accept it. Daphne knows that she is not aging like most of her peers. She
is composing a life in which age doesn't much matter. Her evolving identity is measured by her growth, not by external standards.

In addition to recovering her youthfulness, Daphne has discovered a
spiritual aspect in her identity. Her immersion in Indian culture years ago
led to a reworking of her values and her identity. She saw people the rest
of the world considered abysmally poor. Yet to her they were inwardly
rich. Becoming friends with people shaped by a culture very different
from her own challenged her to reexamine her materialistic notions of
success. Influenced by Indians, she started to build an identity as an independent, liberated woman, a person aiming toward an ideal self. In freeing
herself from attachment to materialistic status symbols, her growth took

on what she referred to as a spiritual dimension. She changed her definition of success. She wants "to grow rich spiritually" rather than just mate-
rially.

"What did she mean by that?" I wondered as I thought about her hyper-
active schedule. How could anybody this busy realistically define her
growth as spiritual? She explained to me that her spirituality is deeply
connected to serving other people and to her experiences outdoors, where
she feels connected to the sun, wind, earth, and with her friends. While
she described her growth as spiritual, Daphne did not admit to being the
least bit religious. She attends temple once a year, mainly because "this
would please my mother." It also helps her connect to her roots. But her
spirituality is not located within a religious tradition.

As she talked about her everyday life, I saw more clearly how her spirituality could blossom with people in nature. Camping with good friends
or taking a walk with them can be a spiritual event:

> Just the other day, I got together with a good friend. We met for lunch and
> then hiked along a rough trail overlooking the Pacific Ocean for about six
> miles to talk and catch up. That was such a wonderful time. I do that with
> my younger friends. She is fifty-two. You know, I can't do that with most of
> my old friends my age anymore, though I have been walking several times a
> week with a friend for the past twelve years.

Her spirituality is a rich, paradoxical blend of meditation, hard work,
appreciating nature, vigorous exercise, intimate conversation, and the experience of deeper connections. It also includes a deeply felt gratitude for
what life has given her and a sense of adventure to go beyond those givens.
As she connects with people and nature and devotes herself to environmental causes, she is developing her own brand of ecological spirituality.
When we last spoke, she told me of helping to launch a movement of elders who honor the earth. The spirituality of aging and the spirituality of
practical ecology are two of her current projects.

From her I began to see another dimension of spirituality. While she
did not say so, I think that her sense of spirituality is also related to her attitude toward risks, where she transcends boundaries of the known and
moves into the unknown. Risk taking can propel us into an ecstatic liberation, which we sometimes experience in a moment of flow. When I once
asked her about her attitude toward risk taking, she gushed:

Risks? I love risks. I always risk. I love it, except when I'm on a ski slope and start going too fast. I tighten up because I have broken things. I don't do black diamond trails like I used to. But in matters of the mind, I jump in. When I was fifty-nine and went back to school, that whole process presented a risk. Going to India as a single woman was a risk.

Her risk taking is an expression of her lust for life and her determination to become a fully self-realized person. It is a key factor in her learning, creativity, and reaching out to make deeper connections with people and the earth. It certainly contributes to her being such a free spirit.

Throughout her third age, Daphne has personified vitality. But is all this ebullience real? Could she just be very clever at denying her age? Does she model a realistic alternative to usual aging, or is she living out a pretense like some middle-aged people in the media seem to? In his powerful novel *Miss Lonelyhearts* Nathaniel West portrayed a woman who could not enjoy a full life because she would only accept the bright side. Authentic life involves embracing both light and dark dimensions. Is Daphne open to the shadow dimension of the self and the dark sides of life? Does she live with the pain of life as well as its pleasures? And what about recognition of her mortality? Is she really aware of her own unavoidable death? I pressed hard with these questions, with more truculence than I would want from any interviewer.

I sometimes meet highly active people in midlife who seem to be in denial about the inevitable end of their lives. In a workshop, when I commented that we will not continue growing through midlife without consciously accepting our inevitable death, several participants gasped in shock. Denial will get us nowhere. Is Daphne consciously aware of her own mortality, I wondered, and is she facing the reality of her own death?

I am aware of my death. My mother died at the age of eighty-one. She had a good, long life. I thought that would be about right for me. I accepted it. When I told my children, they hollered, "You can't die that soon." Well, as good as I felt at seventy, I thought I might last until ninety anyway. So I've quieted them, saying I'll live until ninety.

But honestly, if I died on this trip to the Himalayas, I wouldn't have regrets. I wouldn't mind dying on top of a mountain. I've had a very full life. I learned back when I was fifty that it was up to me to take charge of my life. I can see my world positively or negatively. What happens to me in life depends on my perception and my deciding what I want. Knowing my end motivates me to take risks, to go for what I really want.

Acknowledging death as part of life must be an element in our growth. Fear and denial of death diminish the quality of living. Realistic awareness of our boundaries, including death, can help us appreciate the present and embrace life with gratitude and passion. We may soar in our dreams, but real life has boundaries; they can expand, but we must respect their presence. In classical Greece the Delphic oracle's timeless injunction, "know yourself," originally meant to know your limits. Acknowledging the final limit of our lives can be a wake-up call to motivate us to boldly pursue our dreams. What matters as we both pursue our dreams and face the end of life is that we affirm our control of the direction we take.

How about facing the darker sides of life? Usually, Daphne radiates optimism. On an optimism scale ranging from one to ten, she rated herself near the top, about a nine-plus. But, she said, she had not been optimistic in her forties. She has worked on developing a positive, hopeful outlook. Optimism is crucial to growth and successful aging, she believes. Even with her high level of optimism, she experiences suffering and sadness, and at times she loses hope:

> Sometimes I feel near despair, not about myself but about my children. Their pain and setbacks still affect me greatly, though I know I cannot solve their problems. It has to come from them. My son has had a long-term drug problem. Just when we think he's out of it, he slips back. That's so painful, and so hard on his family—and on my grandchildren, whom I love dearly. My oldest daughter, who has done so well, is now very unhappy. She's almost forty, desperately wants a child, but has no man. I feel bad for them. I can't draw the line between them and me. We stay in touch; I listen and try to be supportive.

Daphne was visibly moved as she told me of her pain. Her optimism does not shield her from sadness, especially when the source of it lies in the connection with someone she cares deeply about. She tries to balance hope with care, compassion, and realism. "I do the best I can, but you never know what will happen. That part of my life—it's hard," she said, not able to finish a sentence that had put her on the verge of tears. Her grown-up optimism is hopeful yet realistic. She believes in good but is agnostic about final outcomes, and she is intuitively aware that there is much more to be thankful for than to grieve over.

Acknowledging the dark along with the bright sides of life increases our awareness of meaning. Light needs darkness to become visible. Adults like Daphne have opened up to a full panorama of insights and emotions. They experience purposeful living just when conventional wisdom assumes they should be running mainly on memories. "Where do you find meaning, Daphne?" I asked her.

> Friendships are number one in importance. They have been since my late forties. Along with them, right at the top, are my children, my companion, my work, and my growth. I can't put them in order—but they are what really give my life meaning. By work, I don't mean a job. My work is what I do that brings fulfillment not only to myself but to others.

For Daphne and the others in this study, meaning emerges in the pattern of their lives; it is shaped by freedom and connection, love and friendships, work and play, caring and service, and the myriad other paradoxical dimensions of personal growth.

Daphne's life provides a full portrait of midlife renewal, one that resonates with paradoxes. A dynamic person who experienced a personal renaissance at fifty, she has grown richly for nearly thirty years. This new growth fills the longest and best period of her life. Like others in this study, she can serve as a role model for those of us who want to follow the road never traveled. All the paradoxical principles are here, along with struggles and contentment, heartache and joy, confusion and discovery.

What of importance is missing? What about sex? Why have I said nothing about sex in this narrative about vitality and passion, creativity and love? In spite of conventional notions of aging, sex is certainly important in the second half of life. Where does it fit in this portrait of a fuller life?

At the end of one interview, I asked Daphne, as I did all the others, if there was something important that I had left out. She immediately commented, "You haven't asked about sex. Why not? It's so important." I blushed. Questions about sex are in my research design. I skipped them only a few times, fearing embarrassment—once with a nun, once with an older single woman who had left her husband, and with Daphne. Maybe I had assumed she had passed the point where it counts. Old assumptions die hard.

I asked her to tell me what she thought was significant about her sexuality and how it had changed. Her answer was both an affirmation of the importance of sex after sixty and seventy and an open admission that she has in a fundamental way accepted her own aging process:

> Sex for me is becoming more like that of a senior woman who compared having sex with her occasional enjoyment of steak in a nearly vegetarian diet. As you grow older, lovemaking is as endearing as ever, but there is less of it. There is less desire, probably because of hormones. But my companion and I do make love, and we touch a lot. He has more desire than I do, but we work it out. This also includes sex roles. I am much more liberated than he. But we work that out, too.

What I heard from Daphne I also heard from the others. Sex remains very important for those who continue growing. Like other significant aspects of personal life, it gets redefined. Maturing adults told me that sex after fifty or even seventy was sometimes the best they had experienced—more personal and intimate, more complex and more fulfilling. One man in his late seventies confided, "I'm certainly no Don Juan, never was. But sometimes my wife and I surprise ourselves by how we get it on, even after fifty-five years." He smiled coyly and then a tear appeared in the corner of one eye. For all his impressive accomplishments, he told me that his wife was his "whole life."

In making love we can connect with that special person who is the love of our life and who shares the core of our being. Love making can also free us from old scripts and rejuvenate us with youthful passion. It can be a primary way to experience flow. In affirming what we want in making love, we also contribute to the realization as well as the pleasure of our partner. The ecstasy of physical and spiritual intimacy is something wonderful to add to our dreams of a fulfilling third age.

Daphne's story shows us a creative alternative to the usual patterns of midlife and aging. Her growth has broken the mold of middle-aging as it has transformed the process of aging. Her initiatives model the principles of second growth. In her life story we can see all six of them: reflection and risk taking, building realistic optimism, creating a positive identity, enlarging freedom and intimacy, redefining work and play, and building a more caring life. The mosaic of her life results from the art of creative balancing. Her young/old life illustrates a new scenario for a greatly extended, more expansive, more vibrant, and more purposeful life for the second half. She, like the others in the study, serves as a trailblazer across the new terrain that lies before us.

THE INVITATION OF A LIFETIME

What should we make of these two lives? Ted and Daphne are two very different people. They have had similar careers; both have been creative designers. Perhaps this talent gave them an edge in learning to design creatively the second halves of their lives. Another common feature is that in their late forties, both began a process of mindful reflection that pointed them in new directions. They have continued to question, explore, and invent. Over the years they have grown significantly, fashioning their lives with a dynamic new pattern of paradoxes that I have called second growth. They have discovered exciting potential and new possibilities, and have known impressive personal achievements, followed by setbacks and still more growth. They have experienced expanding personal complexity and integration, which defines adult growth, and an increased sense of purpose and satisfaction that they would not have predicted when they reached fifty. Both claim that as they have added years, they have grown better. In committing themselves to their own growth, they have also contributed to the well-being of others. Their course through the third age of life shows what is now possible for us.

You might read these stories as inspirational. I see them as having much greater importance. They reflect our new option. They should not inspire us to hold our course but to change it. Second growth represents an alternative to aging as we have known it. We have not discovered a fountain of youth. Biology still prevails, yet it alone is not our destiny. Social structures still shape us, but they do not have the final word about who we will become. We have the capacity to shape our destiny and influence our future. Having followed the development of several dozen adults, we can now better apply this insight to our lives as we face the reality of getting older.

In the past two decades other scientists have discovered significant variables that influence aging, but in fixing on a broad canvas, most have missed this exception to the general rule. In the 1960s Professor Bernice Neugarten, one of the most astute investigators of middle age and aging, shook common presumptions about later life. In a study of adults she showed that not everybody ages in the same way, though at that time it was assumed that nearly everybody started to age at around fifty. She concluded that the way people experience aging depends in part on their personalities. She identified eight types. By age fifty-five, seven of the types were slowing down, living with their throttles depressed, and becoming dissatisfied. Only one type, the "integrated personality," had a positive experience of growing older, forming a new category of elders, whom she later called the "young/old." She detected the first signs of what I have called second growth. Research done in the 1980s was consistent with her general findings, but it did not identify anything like second growth. I have seen healthy adaptation mentioned here and there; but rarely in portraits of people between midforties and eighty have I seen the extended, vital, creative growth that the adults in this study manifested.

A good friend of mine, who has headed an innovative gerontology program for two decades, confided some startling statistics. Among the elderly he has studied, about half degenerated and many suffered premature death. About 40 percent adapted to their changing circumstances and functioned fairly well, with diminishing returns. Fewer than 10 percent have generated self-actualization after age fifty-five. In general, while aging overtakes and then overwhelms multitudes, only a few so far experience renewal and rejuvenation. Most humans live fully for only a short time and extend the dying process way too long. With the advent of a third age, we need not go that route. Second growth provides us with an alternative. It enables us, for a long time after fifty, to live with our throttles wide open.

To activate the message of this book, we have to shed old assumptions, expand our limits, think creatively, and live differently. We cannot rely on past accomplishments. Invention is called for. Our way forward is dimly seen. The opportunity has only just knocked. We have so much more life in front of us. We can make of it what we want. Right now we have the invitation of a lifetime for new growth, enrichment, and purposeful living. Ted, Daphne, and the others have pointed the way. The next step is ours to take.

Afterword:
On the Meaning of
the Third Age

AN ERA OF SOCIAL DISCONTINUITY

Throughout this book I have emphasized the importance of the longevity revolution because it is changing the woof and warp of our lives. But longevity alone has not made all the difference. What compounds our experience of greater longevity is the rate and nature of vast social changes. Our prospects for living much longer than previous generations have emerged in an era marked by social discontinuity. Changing social conditions have virtually ripped apart assumptions about expected paths into the future and the standards by which to guide and interpret midlife experience. This makes our life bonus both more liberating and more confusing.

The adult life course is less predictable than ever. In the last generation adult life was structured largely by age, education, work, and family. A normal American male sequence included graduation, finding work, getting married, raising a family, concluding work, and entering retirement. For women, the pattern was similar, except that work was often confined to the home. Our lives and careers have been graded by age and constrained by roles. This sequence of social roles has been scrambled for many people. Adults often leave school, work, marry, raise children, and then become students again by returning to school to go on with a new career. Education used to be primarily for the first age; it is now a lifelong necessity. Parents and grandparents are becoming students and novices again. Age is increasingly irrelevant to how we live, what we experience, and who we are becoming.

Related to this upheaval is a changing view of success, which also affects our lives in several ways. People used to measure success by establishing a position in a lifetime career or job and carrying that as far as they could. The average adult today can contemplate changing careers five times. Success today might better be measured by how adept we are in switching careers. Greater longevity further complicates our sense of satisfactory work completion. Midlife used to be a time to start winding down one's career. Now many people embark on promising careers at fifty, sixty, and even seventy. The longer we live, the more likely people are to have serial careers (not to mention serial marriages). Many expectations have been turned upside down. What do we want on our epitaph?

Structures and sequence in family life have also altered the adult life course and our personal identities. Families in the midtwentieth century were usually thought of as bastions of security, providing a clear pattern of social roles. Today, most families have been splintered by moves, separation, and divorce. More than half of the marriages in the United States end in separation and divorce. Once-married people usually remarry, which complicates not only the structure of those families but also the responsibilities and identities of those affected. In addition to their own children, parents now care for stepchildren, in-laws, grandchildren, and even their own parents. Adults saying good-bye to the last child to leave home, anticipating the peace and quiet of an empty nest, sometimes find parents and older children moving back in. Family life for maturing adults involves constant renegotiation of roles and expectations. The shifting scope of our responsibilities to those we have been connected to forces us to rethink the goal of our personal development. Furthermore, changing gender roles have drastically altered lifestyles as well as life in the family. Being the man or woman of the house does not mean what it used to mean. What seemed normal in our parents' generation now appears hopelessly outdated.

Adult life increasingly develops to different rhythms. Some people start new careers when others their age are concluding their last one. Some start making families at the same age that others are saying good-bye to children. Men have been known to marry younger women and start a new family at the same time their adult children are giving them grandchildren. Women are starting to do the same. Thanks to biotechnology, women have a chance to experience maternity well past the conventional time limit. As I was working on this material, the newspapers reported that a sixty-two-year-old Italian woman gave birth to a son. Her physician defended implanting an embryo in her, saying she had the body of a forty-year-old woman. Her chances to live a very long life are good. At the age of ninety-two, she can celebrate the thirtieth birthday of her son, who is younger than her grandchildren. In this era of discontinuity, confusion, perplexity, and surprise are normal ingredients in growing older.

As these changes break up old expectations they also produce novel possibilities. They can free us to experiment with new ways to mature. We are just beginning to see extraordinary diversity among the elderly. Some adults become physically active and even start to train for athletic events, whereas in a previous generation they would have been heading toward rocking chairs. Who would have thought that eighty- and ninety-year-olds would be running marathons, competing in swimming and downhill ski races, and trekking through wilderness areas? Who could have imagined sixty- and seventy-year-olds building new careers and producing some of their most creative work? Who would have dreamed that a seventy-seven-year-old former astronaut would take another test ride in outer space? Who could have foreseen liberation and the blossoming of new love in people over sixty and seventy? If such novelties are possible for elders, just imagine what could be in store for younger adults in their fifties and sixties. We shall witness much more diversity in adult development in the future. The possibilities for new lifestyles in the second half of life seem limitless.

It is easy to lament discontinuity and to wish for a return to simpler, more stable times. Sometimes politicians, preachers, and writers cash in on such wishes. But we cannot go back, even if we might want to. If ever there was a shared, clear expectation about what it means to be a mature adult, it has disintegrated. Experiencing chaos is discomforting; but it can also stimulate creative questioning. As we learned from the adults I have studied, this can free us to build new life models. At what age should we assume that we have grown up? And how should we conceive of maturity? Our parents considered thirty to be a grown-up age. I have heard thoughtful people at fifty and sixty wonder aloud what they will be like when they have grown up.

Our chance for greater longevity in an era of discontinuity makes it imperative that we search for new models of maturity. A positive response to all of this discontinuity is to see our unsettling situation as providing opportunities for creative redefinition of adult life. That to me is what the third age means. As social discontinuities shatter old models, they also can open the way to a fulfilling third age. We have an opportunity of a lifetime.

CREATING AN OBJECTIVE CORRELATIVE WITHIN THE THIRD AGE

The third age has emerged so recently that most of us are not prepared for it. What we have prepared for is middle age and aging in retirement, in large part because of a modern social security system that was designed according to an old model of aging. That expectation is just not appropriate any longer. When social security was established in America as part of the New Deal, most people, especially men, were not expected to receive its benefits for more than a few years, if at all. President Franklin Roosevelt, who established the system, ironically enough never benefited from it. He died at the age of sixty-three, although he lived longer than his hardier relative, Theodore, who died at sixty-one. They were thought to be old when they died. Unlike previous generations, we now not only live longer, but we also confront a structural change in the middle years not imagined fifty years ago.

We can better understand what this structural change in the life course can mean to us personally by comparing it with two dramatic developments in the last century that transformed the first age of human life. We assume today that childhood lasts at least a dozen years, and that it contains universal developmental stages that parents and teachers need to be aware of. Yet historical studies have shown that childhood as we know it simply did not exist for most people before the eighteenth century. Childhood previously was thought to last for about the first seven years, and even then children were regarded as little adults. The inner development of childhood that we take for granted was actually called into existence by the social, political, cultural, and economic changes of the modern world.

An insight from dramatic criticism will clarify this point. In writing about Shakespeare's *Hamlet*, T. S. Eliot suggested that in a successful drama we should discern an objective correlative. The term refers to a situation in which an appropriate inner development of character is elicited by changing external circumstances. When there is congruence between internal and external developments within a drama, we discover an objective correlative.

Something like this happens in real life. Changing circumstances in the last two centuries have opened up the potential complexities of childhood. The new structure of childhood presents children with specific challenges that normally must be met to fulfill their emergent potential. When children respond appropriately, we can discern an objective correlative between healthy childhood growth and the changing conditions of society. Their growth expresses a congruence between inner life structure and external circumstances.

A similar phenomenon has occurred in the development of another supposedly universal life stage. Modern adolescence has also been produced by drastically changing circumstances. It is not a built-in life structure. We assume it to be a universal stage of life, with its special issues and tasks. But actually it has emerged in industrialized nations only since the nineteenth century. Just a hundred years ago the American psychologist G. Stanley Hall had to invent a new term for the strange phenomena parents and educators were noticing in young people. He called it adolescence, which means literally "growing up into adulthood." This period of growth evolved out of a drastically changing social situation that included democratic political structures, formal education, work patterns, greater affluence, a rising middle class, and such cultural values as individualism, smaller families, delayed marriages, and better health care. What used to be a brief period of puberty in which children quickly skipped into adult roles now stretches through the teens and even into the twenties. Growing up now not only takes much longer, but it has also become a more complex process than the *rite de passage* of puberty. Successful adolescence calls for developing life skills of independence, intimacy, and a healthy personal identity. When adolescents adapt appropriately to the complexities of modern life, we can discern another objective correlative.

The point of view I am presenting here is called life course theory. It sees individual lives socially organized in response to historical forces. One aim of this theory is to relate lives to an ever changing society, to grasp the effects of changing circumstances on individual development in contrast to theories that assume a universal life structure. As new human potential in the expanding periods of childhood and adolescence has emerged from the interaction between internal life, both physical and mental, and changing external social conditions, a similar development is occurring today in adult life. Old patterns of middle age and aging are also not built-in life structures.

Changing historical circumstances, especially social discontinuity interacting with greater longevity, have produced a new period of adult life reminiscent of what we noticed happening in childhood and adolescence. Like those two early periods, our middle years have been stretching out. Within this extended middle period, we have potential for growth that previous generations never realized. That is the promise of the third age. Until now, midlife was shaped largely by the aging process. But as young growth concludes and second growth responds to changing circumstances, we can discern in a growing number of people another objective correlative. The third age sets the stage for a different kind of experience of the middle years; second growth fills it with decades of life renewal.

In this book I have concentrated on new growth in the third age. I am beginning to see that the final period of aging can also be much more vital and fulfilling than we had thought. The fourth age has been until now defined by the degeneration of aging. Other research is showing the possibility of another new growth curve starting near the end of the third age. I believe that a fulfilling third age contains potential to transform the fourth age. We shall have to modify our scenario of adult life once again to account for a later life option. During the past two decades, the concept of successful aging has emerged in contrast to the usual mode of decline. There are possibilities for the final period of aging that we have just begun to tap. Second growth for thirty or more years will provide a foundation for unprecedented creative, successful aging on a new growth curve.

With continued interaction between social discontinuities and longevity, we might begin to visualize optimal experience throughout the life course as a series of objective correlatives. In the figure below four overlapping sigmoid curves represent possibilities within the four ages of our lives. The first age is a long period of growing up. The second age is organized around productivity (jobs, incomes, adult challenges) and settling in (family, organizations, community). The third age, the longest of the periods, has the potential for the kind of self-actualization through second growth that I have discovered. The fourth age, which traditionally has been seen as a downward slope of increasing decrepitude, might be represented by still another sigmoid curve signifying successful aging. A goal for the fourth age might be to live young while growing older and to die young as late as possible. Here is how I see the new possibility for a fulfilling life course:

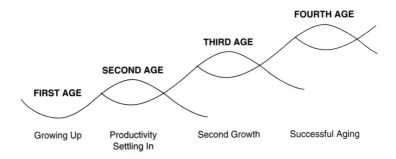

With respect to discoveries about human development, the twentieth century has been the age of childhood and youth. The twenty-first century promises to be the age of adulthood and maturity. I see second growth in the third age transforming everything we previously imagined about the second half of life. That is why we should prepare to take off, with anticipation and hope, in the second half of our lives.

Notes

INTRODUCTION

xiii   More recently, anthropologists have made a similar point about different life experiences and developmental patterns in societies quite distinct from our own. For example, just when women in our society expect to experience a downward trend, women in some preindustrial cultures experience the prime of their lives. See the articles about women in several nonindustrial societies in Judith K. Brown et al., eds., *In Her Prime: A New View of Middle-Aged Women* (Granby, MA: Bergin and Garvey, 1985).

xiv   Erica Jong, *Fear of Fifty* (New York: HarperCollins, 1994), xxxii.

CHAPTER 1

1   While the average life span is increasing, the optimal life span remains about 115 to 120 years. The oldest living person in our time celebrated her 122nd birthday before her death in 1997. Walter M. Bortz, M.D., discusses the biogenetic potential for a maximum life span of 120 years. See his *We Live Too Short and Die Too Long: How to Achieve Your Natural 100-Year-Plus Life Span* (New York: Bantam, 1992).

1   Judith Treas, "Older Americans in the 1990s and Beyond," *Population Bulletin* (Washington, DC) 50, no. 2 (May 1995): 14. More recent statistics indicate that the average has climbed even faster than expected, which supports my suggestion that we now have a thirty-year life bonus.

1   Walter M. Bortz, M.D., *Dare to Be 100* (New York: Fireside, 1996).

2   Thomas T. Perls, M.D., "The Oldest Old," *Scientific American* (January 1995): 70–75.

2   See Alan Pifer and Lydia Bronte, eds., *Our Aging Society* (New York: Norton, 1986). Pifer's introduction and concluding chapter dealing with public policy deserve careful rereading. In the decade following the publication of this volume, predictions about the increase in longevity in America have been revised. Already the demographic forecasts made in the 1980s seem

too cautious. One 1995 forecast for average American life expectancy in 2020 suggested eighty-five, several years higher than earlier conservative estimates. The average life span in Japan is now over eighty. But there is a reverse trend occurring in other parts of the world. The average life span in Africa is still about fifty, and that of Russia has declined to below sixty.

2   See Ken Dychtwald and Joe Flower, *Age Wave* (Los Angeles: Tarcher, 1989).

2   Alan Pifer, introduction to Pifer and Bronte, eds., *Our Aging Society*. While I agree with Pifer that we have a new period added to the adult years, I prefer *third age* to a third quarter, because the former term suggests greater flexibility; in fact, this period may well be the longest in the life course, with ten years more than a quarter of a century.

2   See Harry R. Moody, "Education as a Lifelong Process," in *Our Aging Society*. Moody sees the need for extensive lifelong learning, which challenges not only individuals but colleges and universities to make some changes.

3   The word *paradigm* has been used recently in several contexts. While in general use it refers to a mental model used to categorize and explain phenomena, it has a more specific meaning as a set of assumptions used to interpret data. As changes occur within a given set of explanatory ideas, we experience a paradigm shift. There has been a paradigm shift, for example, in the physical sciences from Newtonian physics to quantum mechanics, relativity theory, and the science of chaos. See the pivotal work by Thomas S. Kuhn, *The Structure of Scientific Revolutions* (Chicago: The University of Chicago Press, 1962). The introduction to the second edition (1970) contains a helpful discussion of paradigm usage. More recently, some writers have argued that there has been a paradigm shift in the business world, moving from a narrowly focused profit orientation to one that promotes social responsibility using a multiple stakeholder model. See Michael Ray and Alan Rinzler, eds., *The New Paradigm in Business* (New York: Tarcher/Perigee, 1993). I am using the term to refer to a set of assumptions and an overall framework of ideas to envision and reinterpret adult development in the second half of life.

3   T. S. Eliot, quoted in the *New York Times,* September 23, 1958.

3   See Theodore Lidz, *The Person* (New York: Basic Books, 1968), 458, 460. Fifteen years later, another doctor argued that all males between the ages of forty-five and fifty-five have a crisis that acts like a disease, perhaps caused by changes in brain chemistry. See William A. Nolen, *Crisis Time* (New York: Dodd, Mead, 1984). More recently, a psychologist has argued that "after the age of thirty-five or forty years, the human psychological organism undergoes a crisis: a more or less abrupt decrement in the power of silent hardware operators." See Jaun Pascual-Leone, "Reflections on Life-Span, Intelligence, Consciousness, and Ego-Development" in Charles Alexander and Ellen Langer, eds., *Higher Stages of Human Development* (New York: Oxford University Press, 1990). These old paradigm statements do manage to put a positive view on middle-age breakdown, seeing the loss of hard-

ware operators, such as energy, learning, libido, and so on, leading to greater reflection, spirituality, and wisdom. However, this vision is blind to the greater opportunity of second growth.

4   Thirty years after exposing the "feminine mystique," Betty Friedan launched a massive attack on the conventional attitude toward and perspective on aging. She has referred to the power of this conventional notion of our mature years as the "mystique of aging." See her *The Fountain of Age* (New York: Simon and Schuster, 1993).

4   In addition to selected references provided in notes, interested readers may wish to consult an excellent summary article by Winifred Gallagher, "Midlife Myths," *The Atlantic Monthly* 271, no. 5 (May 1993): 51–68. See also an important article by John W. Rowe, M.D., and Robert L. Kahn, "Human Aging: Usual and Successful," *Science* 237 (July 10, 1987): 143–149 and their recent book *Successful Aging* (New York: Pantheon, 1998). See also Melinda Beck's report, "The New Middle Age," *Newsweek* (December 7, 1992): 50–56.

5   For a study of healthy adaptation among adult men, see George E. Vaillant, *Adaptation to Life* (New York: Little, Brown, 1977). As a director of the famous longitudinal Harvard Study, Vaillant followed the development of about one hundred men from childhood through their forties. When the book was published, the men were in their fifties. Using his criteria, I concluded that the two men in my interview both exhibited traits of healthy adaptation. However, Vaillant's criteria for healthy adaptation did not account for the exceptional growth of one of them. As I uncovered second growth, I found that it built on but could be distinguished from healthy adaptation.

7   The term *life structure* has been used by Daniel Levinson to refer specifically to a supposedly universal pattern in adult development. See his *The Seasons of a Man's Life* (New York: Knopf, 1978). I did not find his life structure model to be applicable to the people I studied. The ideas of life stages and life structure may better be thought of as cultural artifacts rather than as valid generalizations that apply to all adults. They do not accurately describe human development in many cultures, nor do they account for the interplay between social situations and internal human development. I prefer the sociological term *life course*, which suggests both the fluidity and flexibility that we have discovered in human development as well as situational determinants and variations. See my afterword for a fuller discussion.

8   The procedures I followed generally fall within the model of grounded theory in qualitative research. See Anselm Strauss and Juliet Corbin, *Basics of Qualitative Research: Grounded Theory Procedures and Techniques* (Newbury Park, CA: Sage, 1990). Thanks to the coaching of the late John Clausen, a former director of the Institute of Human Development at the University of California, Berkeley, I was able to turn my research into a longitudinal study that extended over a dozen years.

9   Robert Browning, *Selected Poetry* (New York: Modern Library, 1951), 479.
        Anthropological studies have suggested that in some cultures, women expe-
        rience the prime of life after menopause. See the citation of Judith Brown
        in the notes to the introduction.

9   See B. F. Skinner and M. E. Vaughan, *Enjoy Old Age* (New York: Norton,
        1983), 28.

9   Gail Sheehy once argued that adult life was controlled by a biological clock
        that went off like an oven timer about every seven years, causing a signifi-
        cant change in experience and behavior. (See her *Passages* [New York: Dut-
        ton, 1976.]) This opinion has not been supported by scientific research.
        Biology limits but does not control adult development. Twenty years later,
        she herself questioned the strict life stage model, which she borrowed from
        the writings of psychologist Daniel Levinson. In *The Silent Passage* (New
        York: Random House, 1992), she argues that even menopause should no
        longer be considered a biologically tied marker. Still, she portrays the adult
        life course as having distinct stages, with each stage entered only through a
        predictable crisis, which is what the term passage refers to. In her *New Pas-
        sages: Mapping Your Life Across Time* (New York: Random House, 1995), she
        extends the seven-year stages to decades and adds a new stage. But she reaf-
        firms a fixed-stage life structure with inevitable crises: "Despite the recent
        shifts in the life cycle, there are still broad, general stages of adulthood with
        predictable passages between them" (page 13). Like many other social sci-
        entists, I have found neither predictable, inevitable crises in the life course
        nor a set of life stages that has become so popular. In contrast to the above
        models, life course theory is more sensitive to social and cultural factors
        that influence the evolution of individual lives.

9   While chronology does not predict how adults pass through midlife, there
        is evidence that social class can significantly influence development. In
        summarizing a debate about the validity of life stages in adult development,
        the sociologist Janet Zollinger Giele made this interesting observation
        about the relationship between adult experience and adult development:

> Evidently some people experience distinct stages of adult development while
> others do not. It is the degree of social complexity on the job or in other as-
> pects of everyday life that appears critical. Those who must learn a great deal
> and adapt to many different roles seem to be the most concerned with trying
> to evolve an abstract self, conscience, or life structure that can integrate all
> these discrete events. By contrast, those with a simple job, limited by meager
> education and narrow contacts, are less apt to experience aging as a process
> that enhances autonomy or elaborates one's mental powers. . . . Identifiable
> developmental stages thus appear more likely to occur in some persons and in
> some social settings than in others. Absence of stages is the norm among their
> opposites. (Janet Zollinger Giele, *Women in the Middle Years* [New York: John
> Wiley and Sons, 1982], 8.)

As we shall see in the following chapters, people can and do break out of situational restrictions to become mindful of their human resources and life possibilities. Class influences but does not ultimately determine who we become. In fact, even age and gender are not as influential as they used to be. In another book, Giele suggests that our current redefinitions of age and gender have transformed traditional assumptions so much that they have provided a new concept of adulthood. See her "Adulthood as Transcendence of Age and Sex," in Neil J. Smelser and Erik H. Erikson, eds., *Themes of Work and Love in Adulthood* (Cambridge: Harvard University Press, 1980). Since the time of that writing, adult transformation has continued to the point where we are discovering a whole new paradigm of adult development.

9   Recent medical research has demonstrated both biological variability and physiological plasticity. See, for example, the studies on the effects of exercise on aging: Walter R. Frontera et al., "Strength Conditioning in Older Men: Skeletal Muscle Hypertrophy and Improved Function," *Journal of Applied Physiology* 64 (1988): 1038–1044; and Frontera and C. N. Meredith, "Exercise in the Rehabilitation of the Elderly," in G. Felsenthat, S. Garrison, and F. Steinberg, eds., *Rehabilitation of the Aging and Elderly Patient* (Baltimore: Williams and Wilkins, 1994), 35–46.

10   See Daniel J. Levinson, *The Seasons of a Man's Life*, 57.

11   Charles Handy, *The Age of Paradox* (Boston: Harvard Business School Press, 1995), 50–56. Handy borrowed and adapted this two-curve model from John R. O'Neil's book about business leaders. See O'Neil's *The Paradox of Success: When Winning at Work Means Losing at Life* (New York: Tarcher/Putnam, 1994), 127–131. O'Neil actually is using an idea developed by Jonas Salk, in which two overlapping sigmoid curves illustrate how new learning emerges. The second curve represents a departure from what is known. This model of overlapping sigmoid curves suggests that it is best to plan for renewal before we peak.

12   The psychologist Mihaly Csikszentmihalyi also argues that personal growth and happiness occur as we fulfill the potential complexity of our lives. See especially two recent books: *The Evolving Self: A Psychology for the Third Millennium* (New York: HarperCollins, 1993) and *Flow: The Psychology of Optimal Experience* (New York: Harper and Row, 1990). The late Gordon Allport, who supervised my graduate program at Harvard University, espoused a similar view. The process of becoming fully human entails the development and organization of greater personal complexity, in contrast to B. F. Skinner's notion that to enjoy aging we need to strip down to greater simplicity. This view has recently found support from astrophysics. When considering our smallness in relation to the vastness of the cosmos, it "is not the quantity of space and time which matter, but the quality of complexity that our existence manifests." See Bruno Guideroni of the Institut d'Astrophysique de Paris, "Modern Cosmology in the Islamic Worldview,"

in *Science and the Spirtual Quest,* conference papers (Berkeley: Center for Theology and the Natural Sciences, 1998).

12   The Harvard psychologist Howard Gardner has developed a complex view of human intelligence. See his *Frames of Mind: The Theory of Multiple Intelligences* (New York: Basic Books, 1983). In this book he argued that there are seven different kinds of intelligence; since then he has expanded the list. His theory has been used to develop curricula and pedagogy in schools, but I find that it also helps explain untapped potential and some features of second growth. For example, I see adults developing emotional, interpersonal, creative, and existential intelligence. Especially relevant to some key aspects of new growth is the concept later developed by Daniel Goleman. See his *Emotional Intelligence* (New York: Bantam Books, 1995). The key aspect of emotional intelligence is awareness of and access to one's feelings and an ability to draw upon them to guide behavior; it also includes empathy and interpersonal and social skills. Emotional intelligence is present in mindful reflection as well as in other second growth principles that are operative in building a renewed identity, developing new forms of intimacy, and increasing a capacity of caring.

13   See Martin Rees, *Before the Beginning: Our Universe and Others* (Reading, MA: Addison-Wesley, 1997). Rees's description of our unfolding universe points to both paradox and a tendency towards greater complexity.

14   O'Neil, *The Paradox of Success.*

14   See James C. Collins and Jerry I. Porras, *Built to Last: Successful Habits of Visionary Companies* (New York: HarperCollins, 1994). Part of their argument emphasizes the "genius" of *and,* rather than *either/or,* which in effect advocates adhering to paradox.

14   See Robert Quinn et al., *Becoming a Master Manager,* 2d ed. (New York: John Wiley & Sons, 1996), 391.

14   See, for example, James O'Toole, *Leading Change: The Argument for Values-Based Leadership* (San Francisco: Jossey-Bass, 1995), and James A. Autry, *Life and Work* (New York: Avon, 1994).

14   See Charles Handy, *The Age of Paradox.*

14   Other writers have also developed a nonlinear approach to human development. See, for example, Ellen Langer, Mihaly Csikszentmihalyi, George Vaillant, and John Clausen, whose works are cited in other parts of this book. Another writer has developed a cyclical model. See Frederic Hudson, *The Adult Years: Mastering the Art of Self Renewal* (San Francisco: Jossey-Bass, 1991). None has specifically pointed to the phenomenon of second growth, though their ideas have helped me understand the six principles of it more clearly.

15   See especially Martin Buber's classic works, such as *I and Thou* and *Between Man and Man.* I discussed this paradox in Buber's writings in a previous

book. See William A. Sadler, Jr., *Existence and Love* (New York: Charles Scribner's Sons, 1970), Chapter 5.

15   See, for example, Deepak Chopra, *Ageless Body, Timeless Mind: The Quantum Alternative to Growing Old* (New York: Harmony, 1993) and Thomas Moore, *Care of the Soul: A Guide for Cultivating Depth and Sacredness in Everyday Life* (New York: HarperCollins, 1992).

17   See the afterword for a fuller discussion of the meaning of the third age for the life course.

17   See Peter Laslett, *A Fresh Map of Life* (London: Weidenfeld and Nicolson, 1989). Gail Sheehy has applied the map metaphor to an American setting. See her *New Passages*.

18   See the now-classic article by Bernice Neugarten with J. Moore and J. Lowe, "Age Norms, Age Constraints, and Adult Socialization," *The American Journal of Sociology* (1965): 70. Reprinted in Neugarten, ed., *Middle Age and Aging* (Chicago: University of Chicago Press, 1968), and in James Birren and Diana Woodruff, eds., *Aging: Scientific Perspectives and Social Issues*, 2d ed. (Monterey, CA: Brooks/Cole, 1983).

18   Bernice Neugarten and Associates, *Personality in Middle and Late Life: Empirical Studies* (New York: Atherton, 1964).

19   Ellen Langer recommends that individuals make the opportunity to create their own development by exercising choice and acting mindfully. Her experiments suggest that the presumed irreversible cycle of decline is reversible. Langer et al., "Nonsequential Development and Aging," in Charles Alexander and Ellen Langer, eds., *Higher Stages of Human Development*.

19   Lydia Bronte has suggested that people today can have a second middle age after sixty. (*The Longevity Factor* [New York: HarperCollins, 1993].) Other writers, like Sheehy, have similarly suggested that there are young and old stages within middle age. As I suggest in the afterword, instead of stages and ages, we might better understand the *life course* as a continuing process of transitions with very fluid boundaries.

19   In March 1994 I chaired a fascinating symposium on creative aging at the annual meeting of the American Society on Aging. Reports from four studies had amazingly similar findings on the qualities of successful aging, which was found to emerge from a creative growth process sustained or begun in middle age. All of the traits of successful aging were nurtured during a vital age marked by second growth, which I believe provides the best foundation for successful aging.

21   See for example, Robert Bellah et al., *Habits of the Heart: Individualism and Commitment in American Life*, 2d ed. (Berkeley: University of California Press, 1996).

21   See a similar argument made by Charles Handy in his *The Hungry Spirit* (New York: Broadway Books, 1998).

CHAPTER 2

27   Ellen Langer, *Mindfulness* (Reading, MA: Addison-Wesley, 1989). This con-
      cept elaborated by Langer is particularly powerful in explaining a key factor
      in personal growth. Others have found it under different names. For exam-
      ple, the late John Clausen, of the University of California, Berkeley, years
      ago coined the term *planful competence* to describe a similar trait. See his
      book describing lives over a sixty-year period as studied by the Institute of
      Human Development at Berkeley: *American Lives* (New York: The Free
      Press, 1993). He traced this trait in successful seventy-year-olds back to
      their teenage years. He showed how this trait, developed in adolescence,
      continued through their lives to support growth. Though it can start early,
      we both agreed that planful competence, or mindfulness, can be developed
      in one's mature adult years. The two American women in this chapter both
      developed traits for growth in their forties and fifties.

27   In *Mindfulness* and subsequent work, Langer also applies the term to other
      areas of life, such as education, race relations, work, and business.

29   See Vietnamese Buddhist writer Thich Nhat Hanh, *Peace Is Every Step: The
      Path of Mindfulness in Everyday Life* (New York: Bantam, 1992).

29   Thomas Moore has written extensively about this reflective process, which
      he describes as recovering one's soul. See his *Care of the Soul.*

30   Csikszentmihalyi, *Flow*, 83.

30   See two more recent books. Mihaly Csikszentmihalyi, *The Evolving Self* and
      Creativity (New York: HarperCollins, 1996).

30   *The Evolving Self*, 237–238. See also *Flow*, especially Chapters 3 and 9.

30   Csikszentmihalyi also sees the need to embrace paradox in meaningful
      growth. He writes of self-fulfilling people that their growth combines op-
      posite tendencies, such as independence and responsibility for others, intu-
      ition and discipline: "Only when the apparent antinomy of these two
      processes is resolved can a self fully participate in the flow of evolution."
      (*The Evolving Self*, 238.)

31   John Steinbeck, quoted in Michael Hammer and James Champy, *Reengi-
      neering the Corporation* (New York: HarperCollins, 1993).

31   A cardinal rule in change management stemming from the powerful in-
      sights of Kurt Lewin has been to unfreeze a situation by performing a care-
      ful analysis and comparing it with the desired situation. What works for
      organizations also works for individuals, because that is where change re-
      ally needs to be focused.

31   Daryl R. Conner, more clearly than most change agents, has emphasized
      the importance of assessing the costs involved in a change process. See his
      *Managing at the Speed of Change: How Resilient Managers Succeed and Pros-
      per Where Others Fail* (New York: Villard, 1993), Chapter 6.

41   Outward Bound is an international educational program offering courses
      designed to develop character in challenging outdoor settings. Though

originally designed for adolescents during World War II, it now enrolls many adults in a wide variety of courses.

42   Kurt Hahn, quoted in Joshua L. Miner, *Outward Bound USA* (New York: William Morrow, 1981), 27.

45   Vaillant, *Adaptation to Life*, 359.

CHAPTER 3

47   See, for example, Bill D. Moyers and Betty Flowers, *Healing and the Mind* (New York: Doubleday, 1993). This book coincided with the television series of the same name.

48   Some scientists have written popular books stressing the connections among positive attitude, healing, and health. For example, see Bernie Segal, *Love, Medicine, and Miracles* (New York: Harper and Row, 1989); Joan Borysenko, *Minding the Body, Mending the Mind* (Reading: Addison-Wesley, 1987); Martin E. Seligman, *Learned Optimism* (New York: Pocket Books, 1992). The latter book is particularly helpful; we shall explore its central message later in this chapter.

Psychologists have shown a strong correlation between a positive attitude toward adversity and well-being. See Suzanne C. Thompson, "Will It Hurt Less If I Can Control It?" *Psychological Bulletin* 90, no. 1 (1981): 89–101; Shelly E. Taylor, "Adjustment to Threatening Events: A Theory of Cognitive Adaptation," *American Psychologist* (November 1983): 1, 161–173; and Suzanne C. Kobasa, Salvatore Maddi, and Sheila Courington, "Personality and Constitution as Mediators in the Stress-Illness Relationship," *Journal of Health and Social Behavior* 22 (1981): 368–378.

Optimism is now recognized as an important ingredient in healthy aging. A few years ago I chaired a symposium on creative aging, and all of the researchers pointed to optimism as a significant ingredient. Gary Reker, a Canadian psychologist, has also been studying the beneficial effects of optimism on aging. See Reker and Paul T. Wong, "Personal Optimism, Physical and Mental Health," in James Birren and Judy Livingston, eds., *Cognition, Stress, and Aging* (Englewood Cliffs, NJ: Prentice Hall, 1988). In recent work, Reker shows how optimism protects and promotes health in the elderly, and how it can be learned.

48   Bill Moyers, "Let There Be Light," keynote speech to the Religion Newswriters Association, in *Religion and Values in Public Life* 2, no. 3/4 (spring/summer 1994): 4.

49   Peter Drucker, *Post-Capitalist Society* (New York: Harper/Business, 1994), 15. Drucker's remark, while apparently disparaging optimism, is actually inconsistent with his argument, which calls for leadership to move forward to a better society. I believe that Drucker would endorse the kind of realistic optimism described in this chapter.

50   Julian of Norwich, *Revelations of Divine Love* (London: Methuen, 1952), 54–65.

50   Norman Vincent Peale, *The Power of Positive Thinking* (Greenwich: Fawcett, 1969).

51   See Martin Seligman's *Learned Optimism*, a very rich, detailed account of optimism and how to acquire it. For twenty-five years, he has worked to develop a science of personal control. As both a researcher and a therapist, he tries to help people recover from depression caused by pessimism through the technique of cognitive therapy. In previous work, he showed how people become self-defeating through learned helplessness. (Martin E. Seligman, *Helplessness* [San Francisco: W. H. Freeman, 1975].)

      Seligman has developed a scientifically based method of teaching people how to become optimists by changing "the way [they] think about their failures." In *Learned Optimism* he describes pessimism and optimism as models people use to explain failure. He maintains that "if you use a different explanatory model, you'll be better equipped to cope with troubled times and keep them from propelling you toward depression" (page 53). In his view, optimism involves primarily a set of skills to explain your experiences positively: "Changing the destructive things you say to yourself when you experience the setbacks that life deals all of us is the central skill of optimism" (page 15). After surveying the research that supports his method, he offers practical exercises to develop optimism. Seligman's model represents a form of behavioral self-management, focusing on how you talk to yourself after setbacks.

      In spite of our similar outlooks, my idea of optimism is more complex and better suited to middle-aged adults who are not seriously depressed. In addition to cognitive reframing and taking charge of one's life, I emphasize interpersonal relationships, life planning, and improving one's sense of humor.

51   Rosabeth Moss Kanter, *When Giants Learn to Dance* (New York: Simon and Schuster, 1989), 18.

54   This view emphasizes the critical importance of good interpersonal relationships in the formation of a healthy individual, a cornerstone in the perspective of the late American psychiatrist Harry Stack Sullivan. See Sullivan, *The Interpersonal Theory of Psychiatry* (New York: Norton, 1953). See also my discussion of Sullivan in Sadler, *Existence and Love*, Chapter 12.

55   I used the phrase pursuit of loneliness in a title for workshops on loneliness in the early 1970s. See also Philip Slater, *The Pursuit of Loneliness* (Boston: Beacon, 1970). In his provocative book, Slater focused on American culture; my studies and workshops focused on the actual experience of loneliness, which I found to be caused by social and cultural as well as psychological factors.

55   For a provocative description of individualism in contemporary America, see Bellah et al., *Habits of the Heart*.

55   William A. Sadler, Jr., with Thomas Johnson, "From Loneliness to Anomia,"
      in Joseph Hartog, M.D., Ralph Audy, and Yehudi Cohen, eds., *The Anatomy
      of Loneliness* (New York: International Universities Press, 1980). See also
      Sadler, "Dimensions in the Problem of Loneliness," *Journal of Phenomeno-
      logical Psychology* 9 (1978):1–2; and Sadler, "On the Verge of a Lonely Life,"
      Humanitas X, no. 3 (1974).

55   James Lynch, M.D., *The Broken Heart: The Medical Consequences of Loneli-
      ness* (New York: Basic Books, 1977).

64   Csikszentmihalyi, *Flow,* 92 and 108.

65   Norman Cousins, *Anatomy of an Illness Perceived by the Patient* (New York:
      Norton, 1979).

67   Garrison Keillor regularly tells the news from this fictitious town on his
      weekly *A Prairie Home Companion* radio show. Some of his early stories are
      included in his *Lake Wobegon Days* (New York: Penguin, 1986).

CHAPTER 4

73   Erik Erikson described the process in his *Childhood and Society*, 2d ed.
      (1963), *Insight and Responsibility* (1964), and *Identity, Youth, and Crisis*
      (1968). He developed the idea of an evolving identity in *The Life Cycle
      Completed* (1982). (All published by Norton, New York.)

73   See for example Roger L. Gould, "Transformation During Early and Middle
      Adult Years," in Neil J. Smelser and Erik H. Erikson, eds., *Themes of Work
      and Love in Adulthood.* See also Gould, *Transformations: Growth and
      Change in Adult Life* (New York: Simon and Schuster, 1978).

74   See John A. Clausen, *American Lives.* In this book he focused on both typi-
      cal and outstanding studies conducted by the Institute of Human Develop-
      ment at the University of California, Berkeley. He told me that those whose
      lives seemed most successful had apparently experienced midlife renewal.

74   See, for example, Orville G. Brim, Jr., and Jerome Kagan, eds., *Constancy
      and Change in Human Development* (Cambridge: Harvard University Press,
      1980).

74   See especially Florine B. Livson, "Paths to Psychological Health in the Mid-
      dle Years," and Harvey Peshin and Norman Livson, "Uses of the Past in
      Adult Psychological Health," both in Dorothy Eichorn et al., eds., *Present
      and Past in Middle Life* (New York: Academic Press, 1981). Their work and
      other articles related to the "Berkeley" studies were part of the ongoing re-
      search conducted by the Institute of Human Development at the University
      of California, Berkeley.

74   Robert Kegan and Lisa L. Lahey, "Adult Leadership and Adult Develop-
      ment," in Barbara Kellerman, ed., *Leadership* (Englewood Cliffs, NJ: Pren-
      tice-Hall), 1984.

75   See the discussion in K. Warner Schaie and Sherry Willis, *Adult Development and Aging* (Boston: Little, Brown, 1986), 139ff.

75   Abraham H. Maslow, *Toward a Psychology of Being* (New York: Van Nostrand Reinhold, 1968). See especially his preface to the second edition and his discussion of ego-centering and ego-transcending, 37.

76   This tale was told by Peter Vaill in his book *Managing as a Performing Art: New Ideas for a World of Chaotic Change* (San Francisco: Jossey-Bass, 1989), 85.

77   James Birren, "Process of Aging: Growing Up and Growing Old," in *Our Aging Society*, 274.

77   Gay Luce, quoted in Ashley Montagu, *Growing Young*, 2d ed., (Granby, MA: Bergin and Garvey, 1989), 181.

77   Betty Friedan, *The Fountain of Age*.

78   John Lennon and Paul McCartney, from the Beatles' album *Sgt. Pepper's Lonely Hearts Club Band*, Capitol Records, 1967.

78   John Updike, *Rabbit at Rest* (New York: Knopf, 1990).

79   Anne Tyler, *Breathing Lessons* (New York: Knopf, 1988).

79   Anne Tyler, *Ladder of Years* (New York: Fawcett Columbine, 1995).

79   A report on Leisure World revealed a rift between members in their sixties and those over seventy. The younger members were "very reluctant to address the issue of aging" and resented the influence of the more senior members. *San Francisco Chronicle*, February 15, 1993, A6.

79   Bernice Neugarten, "Personality: Toward a Psychology of the Life Cycle," in William C. Sze, ed., *Human Life Cycle* (New York: Jason Aronson, 1975).

79   Clausen, *American Lives*, 16.

86   John Fowles, *Daniel Martin* (New York: New American Library, 1978), 578.

87   *Adaptation to Life*, 332.

88   Ashley Montagu, *Growing Young*, 2d ed., 2–5. I find the idea of neoteny much more exciting to work with than a medical idea of growing younger. Robert Morgan, a Canadian doctor, has proposed that we can grow younger by setting goals for our body age and length of life and then changing our lifestyle accordingly. He has run antiaging workshops that focus on diet, lifestyle, self-hypnosis, and meditation. See Robert F. Morgan and Jane Wilson, *Growing Younger* (Toronto: Methuen, 1982).

88   C. G. Jung, "The Development of Personality," in *The Development of Personality* (New York: Pantheon, 1954), 170.

88   David Gutmann, "Beyond Nurture: Developmental Perspectives on the Vital Old Woman," in Judith Brown et al., eds., *In Her Prime*. See also David Gutmann, *Reclaimed Powers* (New York: Basic Books, 1987).

88   Emily Hancock, *The Girl Within* (New York: Ballantine, 1989).

91   Jerome Bruner, *In Search of Mind: Essays in Autobiography* (New York: Harper and Row, 1983), 3–5.

91   Eliot Jacques, "Death and the Midlife Crisis," *International Journal of Psy-choanalysis* 46 (1965): 502–514. The concept of a male midlife crisis has subsequently been blown way out of proportion. Most people do not appear to have a midlife crisis, nor do they have an inevitably anxious response to a realization of their mortality.

91   Irvin D. Yalom, *Love's Executioner* (New York: Basic Books, 1989), 260.

93   Janet Zollinger Giele, *Women in the Middle Years* (New York: John Wiley and Sons, 1982), especially 199–204. See also Giele, "Adulthood as Transcendence of Age and Sex," in Neil J. Smelser and Erik H. Erikson, eds., *Themes of Work and Love.*

CHAPTER 5

98   Peter B. Vaill, *Managing as a Performing Art*, 2ff.

98   See Juliet B. Schor, *The Overworked American: The Unexpected Decline of Leisure* (New York: Basic Books, 1991), 11.

98   Ibid.

98   Schor, quoted in *Harvard Magazine* (September–October 1995): 12–13.

99   *Fortune,* 132, no. 6 (September 18, 1995).

99   See the discussion of work attitudes among fifty-year-olds in W. Berquist, E. Greenberg, and G. A. Klaum, *In Our Fifties* (San Francisco: Jossey-Bass, 1993), 115–135.

99   See the profound and classic discussion of the nature and meaning of work by Hannah Arendt, *The Human Condition* (Garden City, NY: Doubleday Anchor, 1959).

100   That model of success might seem elitist. Admittedly, my sample is very limited. In this chapter, all of my examples are people who are solidly middle class and who have college experience and sometimes advanced degrees. In the course of this research, I have interviewed in depth a few individuals from the working class, such as Ginny in Chapter 1 and Helen in Chapter 4. Other sociological research has suggested that in the working classes and among the poor, potential for growth may become stunted. If so, a success model that is defined by growth may seem unrealistic and socially arrogant. See, for example, Majorie Fiske, "Changing Hierarchies of Commitment in Adulthood," in Neil J. Smelser and Erik H. Erikson, eds., *Themes of Work and Love.*

      While social class has a powerful influence on one's development, the crucial issue is personal resourcefulness. In previously cited research by John Clausen and Ellen Langer, there is evidence that, regardless of social class and life history, people can overcome obstacles and grow. And as George Vaillant's research of Harvard graduates makes clear, privilege, power, and wealth do not guarantee growth, well-being, and happiness. Social deprivation obviously makes the opportunity presented by the third age difficult to respond to; but this fact only points to the need for more learning, liberation, and creative social engagement by those committed to growth through the third age.

100 See Jesse Bernard, "The Good-Provider Role: Its Rise and Fall," *American Psychologist* 36, no. 1 (January 1981): 1–12. Reprinted in Arlene Skolnick and Jerome Skolnick, eds., *Family in Transition,* 8th edition (New York: HarperCollins, 1994).

100 See the helpful book about transforming your work by William Bridges, *Job Shift: How to Prosper in a Workplace without Jobs* (Reading: Addison-Wesley, 1994). See also Jeremy Rifkin, *The End of Work* (New York: G. P. Putnam's Sons, 1995).

100 Kathy Kolbe, *Pure Instinct: Business' Untapped Resource* (New York: Times Books, 1993).

100 See Csikszentmihalyi, *Flow.*

101 While ostensibly about the radical organizational changes that affect the meaning and patterns of work, Handy's book is also about developing a more creative lifestyle, especially in the third age. See his *The Age of Unreason.*

101 John R. O'Neil, *The Paradox of Success.*

108 See the classic study by the sociologist Max Weber, *The Protestant Ethic and the Spirit of Capitalism* (New York: Charles Scribner's Sons, 1930).

110 Research into work satisfaction has repeatedly found goals like Judy's important. See Chris Argyris, *Personality and Organization* (New York: Harper and Row, 1957); Frederick Herzberg, *Work and the Nature of Man* (Cleveland: World Publishing, 1966); Douglas McGregor, *The Human Side of Enterprise* (New York: McGraw-Hill, 1960); Thomas Peters and Robert Waterman, Jr., *In Search of Excellence* (New York: Warner, 1982); Edgar H. Schein, *Organizational Psychology* 3d ed. (Englewood Cliffs, NJ: Prentice-Hall, 1980); and J. R. Hackman and G. R. Oldham, "Motivation through the Design of Work," *Organizational and Human Performance* (August 1976): 250–279.

117 See my earlier articles on play, especially William A. Sadler, Jr., "Creative Existence: Play as a Pathway to Personal Freedom and Community," *Humanitas* 1 (1969). Reprinted in F. Severin, ed., *Discovering Man in Psychology* (New York: McGraw-Hill, 1973). Also Sadler, *Existence and Love* (New York: Charles Scribner's Sons, 1969), Chapter 9.

117 The importance of playtime, vacations, and humor is a theme that runs through Vaillant's study of healthy adaptation. See his *Adaptation to Life.*

117 Peter Chew, *The Inner World of the Middle-Aged Man* (Boston: Houghton Mifflin, 1977), 230.

117 See the classic work by Johan Huizinga, *Homo Ludens: A Study of the Play Element in Culture* (Boston: Beacon, 1955).

123 Irving Rosow, *Socialization in Old Age* (Berkeley: University of California Press, 1974).

123 E. Cumming and W. Henry, *Growing Old: The Process of Disengagement* (New York: Basic Books, 1961).

123 Charles Handy, *The Age of Unreason*, 180.

124 See his autobiographical statement, "Former College President as Vermont Innkeeper," *The Chronicle of Higher Education* (August 15, 1990): Section B, 2–3.

127 Melissa Everett has shown how many people are redesigning their work lives in order to make valuable social contributions. See her *Making a Living While Making a Difference: A Guide to Creating Careers with a Conscience* (New York: Bantam, 1995).

127 I think of "retired" President Jimmy Carter, who, in his midlife career since leaving the office of president, has enriched countless lives in many countries by contributing to important social and environmental causes and by adding a dimension of integrity to domestic and international political debates and policies. Some of the "retired" people in my study are using their free time in a similar way. See President Carter's portrayal of his own midlife renewal in his *The Virtues of Aging* (New York: Ballantine Books, 1998).

CHAPTER 6

129 Kahlil Gibran, "On Marriage," *The Prophet* (New York: Knopf, 1963), 15.

130 Some writers have tried to explain the midlife crisis as being part of normal adult development. See, for example, the previously cited works by Daniel Levinson and Gail Sheehy. A British psychoanalyst coined the term to describe what he saw in a few patients. See Eliot Jacques, "Death and the Midlife Crisis," *International Journal of Psycho-Analysis* 46 (1965): 501–514.

134 Csikszentmihalyi, *Flow*, 19–21.

135 In her study of ego development, Jane Loevinger ponders why "the vast majority of the population stabilizes at some stage far below the maximum compatible with their intellectual and other development" (page 311). She acknowledges that this question has not been sufficiently researched, but she proposes an answer. Borrowing from Piaget, she suggests that growth, like learning, requires an experience of disequilibration in which a person's expectations are disconfirmed. As long as a person experiences a challenge or contradiction to his expectations, "he has the potential for further

growth." When equilibration is achieved, the likelihood of change is small. Loevinger, *Ego Development* (San Francisco: Jossey-Bass, 1976).

136   See the criticisms of exaggerated individualism in Robert Bellah et al., *Habits of the Heart*, and Christopher Lasch, *The Culture of Narcissism* (New York: Norton, 1979).

138   See Sam Keen, *Fire in the Belly: On Being a Man* (New York: Bantam, 1991).

138   Deborah Tannen, *You Just Don't Understand* (New York: Ballantine, 1990).

138   Arlene Skolnick, *The Embattled Paradise* (New York: Basic Books, 1991), 203.

138   In defining maturity, we need to question the end state, or final outcome, assumed by theories of development. The father of the cognitive develop-ment model, Jean Piaget, saw autonomy of the individual who had reached the stage of formal operational thinking as a final desired outcome. Most psychologists seem to have assumed that there is no qualitatively significant change beyond that stage. I have argued that second growth challenges that assumption and provides us with a new developmental model.

Recently, others have also suggested that there are other possible out-comes. The goal of autonomy can be superseded by individuals who are more open, more giving, and more closely connected to others. The end state is an "interindividual self," similar to the mature self I have depicted, who integrates autonomy and interdependence. See Emily Sourvaine, Lisa L. Lahey, and Robert Kegan, "Life After Formal Operations: Implications for a Psychology of the Self," in Charles Alexander and Helen Langer, eds., *Higher Stages of Human Development* (New York: Oxford University Press, 1990).

Earlier in this century two influential philosophers also criticized an as-sumption that the self as autonomous agent is a final outcome. Our goal, they believed, was to develop "I-Thou" relationships. See my discussion of Martin Buber and Gabriel Marcel in William A. Sadler, Jr., *Existence and Love*, Chapter 5. See also the argument by psychologist David Bakan, *The Duality of Existence* (Chicago: Rand McNally, 1967).

138   See Judith S. Wallerstein and Sandra Blakeslee, *The Good Marriage* (New York: Houghton Mifflin, 1995), 154–158 and 272–275.

139   Francesca M. Cancian, *Love in America: Gender and Self-Development* (Cambridge: Cambridge University Press, 1987).

139   Maggie Scarf, *Intimate Partners* (New York: Ballantine Books, 1988), 401–402.

140   Writing about his own marriage and the relationships of several other cou-ples, Carl Rogers made similar observations. See his *Becoming Partners* (New York: Dell, 1972).

144   See Daniel Goleman, *Emotional Intelligence* (New York: Bantam, 1995).

145   The psychology of women has discovered a basic difference between men's and women's outlook and adaptational styles. Whereas men are more ori-ented toward independence and individual achievement, women are more oriented toward relationships. See, for example, the pioneering study of

women's moral development by Carol Gilligan, *In a Different Voice* (Cambridge: Harvard University Press, 1983). Another research project independent of Gilligan's work is even more explicit in defining these differences and women's interpersonal skills. See Deborah Tannen, *You Just Don't Understand.*

146   Aristotle, *Nichomachean Ethics*, trans. Martin Ostwald (Indianapolis: Bobbs-Merrill, 1962). Aristotle argued that to be a good friend one must have a good character. Friendship in his scheme is a culmination of the development of virtues.

147   Tannen, *You Just Don't Understand.* Tannen's portrait of men applies to Americans. The interpersonal rapport between men I have observed in Africa and Turkey suggests these male traits are not implanted in genes but are cultural byproducts.

147   I sketched out basic elements in close friendships using a phenomenological approach a number of years ago. William A. Sadler, Jr., "The Experience of Friendship," *Humanitas* 2 (Fall 1970). The elements include enjoyment of the friend and the relationship; truthfulness; a deep level of sharing; recognition and support of the friend's freedom and individuality; and willingness to sacrifice for the friend. I believe these elements exist in the close friendships that men and women have described to me in this study.

149   My previous book explores the relationship between freedom, growth, and love in considerable detail. See Sadler, *Existence and Love.*

CHAPTER 7

151   According to Erikson, middle-aged adults must become "generative" if they are to avoid stagnation and achieve the ultimate virtue of integrity. See Erik H. Erikson, *Childhood and Society,* 2d ed. (New York: Norton, 1963). Originally, he meant that adults should become more caring about the generations that followed. Later, the term was expanded to mean caring for and involvement with people, not just a younger generation. See Erikson, *The Life Cycle Completed* (New York: Norton, 1982). Researchers who have followed the development of adults through their forties and fifties have found that healthy adapters, those who have consolidated their careers and established intimate relationships, become more caring. The journalist Daniel Goleman summarized research up to 1990, indicating that many adults see middle age as a time of emotional richness, deepening relationships, and greater altruism, generosity, and compassion. In *The New York Times*, February 6, 1990, sec. C, 1.

151   Two thinkers who influenced my early thinking about caring were Martin Heidegger and Paul Tillich. See Heidegger's *Being and Time* (New York: Harper and Row, 1964) and my discussion of Heidegger's existential phi-

losophy in William A. Sadler, Jr., *Existence and Love*, Chapter 4. Heidegger's brilliant description of the structure of human care did not pay sufficient attention to the special form of care found in love and intimacy. See Paul Tillich, *The Protestant Era* (Chicago: University of Chicago Press, 1951); *The Courage to Be* (New Haven: Yale University Press, 1953); and *Dynamics of Faith* (New York: Harper and Row, 1957). I discussed and critiqued Tillich's ontological ideas in my dissertation. (William A. Sadler, Jr., *Ludwig Binswanger's Existential Phenomenology*, Ph.D. diss., Harvard University, 1962.)

152   While popular literature suggests that self-centered individualism is a recent phenomenon, sociology has, in fact, been tracking individualism since its inception in the eighteenth century. For a brief, insightful discussion of a social trend toward greater self-centeredness see Alice Rossi, "Sex and Gender in the Aging Society," in Alan Pifer and Lydia Bronte, eds., *Our Aging Society*.

152   Jeremy Rifkin, *The End of Work*, 21.

159   See the argument made by Matthew Fox in his *Original Blessing* (Santa Fe: Bear and Co., 1981).

159   See Robert M. Grant and David N. Freedman. *The Secret Sayings of Jesus (The Gospel According to Thomas)* (London: Fontana Books, 1960), 164. Charles Handy provided the rendering that I have given here in his *The Hungry Spirit*, 103.

163   See Kenneth Pelletier (*Sound Body/Sound Mind*, New York: Simon and Schuster, 1994). Pelletier defines health holistically, emphasizing optimal health. Although he recognizes the importance of physical activity and a healthy lifestyle, he believes that optimal health starts in the mind. Jogging and diet alone will not bring good health throughout our adult years.

164   See Robert N. Butler, *Why Survive? Being Old in America* (New York: Harper and Row, 1975). The advice he gave twenty years ago is as relevant as ever.

164   See Kenneth H. Cooper, *The Aerobics Way* (New York: Bantam, 1978). This book has detailed plans, charts, and practical information about various forms of exercise and diets.

165   See, for example, Walter R. Frontera and Carol N. Meredith, "Exercise in the Rehabilitation of the Elderly," in G. Felsentha, S. Garrison, and F. Steinberg, eds., *Rehabilitation of the Aging and Elderly Patient*, Baltimore: Williams and Wilkins, 1994, and Frontera et al., "Strength Conditioning in Older Men: Skeletal Muscle Hypertrophy and Improved Function," *Journal of Applied Physiology*, 64 (1988): 1039–1044.

165   "Walking: The Ideal Exercise?" *The Harvard Health Letter* 3, no. 3 (November 1992). This article extols the benefits of walking and suggests that it may be the best way to start an exercise program. Later research suggests that biking, jogging, swimming, and aerobics can be more effective.

165 Jane E. Brody reported on a recent Harvard study that found that middle-aged men who engaged in strenuous physical activity over a twenty-year period experienced greater longevity. Those men who did only moderate activity, such as golf, showed no such benefits. *San Francisco Chronicle*, April 19, 1995, sec. A, 8.

167 Alfred Einstein, quoted in Peter Senge, *The Fifth Discipline* (New York: Doubleday/Bantam, 1990), 170.

168 See, for example, Thomas Berry, *Befriending the Earth* (Mystic, CT: Twenty-third, 1992), and *The Dream of the Earth* (San Francisco: Sierra Club, 1988). See also James Conlon, *Geo-Justice*, (Winfield, B.C.: Wood 1990) and *Earth Story/Sacred Story* (Mystic, CT: Twenty-third, 1993); and Matthew Fox, *Creation Spirituality* (New York: HarperCollins, 1991). Holy Names College in Oakland, California, has been a vital center for creation spirituality for nearly twenty years.

170 See the optimistic vision of a new era of caring by Vice President Al Gore in the conclusion of his book *Earth in the Balance: Ecology and the Human Spirit* (New York: Houghton Mifflin, 1992). Models of third-age caring have been provided by a host of famous individuals like Jimmy and Rosalynn Carter and by John Gardner, who formed the Experience Corps of Volunteers in Palo Alto, California. They have also, of course, been provided by many ordinary individuals, such as the adults I have been studying for the last thirteen years.

CHAPTER 8

171 Many textbooks on adult development and aging lay out the conventional pattern. Popular books do as well. For example, Gail Sheehy recently wrote, "Despite the recent shifts in the life cycle, there are still broad, general stages of adulthood with predictable passages between them." See her *New Passages*, 13. In contrast to this view, many social scientists now recognize no broad, general stages and certainly no predictable crises. The life course theory, which is what I am most comfortable with in assessing human development, sees individual lives affected by social patterns and historical forces. With this perspective we are more likely to observe many patterns and a host of possibilities in human development and aging. What I have focused on in this book is just one possibility that emerges from a new historical setting, which in turn offers us an opportunity to change the way we age.

172 See Handy, *The Age of Unreason*, 260, and his *The Hungry Spirit* (New York: Broadway Books, 1997).

181 *Down east* is a nautical term referring to the prevailing wind off the coast of Maine. It is also a symbolic phrase referring to the lifestyle in the state. Sail-

ing "on a reach" refers to a point of sail, with the wind crossing the side of a sailboat, in contrast to sailing upwind (beating) or running, with the wind directly behind the stern.

192   Nathaniel West, *Miss Lonelyhearts* (New York: Chelsea House, 1987).

197   Bernice Neugarten and Associates, *Personality in Middle and Late Life: Empirical Studies* (New York: Atherton, 1964).

197   See, for example, Margaret N. Reedy, "Personality and Aging," and Vern Benston and David Haber, "Sociological Perspectives on Aging," both in James E. Birren and Diana S. Woodruff, eds., *Aging: Scientific and Social Issues*, 2d ed. (Brooks/Cole, 1993). An exception to the view of usual aging is the idea of successful aging. See John Rowe and Robert L. Kahn, *Successful Aging* (New York: Pantheon Books, 1998).

AFTERWORD

199   See the provacative analysis by Charles Handy, *The Age of Unreason* (Boston: Harvard Business School Press, 1990). See also the now classical analysis of contemporary social disorder by Peter Drucker, The Age of Discontinuity (New York: Harper and Row, 1969), and Daniel Bell's tremendously insightful *The Cultural Contradictions of Capitalism* (New York: Basic Books, 1976). Bell's book is well worth examining, especially for its discussion of how modern social structures have laid the groundwork for some of the paradoxes we encounter in our own experiences.

202   See Philip Aries, *Centuries of Childhood* (New York: Vintage, 1962). This classic study has been critiqued in terms of details in the argument. I believe the general thesis about the emergence of the modern experience of childhood stands.

202   T. S. Eliot, Selected Essays (New York: Harcourt Brace, 1950). See the essay "Hamlet," 124. Eliot invented this term to explain why, in his view, Shakespeare's Hamlet was not a successful play.

203   The late Erik Erikson was perhaps the leading example of social science thinking about the link between personal development and social/cultural forces. See his now classic study, *Childhood and Society*. From this approach we now have a life stage model that maps out distinct experiences as normal within the development of each person. Ironically, this model now fails to appreciate the basic insight that an internal stage is in part a response to an external condition. Change the situation radically enough and the stage may disappear. The point I wish to make here is that what is generally regarded as a universal life stage, particularly an adult life stage, is actually specific to a particular situation. Circumstances have been changing so rapidly that new inner possibilities are emerging. A life course theory is better suited to appreciate situational contingencies than theories of the life cycle or life stages.

203   For a definitive presentation of life course theory, see Glen H. Elder, Jr., *Children of the Great Depression: Social Change in Life Experience (revised)* (Boulder, CO: Westview Press, 1998), Chapter 11; also his article "The Life Course and Human Development," in Richard M. Lerner, ed., *Handbook of Child Psychology*, Vol. I (New York: Wiley, 1998), 939–991.

     See the important article that reports on interdisciplinary research on successful aging: John Rowe and Robert Kahn, "Human Aging: Unusual and Successful," *Science* 237 (1987): 143–49, and their recent book *Successful Aging*. See also Matilda Riley and John Riley, "Longevity and Social Structure: The Potential of the Added Years," and Bernice Neugarten and Dail Neugarten, "Changing Meanings of Age in the Aging Society," both in Alan Pifer and Lydia Bronte, eds., *Our Aging Society*. Psychologist Ellen Langer's experiments have provided evidence to support the view that ongoing growth is a possibility in old age, and that decline and debility are not inevitable features of human aging. See Langer et al., "Nonsequential Development and Aging," in Charles Alexander and Ellen Langer, eds., *Higher Stages of Human Development*.

Index